Secession

Secession

The Legitimacy of Self-Determination

Lee C. Buchheit

New Haven and London   Yale University Press

1978

Designed by John O. C. McCrillis and set in Baskerville type. Printed in the United States of America by The Murray Printing Co., Westford, Massachusetts.

Published in Great Britain, Europe, Africa, and Asia (except Japan) by Yale University Press, Ltd., London. Distributed in Latin America by Kaiman & Polon, Inc., New York City; in Australia and New Zealand by Book & Film Services, Artarmon, N.S.W., Australia; and in Japan by Harper & Row, Publishers, Tokyo Office.

Library of Congress Cataloging in Publication Data
Buchheit, Lee C   1950–
Secession.

Includes index.
1. Self-determination, National.   2. Secession.
I. Title.
JX4054.B8   341.26   77-20687
ISBN 0-300-02182-8

To
Charles and Helen Buchheit
for their understanding
that the child
would be the
father of
the man

Contents

MAPS

Preface

At the time of this writing, newspaper columns are filled with dire predictions regarding the possible secession of Quebec from Canada in light of the decisive victory of the separatist Parti Québecois in November 1976. With a strong sense of déjà vu, one also reads of an invasion of the Shaba Province of Zaire (formerly the Katanga Province of the Belgian Congo) and the renewal of a secessionist struggle that was thought to have been laid to rest by the United Nations over a decade ago.

Eritrean guerrillas are reported close to accomplishing the separation of that area from Ethiopia while insurgents backed by neighboring Somalia are proclaiming their control over the long-disputed Ogaden region in southeast Ethiopia. Basque and Catalan nationalist sentiment continues to simmer in Spain. The United Kingdom warily watches the growing popularity of certain Scottish and Welsh separatist groups. France is made continually uneasy by the demands of Bretons and Corsicans. Italy contends with separatist movements in Sicily and the South Tyrol. Belgium is a less than harmonious union of French-speaking Walloons and a Flemish-speaking minority. Portugal is importuned by the inhabitants of the Azores to grant independence to those islands, and neighboring Spain is similarly troubled by a group calling itself the "Movement for Self-Determination and Independence of the Canary Islands."

One even hears occasionally of entities such as the Hutt River Province—a twenty-nine-square-mile section of Western Australia whose thirty inhabitants served a formal notice of secession on the Australian government in 1970.

The presence of a separatist movement is typically a matter of acute concern to the unified State likely to be dismembered by the secession of the disaffected province. Legal arguments for a right to secede, such as those hotly debated in the years preceding the secession of the Confederacy in the United States, may raise fundamental issues regarding the internal constitutional framework of the country.

In addition to its significance for the unified State, however, a secessionist movement may also be a matter of practical and legal concern for the international community as a whole. When such a movement erupts into open warfare, as in the Katanga, Biafra, or Bangla Desh, it may constitute a serious threat to international peace. Should the secessionist group be the victim of minority oppression, violations of human rights, or genocide, international concern may also be generated. Finally, the tendency of modern secessionist movements to seek to establish the legal legitimacy of their claims by invoking the international doctrine of self-determination raises thorny legal problems relating to the applicability of this doctrine to minority groups within unified States.

The focus of this book is on the implications for the international community of appeals to the principle of self-determination by secessionist groups within independent States. In particular, an attempt is made to explore the status within international law of claims to secessionist self-determination and to suggest considerations that might influence a collective decision regarding the legitimacy of such claims. Because the emphasis of this book is on the implications of these phenomena for the world community as a whole, no effort has been made to consider in detail the legal or constitutional validity of particular secessionist claims within the context of domestic legal systems.

The major part of this book was written during the 1975–76 academic year while I was in residence at Trinity College, Cambridge. My presence there would not have been possible without the financial assistance of a Franklin B. Gowen Memorial Fellowship from the University of Pennsylvania Law School, and I gratefully acknowledge this crucial support.

I am deeply indebted to several people who have offered guidance and constructive criticism during all phases of my preparation of this work. Professor Noyes Leech of the University of Pennsylvania Law School generated the kind of infectious enthusiasm for the topic that has always seemed to me to represent the highest form of the professorial art. Dr. D. W. Bowett of Queens' College, Cambridge, stoically confronted the reams of typescript that regularly appeared in his mailbox and offered invaluable suggestions for improvement with an unfailing cheerfulness. Dr. Walter Ullmann of Trinity College, Cambridge, read the portion of the typescript dealing with natural law, and I benefited greatly from his advice in this area.

I am grateful to Mrs. Colin Serby and Ms. Carol Cramer for their efforts in preparing the typescript for publication.

Finally, I am most deeply indebted to my wife, Roberta, not only for her perceptive criticism of each paragraph, page, and chapter, but also for her quiet optimism and unfaltering confidence, without which I should never have been able to finish the book.

LCB

Springfield, Virginia
June 1977

1 Self-Determination and the Problem of Secession

Even so celebrated a thinker as Aristotle is reported to have instructed the youthful Alexander of Macedonia that the Persians were by nature slaves and ungovernable in the Greek sense. Aristotle's advice comported with a distinction clearly perceived by the ancient Greeks (among others) between themselves and their "barbarian" neighbors. It is a negative expression of the same sentiment that prompts some groups of Eskimos to refer to themselves confidently as "Inuits," or "the people."

The world view explaining these phenomena, which divides the whole of human society into those with whom one shares certain noticeable ties of kinship or culture and those with whom one does not, is oddly enough one of the few really panhuman traits cherished by most of mankind. Historically, social leaders have found this division into "us" and "them" a useful, if not always defensible, outlook on human existence. It provides a comforting psychological reinforcement for the self-image of the society; fosters the belief that indigenous culture is unique (thus paving the way for the curious leap to the conclusion that it is superior); and reassures the group of its privileged status within the cosmos. Although many societies have artificially cultivated this attitude to preserve their own cultural identity or to justify their dominance over other cultures, it is nevertheless clear that such "parochial" sentiments are deeply embedded in human psychology. Even as a citizen in this cosmopolitan age, one often finds the symptoms of a parochial bent intruding into one's personal judgments and preferences. Thus, our own mother tongue, and preferably our own dialect, usually sounds sweetest; our own customs seem more decorous; our native cuisine more palatable; and our own racial features more regular. Moreover, to the extent that we are parochial in our outlook, there is a temptation to be xenophobic—foreign accents sounding strident, alien customs curious, food indigestible, and faces unattractive.

The student of what has come to be called the doctrine of self-determination must begin with the fact of entrenched parochial sentiment. The psychological force of the principle of self-determination lies in a basic human desire to associate primarily with one's immediate fellows (family, clan, tribe, or village). The moral appeal of the principle seems to arise from a recognition of the harsh treatment and exploitation that have historically been the fate of groups ruled by an "alien" people. The anthropologist may tell us that our tribal ancestors gradually acquired a knowledge which equated the unfamiliar with the hostile, and which taught that whatever small security could be found in life would come from a close association with one's insular group. Whether we are now heirs to a legacy of collective consciousness in which these reactions have become instinctive, or whether we have deduced them from the ample data of recorded history, is of no particular moment here.[1] It is sufficient to recognize that a demand for self-determination will often be deeply rooted in a wish to perpetuate the sense of comfort and security that attends a parochial environment including local self-government, and it may be reinforced by a prejudice that "alien" government will always be harsher, less receptive, and, by definition, supportive of alien values.

This tendency to preserve a parochial environment will of course frequently be at odds with a conflicting desire for the economic, social, and military benefits conveyed by wider participation in a larger grouping such as a city, province, or State. The urge to parochialism suggests a political structure which satisfies an emotional need for self-government while avoiding the dangers and awkwardness involved in association with other, dissimilar, groups.[2] In contrast, the desire for unification or integration with a wider political or economic entity encourages policies calculated to further the aims of conquest, defense,

---

1. *Cf.* F. HERTZ, NATIONALITY IN HISTORY AND POLITICS 17 (1945):

> That the motives of human groups are to some extent offshoots of a gregarious instinct is made probable by the example of many animals living in herds or groups. Gregariousness consists not only in associating with others but also in excluding outsiders, and this tendency often leads to conflicts without any other motive than group feeling. Many animals live in closed societies. A stranger, though of the same species, getting somehow among a group, is attacked, roughly treated or killed. [footnotes omitted]

2. Patricia Elton Mayo has argued that the insistence by polyethnic States on unitary, centralized government at the expense of a communal sentiment among their ethnic minorities contributes to social maladjustment.

> Today many disturbing social symptoms—violence, the lack of civic responsibility shown in certain strikes and elsewhere, the lack of interest in the political life of a country—are caused in part by the destruction of community life. To be happy and

liberation, social advancement, or economic well-being. If left entirely alone, therefore, the centripetal effect of the desire for economic or military strength will presumably be occasionally offset by the centrifugal demands of parochialism whenever the loss of group identity or the fear of alien domination becomes unbearable for the people concerned. It may be expected that this situation will, in turn, be followed by a felt need for a wider association to achieve certain social or military goals, and so on. In practice, of course, these forces have rarely been left alone to operate in this manner.

If history were a chronicle of the voluntary association and disassociation of human groups, there would be no need for a doctrine of self-determination. Without the effects of conquest, forced annexation, subjugation, dynastic union, and colonial expansion, the world's peoples would presumably now be arranged into freely chosen political units. It is the distinct absence of such a peaceful evolution of mankind's social organization which ultimately gave rise to the principle of self-determination as the twentieth century's primary expression of disapproval of involuntary political association.

When it was first articulated during the period of the First World War, the principle of self-determination was not an entirely novel concept in European political thought. Ever since the French Revolution of 1789 many European statesmen had recognized the emergent phenomenon of nationalism as a factor in international relations. During this era there were noticeable instances of plebiscites accompanying territorial transfers; some States openly preached (in the abstract) the virtues of nationalism; and a few even attempted to incorporate the doctrine into their foreign policy. On the whole, however, European statesmen regarded the nationalistic sentiment with suspicion.[3] That it

---

balanced man must have his roots in a living social group, and this informal group to function well should be recognized by the government, although it may be the smallest element in the social structure.

P. MAYO, THE ROOTS OF IDENTITY: THREE NATIONAL MOVEMENTS IN CONTEMPORARY EUROPEAN POLITICS 156 (1974). The Permanent Court of International Justice in the *Greco-Bulgarian "Communities"* case [1930] P.C.I.J., ser. B, No. 17, at 20, opined that "the material benefits which from time immemorial in the East individuals of the same race, religion, language and traditions, have derived from uniting into communities, are well known."

3. Even Bismarck as a young statesman in the previous century had expressed a belief that Europe would not achieve peace until she had been sorted out into her nationalities, or, in Bismarck's word, her "tribes." He did not, however, mean by this to endorse any *moral* superiority of nationalism, only its apparent historical inevitability. *See* A. J. P. TAYLOR, BISMARCK 50 (1974).

existed was indisputable, and that foreign nationalistic eruptions occasionally served a State's purposes was certainly a pleasant enough fact; but for most statesmen nationalism was a dangerously volatile emotion to be discouraged wherever possible. Few regarded its growth as a healthy development, and it seems safe to assert that even fewer thought of it as a "first principle" of international relations. When the doctrine of national self-determination was articulated in just such terms after World War I, therefore, a remarkable innovation had taken place.

The focus of national self-determination was largely the result of historical accident. The doctrine was shaped by two factors of overwhelming importance. First, it was articulated after two centuries in which nationalism had become the foremost expression of rebellion against "artificial" multinational empires. Self-determination was therefore to borrow from nationalism the conviction that societies could be broken down into "natural" political units, loosely given the title of "nations." Second, the doctrine won adherents among the generation saddled with the task of reorganizing Europe after the First World War. This generation was thus given a unique (and irresistible) chance to test on a vast scale the fundamental promise of self-determination, namely, that a rearrangement of political frontiers corresponding to the associational desires of the inhabitants would significantly reduce social and international unrest.

Reflecting the influence of these two factors, the doctrine of national self-determination embraced the proposition that the only legitimate form of government was self-government by natural political units, with its corollary that multinational States or empires, the products of conquest or dynastic union, were ultimately illegitimate political entities. On the theoretical level, legitimacy was seen to derive from the consent of the governed, reinforced by the practical realization that government without consent meant constant unrest (as, for example, in the Balkans), disturbing the internal order of a State, and ultimately threatening international peace. In addition, the self-determination theorists after the First World War were resolved to implement their view of governmental legitimacy as an operational tenet of international relations. There was nothing new in arguing for the moral correctness of the principle of national self-determination; this was, after all, the heart of the nationalist's demand. The crucial innovation after World War I was its elevation to the status of an *international* touchstone of governmental legitimacy which could properly be encouraged or even enforced by the international community.

Unfortunately, the principle of national self-determination as articulated during this era had several practical and theoretical flaws. First, its inheritance from the doctrine of nationalism included the notoriously difficult problem of adequately defining or identifying a "nation" that would then be entitled to "national" self-determination. Second, even if one arbitrarily relied on history to establish a nation as an entity that had once enjoyed a measure of self-government, it was unclear how far back into the past one should search for this characteristic. Third, although nationalism is undeniably a political urge, it is not necessarily the basic political urge. The "nation," a narrower political entity than the multinational State or empire, may nevertheless often be an integration of still narrower parochial loyalties. It is thus frequently true that a successful nationalistic movement must overcome the regional sentiments of its constituents and that these parochial attachments are always liable to recur when the object of nationalistic fervor has been achieved. To the staunch parochialist, therefore, "the nation" may be a concept almost as artificial as "the empire" is to the nationalist. In many cases the nation was historically a form of compromise: smaller than the offending empire but large enough to be an effective force in throwing off the imperial yoke.

At the end of the First World War, therefore, the principle of self-government by "natural" political communities was transformed into a norm to which the international community openly subscribed. The lethal weaknesses of the doctrine of national self-determination were its assumptions that "nations" would generally be self-evident entities and that only nations, as history had delimited them, would constitute natural political units having a compelling desire for self-government.

The seeds of confusion planted by these weaknesses did not take long to ripen. Even before the process of "national" self-determination as undertaken at the Paris Peace Conference of 1919 could be implemented in a satisfactory manner, distinct ethnic groups such as the Kurds, who had little or no pretension to being autonomous nations with any clear historical antecedents, began to invoke the international norm of self-government as a justification for independence from, or at least regional autonomy within, their governing States. Thus polyethnic States were uncomfortably subjected to the same attack as multinational empires.[4] Furthermore, many groups

---

4. "No tribal entity was too small to have ambition for self-determination," lamented Colonel Edward House in describing the experience of the Paris Peace Conference. "Social and economic considerations were unreckoned with, and the only thought for the moment was to reach back to the centuries when they were nomads and were Masters of their own fortunes and desires." House, *The Versailles Peace in Retrospect*, in WHAT REALLY HAPPENED AT PARIS 425, 431 (E. House, C. Seymour Eds. 1921).

that did have some historic claim to participate in a national entity but that remained within "alien" States after the peace settlement (such as the Alsatians and the South Tyrolese) also sought to redress their "unnatural" condition. In both types of cases, the international community's principle of self-determination was enlisted as justificatory support for claims to regional autonomy or complete independence by minority groups within independent States.

On one level, this confusion was an inevitable result of the failure to specify whether the international community had recognized only *national*-determination (referring to "nations" which had historically enjoyed some measure of self-government[5]), or whether it had endorsed *self*-determination (meaning by this a concept of "natural" political units). Statesmen understandably urged that the focus of the principle should be on the nation as an historically determined phenomenon, regardless of whether it might be an artificial construct of smaller ethnic communities. The parochialists countered by putting the emphasis on self-determination as an international endorsement of self-government by "natural" political communities, against which neither the territorial jealousy of multinational empires *nor* that of polyethnic States should be considered. Theoretically, one could ascertain the nature of these communities simply by applying the consensual principle of governmental legitimacy. The obvious remedies for such communities, they argued, included regional autonomy within the framework of a unified State or secession from their governing States followed by independence or association with a political entity of their choosing.

Clearly the international community had spawned a Frankensteinian monster. The doctrine of self-determination obviously took much of its emotive and moral force from a parochial urge to self-government. Moreover, the legal legitimacy of this fundamental urge to self-government had already received some kind of international blessing after the First World War. Just as clearly, however, the international community did not seem to intend the enthronement of a right of secession exercisable by any minority group within an independent State as a canon of international law. Retrenchment was thus manifestly in order. The overriding question became how to affirm something of the underlying premise of self-determination (consent of the governed) without allowing the wholesale dismemberment of independent States into impossibly small parochial entities.

5. Consider, for example, Charles H. Haskin's scornful dismissal of the suggestion of a "national" movement in Alsace-Lorraine primarily because the region "has no traditions of separate life or national independence." Haskins, *The New Boundaries of Germany*, in WHAT REALLY HAPPENED AT PARIS 37, 47, *id.*

Without a satisfactory answer to this question having been achieved during the interwar years, it was almost with a sense of relief that many statesmen witnessed the principle of self-determination after World War II being conscripted into the cause of decolonization. Colonial self-determination, although not very popular with colonial Powers, did not suffer the political drawback of seeming to offer comfort to disaffected groups within established, independent States. This development, however, which seemed at first heaven-sent to supply a minimally explosive content for the doctrine of self-determination, eventually worked to evolve an even more vague but certainly more incendiary terminology — that of the right of "peoples" to self-determination.

Inevitably, with the gradual achievement of the goal of decolonization in the 1960s and 70s, the more troublesome questions regarding the role of the international community's principle of self-determination as a possible justification for separatist movements within independent States again assumed considerable importance. After struggling to accommodate historic claims for national and colonial self-determination, contemporary history began to be punctuated by frequent and insistent demands for secessionist self-determination. These demands pose a considerable challenge for the international community and the international lawyer. If self-determination is to have a persuasive legal significance that survives its application to the colonial context, the principle must be able to accommodate the demands of "selves'" who are located within an independent State but are clearly governed without their consent. The task of the international lawyer therefore is to suggest acceptable guidelines for the operation of the principle of self-determination which, for obvious reasons, may not accede to the demands of every parochial sentiment but which must also avoid an uncritical affirmation of the supremacy of the "sovereign" State.

This does not promise to be a popular task. Neither the secessionist impulse nor the often singleminded determination of a unified State to resist a separatist movement is a simple or altogether rational emotion. There is an understandable tendency among polyethnic States (which category constitutes the vast majority of the world community) to regard all schemes involving any concession to parochial sentiment with a benumbing dread. In addition, an attempt to impose a legal limitation upon the doctrine of self-determination that suggests criteria for ascertaining a legitimate claimant to the principle other than a simple manifestation of an urge for parochial self-government is unlikely to be popular with groups aspiring to political independence solely on the basis of that urge. It cannot be anticipated that even a demonstration of the reasonableness of a group's remaining within a unified State, or the utter foolishness of its attempting an independent international existence, will always be sufficient to moderate the separatist's demands. The desire for independent self-government may seemingly thrive in the face of irrefutable evidence that the political, economic, and military well-being of the group would be better served by a continuing association with a larger political entity. It appears that many groups would gladly embrace an impoverished, defenseless existence in return for the emotional satisfaction of self-government. There were many expressions of this heroic sentiment in the colonial context, such as the splendidly Miltonic statement of a Filipino senator during the 1920s that "We would prefer a government run like hell by Filipinos to one run like heaven by Americans."[6] It is significant, moreover, that the international community rarely allowed considerations of impending economic or political disruption to negate a colonial people's claim to the "inalienable right of self-determination."

In summary, many secessionist movements in recent years have advanced a claim for legal legitimacy based upon the principle of self-determination of peoples. The apparent task of the international lawyer is to counsel the international community in making its assessment of the validity of these appeals to its principle of self-determination in a secessionist context. Although these claims are frequently proposed and opposed for reasons reflecting some of man's most fundamental desires and fears, an international assessment of their legitimacy must attempt to accommodate, in a rational way, the yearning of peoples for self-government, the interests of unified States, and the legitimate concerns of world order.

THE MEANING OF SELF-DETERMINATION

As a descriptive phrase the title "Holy Roman Empire" was defective, Voltaire noted, inasmuch as it denoted an entity neither holy, nor Roman, nor an empire. As a legal term of art, "the right of self-determination" fails in much the same fashion. The expression itself

6. Quoted in B. SHAFER, FACES OF NATIONALISM: NEW REALITIES AND OLD MYTHS 281 (1972). *Cf.* Satan's comment upon arriving in Hell:

> Here we may reign secure, and in my choice
> To reign is worth ambition though in Hell:
> Better to reign in Hell, than serve in Heaven.

J. MILTON, PARADISE LOST, bk. 1, lines 261–63.

gives no clue to the nature of the self that is to be determined; nor does it provide any enlightenment concerning the process of determination or the source and extent of the self's putative right to this process. Putting aside for the moment the implications of a "right" to self-determination, even a cursory examination of the phrase "self-determination" raises a number of questions. For some, the phrase invokes panoramic connotations while others perceive in it surprisingly little by way of indisputable denotation.

The Self

Just as fairy tales customarily begin with "Once upon a time," treatises on the doctrine of self-determination invariably commence with a discussion of the difficulties involved in delimiting the "self." The deficiency of the Wilsonian doctrine of self-determination is trenchantly summarized in Sir Ivor Jennings's oft-quoted remark: "On the surface it seemed reasonable: let the people decide. It was in fact ridiculous because the people cannot decide until somebody decides who are the people."[7] Some general understanding of the subject or beneficiaries of the right to self-determination — that is, the kinds of groups that may legitimately invoke the principle — is certainly a crucial, and probably a highly controversial, first step in any analysis of these issues. The use of variants of the expression such as "national self-determination" or "self-determination of peoples" merely places the definitional burden onto the words "nation" or "people" and is therefore of very little analytical help in this regard.

The most reasonable starting point here is an assumption that, at a minimum, any "self" must be distinct from the other selves inhabiting the globe.[8] Even at this elementary level, it is clear that there are at least two possible methods for confirming a group's distinctness. First,

7. I. JENNINGS, THE APPROACH TO SELF-GOVERNMENT 56 (1956). To some extent, of course, the issue of selfhood has been clarified by the practice of the United Nations, especially in its task of decolonialization. Nevertheless, the relevance of these precedents (which involved the transformation of colonies into States), is questionable where the claim involves a demand for secession that may or may not result in an independent State. For a discussion of United Nations practice as revealing the bounds of selfhood see A. SUREDA, THE EVOLUTION OF THE RIGHT OF SELF-DETERMINATION: A STUDY OF UNITED NATIONS PRACTICE (1973).

8. For related discussions see Les Objections contra L'Application du Droit des Peuples à Disposer D'eux Mêmes, in S. CALOGEROPOULOS-STRATIS, LE DROIT DES PEUPLES A DISPOSER D'EUX-MEMES 207–49 (1973); J. MOORE, LAW AND THE INDO-CHINA WAR 166–67 (1972). See also U. UMOZURIKE, SELF-DETERMINATION IN INTERNATIONAL LAW 177–203 (1972), where the author concludes optimistically, "The legitimate 'self' that 'determines' is now not so difficult to pinpoint." Id. 195.

it is possible to say that a group of people becomes a self for purposes of this principle as soon as it perceives itself as being reasonably distinct from its neighbors. Although evidence of such "group consciousness" ought certainly to be given weight, and some measure of communal sense is probably an indispensable element of selfhood, nevertheless the utility of employing the group's subjective perception of distinctness as the sole basis for implementing a claim to self-determination is obviously greatly impaired by the sheer number and diversity of perceptions capable of being experienced by a population concurrently. The same individual, for instance, may perceive his personal distinctness in terms of his membership in a fraternity, a church, a village, a commonwealth, a profession, or even a school of thought. In each case he will advance some measure of loyalty, experience some concern for the group's welfare and survival, and, in return, expect to share in a sense of fellowship and collective purpose. Similarly, professions, clubs, fraternities, and religious societies can, and obviously do, perceive themselves as distinct in certain respects from the general population. It cannot seriously be suggested that such collective perceptions of professional, religious, or social affiliation can each be made the basis of a right of the group to political autonomy by providing sufficient evidence of the group's "selfness" for purposes of self-determination. In practice, such perceptions tend to be overlapping, unverifiable, and changeable.[9]

A second and more appealing source for evidence of a group's distinctness may be found in the objective characteristics that distinguish the group from the ambient population. At a minimum these criteria of "selfness" could include elements of a religious, historic, geographic, ethnologic, economic, linguistic, and racial character. This approach has the virtue of supplying the international community with a set of relatively objective, verifiable criteria, some or all of which must be satisfied before a group may legitimately claim to be a self and therefore entitled to the process of "determination."[10]

Obviously, the analysis cannot end here for it is extremely unlikely

9. For a more extended discussion of the elements of group identity see H. Isaacs, Idols of the Tribe 26–45 (1977). *But see* Nayar, *Self-Determination beyond the Colonial Context: Biafra in Retrospect,* 10 Tex. Int'l L. J. 321, 340–41 (1975).

10. For a related discussion of "objective" characteristics of nationhood (such as geography, political history, economic structure) versus "subjective" characteristics (national consciousness, loyalty) *see* Q. Wright, 2 A Study of War 992 (1942); M. St. Korowicz, Introduction to International Law 289–98 (1959); and a criticism of same in D. Rustow, A World of Nations: Problems of Political Modernization 22–23 (1967).

both that a set of "necessary and sufficient" conditions of distinctness can be agreed upon, and that a simple satisfaction of such conditions will always reveal a legitimate claimant to self-determination. Such a coldly empirical approach to the problem tends to ignore the immeasurable factors that together constitute the psychopolitical "realities" of a given situation and thus must influence a decision regarding legitimacy. By way of illustration, the American colonists in 1776 satisfied very few conditions of distinctness vis-à-vis the English population; they shared common elements of language, history, law, and religion. Their separation from England was in fact justified primarily on the basis of geographic isolation, incongruity in the economic interests of the parties, and, above all, a sense of injustice and oppression in the mother country's handling of colonial affairs. In contrast, the German-speaking Swiss probably do satisfy most of the objective conditions of distinctness suggested above, yet it is questionable whether they possess a right, on those grounds alone, to leave the confederacy of which they form a part.

"Determination"

Assuming that one succeeds in isolating a proper self, there remains the question of what this self is entitled to do; that is, what sorts of activities constitute legitimate instances of "determining." This issue can be broken down into questions concerning the nature of the determining process and the frequency with which it must occur. Nothing in the principle of self-determination itself demands that a group achieve absolute autonomy or even a Western-style democracy.[11] Even in the relatively narrow field of decolonization, the advisory opinion of the International Court of Justice in the *Western Sahara* case recognized that "the right of self-determination leaves the General Assembly a measure of discretion with respect to the forms and procedures by which that right is to be realized."[12] The demands of a right to self-determination could conceivably be satisfied by the establishment of a more or less strict federalism, or by the granting of complete freedom

---

11. In contrast, two American jurists have concluded: "The list of concepts covered by the terms "equal rights" and "self-determination" . . . clearly refers to only one principle, the democratic principle; for no other political concept contains within it these essential . . . elements." A., A. J. THOMAS, NON-INTERVENTION: THE LAW AND ITS IMPORT IN THE AMERICAS 369–70 (1956). *See also* HERTZ, *supra* note 1, at 240 "National self-determination is by no means identical with political liberty. It does not necessarily imply a democratic regime, but merely freedom from foreign interference."

12. [1975] I. C. J. 12, 36.

of conscience where the cause of the irritation is religious intolerance. Where the basis of the dispute is economic, a solution might involve allowing what Arnold Toynbee would call a measure of "economic autarky"[13] while retaining political unity; or, as in the General Assembly's plan for Palestine, political separation with economic union.[14]

Similarly, one might query whether the establishment of a participatory democracy vitiates any further right to individual self-determination on the part of those groups participating. Or could, for example, a group legitimately choose as its form of government an enlightened dictatorship or single-party regime where the majority felt that these were less conducive to corruption or better able to achieve social or economic order? Does the principle of self-determination require a system that will be constantly receptive to the wishes of the people or can a majority of the group forego such a system without violating the minority's rights (or their own at some time in the future)?[15]

Finally one must decide how often self-determination demands that this process recur. Is it, for instance, satisfied by plebiscites at ten-year intervals or political elections in four-year cycles? How long may a totalitarian regime continue to justify its rule on the basis of popular support at its inception? The outer limits of uncertainty revealed by these questions are at least fairly easy to identify. On commonsense grounds, the right of a group to self-determination cannot blossom again in full vigor hours after a valid plebiscite or election. Political order demands at least some degree of living with one's choice although most would agree that a choice once made does not bind a group in perpetuity. In addition, an incumbent controlling government would be reluctant to hazard its position in a plebiscite or election when, assuming that it won, it would not even gain a temporary respite from the demands of its adversaries based on a right of self-determination.

The Varieties of Self-Determination

The political desires of a population may be expressed in a number of ways. Periodic elections of legislators or governors according to

13. A. TOYNBEE, 1 A STUDY OF HISTORY 288 (Somervell abridgement, 1947).
14. *See* G. A. Res. 181, *Future Government of Palestine,* 2 U.N. GAOR, U.N. Doc. A/519, at 131 (1947).
15. *See* Rivlin, *Self-Determination and Dependent Areas,* 1955 INT'L CONC. No. 501 at 195, 200: "Self-determination, particularly as it is related to democracy, implies a continuing process. Once a nation or a people has achieved independence through self-determination, it must continue to have the right to maintain this independence and sovereignty."

some prearranged constitutional formula, plebiscites to determine political status or affiliation, the voluntary division of an independent State, or free cession of territory to another State in accordance with the inhabitants' wishes are all instances of a peaceful implementation of self-determination.

Practical and legal difficulties are entailed, however, when an assertion of self-determination is made forcibly by a population or part of the population in a state or territory. Within this category (depending on the size, motives, and success of the claimant group) are instances of rebellion, insurrection, revolution, secession, and movements for colonial independence. Both the world community and the doctrines of international law find some of these forms of contentious self-determination far less objectionable than others. It is of course understandable that a community composed of States and a legal system that purports only to regulate the rights and duties of States would react adversely to any threat to the present State-centered order. To the extent that self-determination assumes the form of a revolution seeking to replace the existing government of the whole State, or a movement to free a colonial people (colonial domination now being widely regarded as an illegitimate exercise of State authority),[16] it does not seriously threaten the foundations of the inter-State order and is therefore more agreeable to members of the world community.[17] Similarly, a localized insurrection or rebellion, by virtue of its limited scope, does not jeopardize the structure of the international system, although it may warrant the attention of the world community where claims of intervention, violation of the laws of war, or genocide are raised.

A secessionist effort, however, does have as its express goal the dismemberment of a previously unified, independent State. As such, it clearly constitutes a matter of concern for the world community on a number of levels. First and foremost is the impact of widespread secession on the present structure of inter-State relations. A proliferation of political entities lacking the accepted requirements of Statehood is a foreseeable result of an unqualified acceptance of a right of secession. This would involve at a minimum some serious rethinking of current practices in the areas of recognition, jurisdiction, diplomatic customs, membership in international organizations, State responsibility, and so on. In addition, the two territories resulting from

16. *See* resolutions cited note 63 *infra*.

17. *See* Matthews, *Domestic and Inter-State Conflict in Africa*, 25 INT'L J. 459, 466 (1970), for a discussion of the tendency among African States to prefer movements challenging the legitimacy of incumbent governors (overthrow of the whole government) rather than challenges to a State's territorial integrity (secession).

a secession may lack, at least in early years, the economic and military strength of the unified State.[18] There is always the danger, therefore, that secession will spawn entities dependent upon international economic charity for their continued viability and upon one of the existing power blocs for defense. Finally, the world community must recognize that a favorable international reaction, even to a single secessionist attempt, may constitute a dangerous precedent potentially applicable to any State containing racial, religious, linguistic, or political minorities.[19]

It has recently become popular to speak of the concept of self-determination as having two component parts: (1) a principle of *external* self-determination whereby a group of people are entitled to pursue their political, cultural, and economic [20] wishes without interference or coercion by outside States, and (2) a principle of *internal* self-determination which encompasses the right of all segments of a population to influence the constitutional and political structure of the system under which they live. In the words of one writer, the two parts of this dichotomy represent the rights to "external independence and internal autonomy."[21]

A very curious use of the terms "internal" and "external" self-determination was made in the 1949 *Special Report of the United Nations Commission for Indonesia*[22]—a fact which may indicate that a greater lat-

18. For a discussion of the relationship between geographic size and economic viability in the context of former colonial territories see Abbot, *Size, Viability, Nationalism, and Politico-Economic Development*, 25 INT'L J. 56, 58–63 (1969–70). *See generally* R. DAHL, E. TUFTE, SIZE AND DEMOCRACY (1974).

19. *See* Matthews, *supra* note 17, at 470: "However justifiable the demands of a separatist group may be, other African States are unlikely to encourage their efforts for fear of opening Pandora's box. As Immanuel Wallerstein has so succinctly put it, 'every African nation . . . has its Katanga. Once the logic of secession is admitted, there is no end except in anarchy' " [footnotes omitted].

20. The expression "economic self-determination," currently in vogue, is often applied to the putative right of a State freely to determine its own economic policies and to maintain permanent sovereignty over its wealth and natural resources. *See Recommendations concerning International Respect for the Right of Peoples and Nations to Self-Determination*, G. A. Res. 1314, 13 U.N. GAOR, Supp. 18, at 27, U.N. Doc. A/4090 (1958); *Charter of Economic Rights and Duties of States*, G. A. Res. 3281 art. 1 (Dec. 12, 1974), reprinted in 14 INT'L LEGAL MAT. 251 (1975). For a more elaborate discussion *see* UMOZURIKE, *supra* note 8, at 204–24.

21. Šuković, *Principle of Equal Rights and Self-Determination of Peoples*, in PRINCIPLES OF INTERNATIONAL LAW CONCERNING FRIENDLY RELATIONS AND COOPERATION 323, 350 (M. Šahović ed. 1972).

22. 4 U.N. SCOR, Spec. Supp. 6, U.N. Doc. S/1417 (1949).

itude for the exercise of minority self-determination may be expected in the formation of a new State than in a forced dismemberment of an existing State. The report summarizes the results of a United Nations Round Table Conference with Netherlands and Indonesian representatives undertaken for the purpose of facilitating the transfer of sovereignty of the Dutch colonies to the Republic of the United States of Indonesia. During the negotiations, it was pointed out that the Provisional Constitution of the republic made reference only to an "internal right of self-determination," which was "the right of populations to determine, by democratic procedure, the status which their respective territories shall occupy within the federal structure of the Republic of the United States of Indonesia."[23] The Netherlands delegation, however, claimed to attach particular importance to an "external right of self-determination, that is, the right of populations to disassociate their respective territories from the Republic of the United States of Indonesia."[24]

When used in this manner, the right of "external" self-determination involved in the formation of a State seems to be the equivalent of what, in an already existing State, would be called a right of secession. In this case, the delegates reached a compromise that managed to encipher their understanding of the actual content of external self-determination. Plebiscites were to be held in certain territories under the auspices of the United Nations Commission for Indonesia to determine whether such territories would form component states of the republic. Each component state would then be given an opportunity to ratify the final constitution of the republic and, in the event a component state decided not to ratify, "it [would] be allowed to negotiate a special relationship with the Republic of the United States of Indonesia and the Kingdom of the Netherlands."[25] Neither the political alternative (should a plebiscite have revealed that a group did not want to become a component state) nor the nature of a "special relationship" was further elaborated.

As can be seen in the Indonesian situation, the problem of a segment of a State wishing to disassociate itself from the unified country falls neatly into an interstice between internal and external self-determination. The seceding province obviously wishes to readjust its political status vis-à-vis the remaining State (which seems an aspect of internal self-determination); yet by proclaiming itself an independent entity it

23. *Id.* 19, para. 52.
24. *Id.*
25. *Id.* 20.

may apparently resist any attempt at forced reunification under the principle of external self-determination (the parent State having become an "outside party").

One can, of course, avoid the particular difficulty posed by secession by restricting the scope of self-determination only to its internal aspect (the right of all groups in a State to influence governmental behavior in accordance with constitutional processes), thus leaving the principle of freedom from external interference to be included within the perhaps more suitable norms of nonintervention and the proscription of the use of force. A second alternative is to confine the meaning of self-determination entirely to its external aspect,[26] and to consider the degree of constitutional indulgence granted by a State to its citizens a matter essentially within its domestic jurisdiction. Neither restrictive approach is likely to find much international support given the tenor of current world opinion. The United Nations reaction to the Rhodesian and South African regimes continues to manifest a consensus that a State's treatment of constituent segments of its population is not always a matter solely within its domestic jurisdiction. Nor is a limitation of the principle of self-determination to internal matters likely to be popular in a climate of world opinion that delights in excoriating the old sin of colonialism and the new sin of "neo-colonialism," both of which are species of external interference with a people's economic and political destiny.

In short, the extraordinarily vague content of self-determination does not seem destined for any clear delimitation in the foreseeable future at the hands of either international jurists or international politicians. Indeed, the extension of the principle to concepts of economic and cultural self-determination (as opposed to political self-determination) portends an even further encroachment of the principle onto ground formerly considered the domain of other norms such as nonintervention and the proscription of force. The singular emotive appeal of the phrase is itself a reasonable guarantee of its future popularity even when the last vestiges of the mountain of colonialism have been swept away.

The Decolonization/Secession Distinction

The major role of the principle of self-determination since 1945 has been to provide a juridical foundation for the process of decolonization. In this task it has been remarkably successful. The United Nations has taken an unequivocal stand against the continuance of colo-

---

26. *See* quotation from HERTZ, *supra* note 11.

nial empires and has annually blessed the struggle of colonial peoples for independence in language that has grown increasingly virulent as more former colonies have become members. It is significant that there has never been an equivalent endorsement of a right of secession or even an expressly stated endorsement limited to circumstances of clear minority oppression.[27]

On grounds of political expediency the reason for this distinction between decolonization and secession is readily apparent. Colonialism has been seen by most members of the international community as a palpable evil. The product of the political thinking of less enlightened centuries, it seemed an ideal candidate for inclusion within the new principle of self-determination which, after all, had to have *some* content. Colonialism could also be denounced by most world leaders with righteous impunity because most were not themselves leaders of colonial Powers. Finally, and most importantly, there were a finite number of colonies on the globe in 1945. As long as it had no colonial possessions, a State embracing colonial self-determination in an ostentatious manner could squeeze a good deal of propaganda mileage out of a relatively harmless principle. Under these conditions, there was no danger that one's rhetoric could come hauntingly back on the lips of a disaffected rebel within one's own country.

The suggestion of an inclusion of a right to secession within the principle of self-determination lacks all of these political benefits. The boundaries of the right are by no means clear and the potential number of groups to which it could apply is vast. What is worse, no State's population is so homogeneous that its leaders may openly embrace the right without some lingering uneasiness. Nor could the United Nations (whose membership, interestingly, is limited to States — not nations or peoples) realistically be expected to advocate a principle that might operate to dismember the territory of its members.

The distinction is therefore easily explicable in terms of the political interests of the world community. One searches in vain, however, for any principled justification of why a colonial people wishing to cast off the domination of its governors has every moral and legal right to do so, but a manifestly distinguishable minority which happens to find itself, pursuant to a paragraph in some medieval territorial settlement or through a fiat of the cartographers, annexed to an independent State must forever remain without the scope of the principle of self-determination.

27. *See* discussion concerning "remedial secession," chapter 4, *infra.*

The evils of colonial status consist in the domination of a people by foreign governors (with its attendant injury to national and cultural pride) and the inability of the colonial subjects to control their own political destiny, often coupled with a degree of economic exploitation and denial of human rights. Should these same circumstances occur in the setting of an independent State exercising repressive control over a national or racial minority within its borders, the same remedy, independence, ought presumably to be accepted. The independent, unified State, whose territorial integrity is so jealously guarded by this restrictive approach to self-determination, may itself be the result of historical, military, and diplomatic fortuities quite unrelated to any cohesive desire of groups making up its population. International law is thus asked to perceive a distinction between the historical subjugation of an alien population living in a different part of the globe and the historical subjugation of an alien population living on a piece of land abutting that of its oppressors. The former can apparently never be legitimated by the mere passage of time, whereas the latter is eventually transformed into a protected status quo.

There have been some valiant, if misguided, attempts to limit the scope of self-determination by reading into the principle arbitrary limitations of some form. The famous "salt-water" test (which required a body of salt water separating the governing Power from the governed colony) was originally suggested as a method of assuring that self-determination would be applied only to overseas, European-type colonial situations. Even less convincing is the recent proposal of circumscribing the doctrine to "pigmentational self-determination"[28] which hopes to find in race the safety earlier pioneers sought in geography.

Despite a significant dearth of theoretical justifications, one must concede some practical considerations supporting the decolonization/secession distinction. Much of the decolonization process succeeded because twentieth-century colonial Powers tended to experience a kind of imperial fatigue in supporting their empires. Colonies that could once be profitably exploited with a minimum of effort

28. *See* A. MAZRUI, TOWARDS A PAX AFRICANA: A STUDY OF IDEOLOGY AND AMBITION 14–15 (1967) for a proposal using these terms. The pigmentation theory has received a scathing criticism in Kamanu, *Secession and the Right of Self-Determination: An O.A.U. Dilemma*, 12 J. MOD. AFRICAN STUDIES 355, 357 (1974): "Japan could colonise Korea, China could dominate Burma, the United States Cuba, and the Soviet Union Poland, without incurring international opprobrium since no breach of the right of pigmentational self-determination or racial sovereignty is involved! It is hard to imagine a better prescription for international chaos."

gradually became drains both upon the imperial Powers' economic and military resources and upon their reserve of international goodwill. As long as the imperial State retained its colonies, its bargaining position within international organizations was impaired and its global initiatives subject to a certain amount of political infirmity. This general predicament often eased the reluctance with which imperial Powers shed their colonies.

Many separatist movements attempt to introduce a corresponding fatigue in the population and ruling class of their governing State. In the majority of cases this takes the form of the separatist group becoming an irritant for its governors, a goal that can be accomplished through a whole spectrum of methods ranging from passive resistance to indiscriminate terrorist attacks. Activities such as terrorism and local resistance tend to embarrass the governing State internationally and encourage political division internally. At a certain point, so the theory goes, the benefits of continued union will be insufficient to outweigh the benefits to be gained from accepting the separatist demands, and the governing State will acquiesce in the secession.

There are, however, a number of crucial differences between the colonial and separatist models. An imperial Power may be willing to divest itself of a colony because the cost of transporting the political and military paraphernalia of government overseas becomes burdensome. They may also be induced to grant independence because current world opinion so overwhelmingly demands it. A polyethnic State, on the other hand, usually will not experience the same logistic difficulties in maintaining control over an area within its own borders. Nor has world opinion been canalized into a general disapproval of maintaining by force the unity of an established State in the face of separatist demands. Finally, rather than inducing a "fatigue" in the governing population, terrorist activities directed against the governing State often serve merely to intensify a desire to suppress the "rebels" and may increase the brutality with which it is done.

In conclusion, the present reluctance to accommodate the claims of secessionist groups within the principle of self-determination seems to be motivated primarily by a fear on the part of most independent States that such a principle would constitute an unmanageable threat to intra-State harmony and consequently have an adverse effect upon the stability of the international system. The recent consensus enjoyed by decolonization has perhaps been a misleading example in this regard. The world community there agreed that all colonial domination was undesirable—thereby imparting to the principle of self-determina-

tion a needlessly "all or nothing" tone. It would seem possible, however, to include within the scope of self-determination only "legitimate" claims to secession and thus shift the emphasis of discussion
onto the standards of legitimacy rather than maintain an unconvincing, inflexible denial of all such claims. Establishing guidelines
that restrict the applicability of the principle would remove the potentially anarchic effect of an unlimited endorsement of secession. Once
the political fears engendered by secession are assuaged, there remains no theoretical objection to its inclusion within the principle of
self-determination.

One final caveat is in order here. It is impossible to know how many
statements containing the phrase "right to self-determination" were *assumed* by their authors to refer only to the process of decolonization
and would be significantly recast under the influence of secessionist
proposals. Where the context does not demonstrate an awareness of
the possibly broader scope of self-determination, it seems wise to refrain from enlisting the statement as supporting a right of secession.
In other instances, the context of a particular pronouncement so
clearly refers to decolonization that, regardless of how broad the terminology or the intentions of *some* of the draftsmen, a cautious reader
must assume it to have a limited import. For purposes of this discussion, this latter category will include, for example, the General Assembly's 1960 *Declaration on the Granting of Independence to Colonial
Countries and Peoples,* which states very expansively that "all peoples
have the right to self-determination; by virtue of that right they freely
determine their own political status."[29]

THE CASE AGAINST SECESSION

Any proposals for the international recognition of secession as a legitimate exercise of self-determination in certain circumstances will
obviously encounter forceful objections from many independent
States. Although all of these objections may emerge from a single, almost visceral dread of secession as a threat to the very existence of
polyethnic States, the objections themselves can be divided into fears
of a psychopolitical nature and arguments more purely legal in character. It is of course very rare that the two kinds of arguments are
clearly distinguished in debates concerning this issue, but it is useful
to isolate their basic features before proceeding to a discussion of the
circumstances in which they have been raised.

29. G. A. Res. 1514, 15 U.N. GAOR, Supp. 16, at 66, U.N. Doc. A/4684 (1960).

The Legal Arguments

THE ARGUMENT FROM THE MAXIM *Pacta Sunt Servanda*

Ever since the heyday of the "social contract" theorists in the seventeenth and eighteenth centuries, it has been quite common to characterize a society as a contract either between the constituent citizens and their sovereign, or between the component groups making up the political association. The use of the contractual metaphor in this regard has led to an application of some maxims of contract law to the social condition, among the most important of which is the maxim *pacta sunt servanda.* Behind the Latin veneer, the law intends by this expression to affirm the rather rudimentary proposition that, all things being equal, contracts should be kept. The import of this principle to the social contract is clear. When a number of groups band together to form a social construct, they commit themselves to stand by their agreement and remain loyal to the social entity in return for the benefits of life in the larger association. To this explanation the self-determination theorist may add a further interpretation that the initial decision to join the society was a legitimate exercise of the right of self-determination by the associating groups. Once it has been exercised, the theorist would contend, these groups do not retain any residual right of self-determination in the form of an option unilaterally to secede from the society and disrupt its existence.[30]

Up to a certain point, this seems an unexceptionable proposition. No one would seriously suggest that self-determination demands that a group be whimsically free to disown a political act like joining an association or electing a government, within hours or days of its undertaking. To suggest, however, that a group has only one chance to exercise a self-determining right, and that once having done so it is forever wedded to its choice, is equally unrealistic. Does the freely chosen decision by a tribal people at the beginning of recorded history to align themselves with a neighboring empire really bind their twentieth-century descendants to an association with the heirs, successors, or assigns of that ancient imperial Power?

As a purported bar to all secessionist claims of legitimacy, this argument has three serious flaws. First, it places an unrealistic emphasis on the temporal identity of a community. For instance, we speak of "the British" fighting the Americans in 1776 but we all know that the ref-

---

30. *See, e.g.,* R. EMERSON, SELF-DETERMINATION REVISITED IN AN ERA OF DECOLONIZATION 28–30, Occasional Papers in International Affairs No. 9 (1964).

erence is to the British living during that period, persons whose temperament and circumstances may have been wholly unlike those of their modern descendants. Surely it is too much to ask that every successive generation patiently accept the "sins of its fathers," committed in some dimly remembered age, in the name of a fiction like the continuing identity of a community. Second, the argument requires at a minimum that the initial political choice should have been freely made. A truly free choice regarding the political destiny of a group is a rare enough occurrence even today to allow much doubt about its frequency in the ruder periods of our past. Third, every lawyer confronted with Latin phrases demanding that contracts once made require faithful adherence will have recourse to the opposing principle that a change in circumstances after the making of the contract permits a modification or abrogation of its terms. This principle, which comfortingly has its own Latin formulation as *rebus sic stantibus,* would seem to allow the renewal of a group's right to self-determination should their political situation radically change.[31]

THE ARGUMENT FROM THE PROBLEMATICAL STATUS OF "PEOPLES" AS SUBJECTS OF AN INTERNATIONAL RIGHT

Strictly speaking, the title "international" law is a misnomer. It is in fact an "inter-State" law which, according to traditional doctrinal teaching, purports to recognize as its subjects only sovereign States and to which individuals or groups have no direct access. If, as this view maintains, only States can have rights or duties under international law, then the so-called right of peoples to self-determination can at best place an obligation upon a State to accord its citizens a measure of self-determination, assuming that it has subscribed to treaties or international agreements requiring that it do so. It cannot

---

31. The Soviet jurist D. B. Levin adopts this position, saying:

When a nation exercises its right to self-determination, form[s] an independent state, voluntarily remains in a multinational state or joins another multinational state, its right to the free determination of its further internal political, economic, social and cultural status passes to the sphere of state law of the state to which the nation now belongs. But this holds good only as long as the conditions on which the nation became part of the given state are not violated by this state and as long as the nation's desire to stay within it remains in force, and it is not compelled to do so by coercive means. As soon as one of these phenomena occurs, the question again passes from the sphere of state law into the sphere of international law.

Levin, *The Principle of Self-Determination of Nations in International Law,* 1962 SOVIET Y.B. INT'L L. 45, 46.

mean, so the argument goes, that the peoples themselves have such a right nor are they in a position to demand that their governing State comply with their self-determining wishes. S. Prakash Sinha articulates the argument in the following way:

> A state's obligation under international law may find its counter-part in another state's right, but not in the right of a people. . . . [I]t is either a state or the community of states forming the United Nations which can seek performance of a state's obligation to accord self-determination to its people, not the people of that state. . . . What is involved here in terms of international law is the international obligation of a state and not the right of its people.[32]

Although confirmed by many venerable jurists over the last few centuries, this doctrine is no longer an accurate description of con-temporary international law (if, indeed, it ever was[33]). The assault on the State-centered prejudice of international law has been pursued on a number of fronts. For example, individuals are now widely consid-ered to be proper subjects of the international law concerned with hu-man rights; transnational corporations are well on the way to being given some form of international personality and made directly re-sponsible for certain obligations under international law, and, despite severe opposition, some so-called national liberation organizations have recently been accorded a representative status within inter-national organizations although they do not speak for independent States. Perhaps most significantly for our purposes, the United Na-tions General Assembly has stopped its previous practice of address-ing its resolutions to States—asking them to respect the right of their citizens or colonial subjects to self-determination—and has begun to affirm directly the right of the peoples themselves to compel the com-pliance of their governors.[34]

THE ARGUMENT FROM MUTUALITY

The final legalistic objection to an unlimited endorsement of seces-sionist legitimacy takes the form of a *tu quoque* argument or, as it is

---

32. Sinha, *Self-Determination in International Law and Its Applicability to the Baltic Peoples*, Res Baltica 256–57 (A. Sprudzs & A. Rusis eds. 1968).

33. *See* St. Korowicz, *supra* note 10, at 327–38. *See also* G. Ezejiofor, Protection of Human Rights under the Law 15–32 (1964); Lauterpacht, *The Subjects of International Law*, 63 Law Q. Rev. 438 (1947), 64 Law Q. Rev. 97 (1948).

34. *See* text accompanying notes 66–67 *infra*.

called here, an argument from mutuality. It begins with a look at the opposite side of the secessionist coin; that is, the legal constraints upon the freedom of the dominant portion of an independent State to oust one of its component provinces.[35] This sort of secession-in-reverse does not require a hostile interregion atmosphere. Consider the situation of a State containing within its borders a province that contributes little or nothing to the economic, political, or strategic welfare of the whole community. This province may also consume, as does Northern Ireland in the United Kingdom, a disproportionate amount of government aid and public resources. In such a case, it is conceivable that the governing State, despite a strong sense of good fellowship toward the people of the burdensome province, might nonetheless feel that it would be better not to be associated with them. Can such a State, in conformity with international law, unilaterally calve off the province without regard for the economic, political, or strategic future of the territory as an independent entity? Does the State have an obligation to the other members of the world community not to clutter the map with helplessly small, powerless political units? In short, is there an international duty to support one's ailing children?

Unfortunately, definitive answers to these questions cannot easily be found. The general territorial acquisitiveness of States coupled with the belief that *any* territory is of some stategic importance, if only as a *cordon sanitaire* around the more valuable regions, makes the voluntary relinquishment of a component province an extremely rare occurrence unless it is ceded to another State in return for some benefits (in which case, of course, these particular questions do not arise). Significantly, the most notable recent example of a voluntary relinquishment of a province (South Africa's creation of the Republic of Transkei in October 1976 out of one of its "black homelands") received a chilly response from the world community. This action was seen as a culmination of South Africa's policy of separate development of its ethnic groups (apartheid) and was disapproved on that basis.[36]

35. One must say "dominant" here rather than simply "majority" in order to avoid confusion with cases involving secession of a segment of a State which contains the majority of the State's population but which has been clearly subservient to the dominant minority. This was, in fact, the situation of the more populous East Pakistan (Bangla Desh) in its secession from West Pakistan in 1971. *See* text accompanying note 203, chapter 3 *infra*.

36. *See* N.Y. Times, Oct. 26, 1976, at 1, cols. 1–3. A second black tribal homeland, Bophuthatswana, is scheduled to achieve independence in December 1977. N.Y. Times, Jan. 25, 1977, at 4, cols. 5–6.

Aside from such rare examples of the actual relinquishment of territory, there are at least five related situations—all of which are arguably regulated by some standards of international conduct—which might suggest some legal constraints on a State's ability to discharge a component province at its pleasure. The first case, which shares some common elements with our example, is that of a colonial Power abandoning its colony without the proper preparation and safeguards for an orderly transfer of government to native authorities. Where this has occurred, as in Belgium's hasty retreat from the Congo in 1960, colonial Powers have been criticized for failing in their international obligation to prepare the territory for self-government.[37]

The second situation is that of a State attempting to cede part of its territory to another State without the consent of the inhabitants. Although occasionally disputed,[38] a growing opinion suggests that a State must consult the wishes of the inhabitants of a region for which a cession is contemplated and that a failure to do so is a violation of their right to self-determination.[39]

The third situation is that of the compulsory transfer or exchange of large populations such as those that took place between Greece and Bulgaria, and Greece and Turkey, during the 1920s.[40] At first, the transfer of populations in this manner was welcomed as an obvious way of achieving national integration without juggling international

37. Of course, there was a tendency on the part of some colonial Powers to abuse this principle by negligently failing to prepare colonial subjects for independence and then using this lack of preparedness as a basis for continuing colonial rule. This prompted the United Nations General Assembly to include in its Resolution 1514 (1960) the following provision: "Inadequacy of political, economic or educational preparedness should never serve as a pretext for delaying independence." 15 U.N. GAOR, Supp. 16, at 66, U.N. Doc. A/4684 (1960).

38. See, e.g., L. OPPENHEIM, 1 INTERNATIONAL LAW: A TREATISE, § 219 (8th ed., H. Lauterpacht ed. 1955): "It is doubtful whether the Law of Nations will ever make it a condition of every cession that it must be ratified by a plebiscite." Cf. I. BROWNLIE, PRINCIPLES OF PUBLIC INTERNATIONAL LAW 174 (2d ed. 1973).

39. For a discussion of juristic opinion on this issue see H. JOHNSON, SELF-DETERMINATION WITHIN THE COMMUNITY OF NATIONS 59–61 (1967). See also Chen, Reisman, Who Owns Taiwan: A Search for International Title, 81 YALE L. J. 599, 638 (1972): "The doctrines of self-determination and the prohibition of the use of force for territorial changes ... [have] transformed the component of acquiescence of the indigenous people into a peremptory aspect, and a virtual requirement of lawful transfers of title" [footnotes omitted].

40. See S. LADAS, THE EXCHANGE OF MINORITIES: BULGARIA, GREECE, AND TURKEY (1932); Séfériadès, L'Echange des Populations, 24 ACADEMIE DE DROIT INTERNATIONAL, RECUEIL DES COURS 311 (1945).

frontiers. However, the enormous hardship it entails for the people involved, added to the unsatisfactory experience with population transfers after the First World War, have made this device the subject of a good deal of juristic criticism.[41] In addition, the same arguments which suggest that a cession, to be in compliance with the principle of self-determination, must be ratified by the local inhabitants, apply mutatis mutandis to a transfer of populations between States.

The deliberate deprivation of large numbers of people of their nationality by a State is also related to the present issue. Although normally the denationalization of an individual person is not a matter for international concern, nevertheless where a minority group is rendered stateless in this manner international interest might be justified in light of the implications of such behavior upon norms protecting human rights and/or self-determination. A clearer breach of international law would attend the simultaneous deprivation of nationality and expulsion of such a group, because foreign States would then be directly burdened with finding a residence for the expelled people.[42]

Finally, the mass expulsion of a minority group who are not nationals of the expelling State is also relevant here, although again this does not involve a transfer of land. A notable example of this was the expulsion by President Idi Amin of the Ugandan Asian minority in 1972. Once again, international law appears to put some serious restrictions on a State's freedom to expel minorities at its pleasure, even minorities that are technically subjects of another Power.[43] Furthermore, at least some of these restrictions may arise from the right of the peoples concerned to self-determination. Thus, one recent study concludes, "A nation intent on expelling a minority would surely deny that this minority is entitled to self-determination, which might well entail secession rather than expulsion! It would appear, however, that under any sensible interpretation of the principle of self-determination, the mass expulsion of a people would be illegal." [44]

If, as these analogies suggest, a State is under certain legal obliga-

41. *See* INSTITUT DE DROIT INTERNATIONAL, 44/2 ANNUAIRE 138–199 (Session de Sienne 1952).

42. For an interesting discussion *see* D. O'CONNELL, 2 INTERNATIONAL LAW 742–43 (1965). *Cf.* U.N. *Convention on the Reduction of Statelessness,* art. 8, in UNITED NATIONS, HUMAN RIGHTS: A COMPILATION OF INTERNATIONAL INSTRUMENTS OF THE UNITED NATIONS 57, 59, U.N. Doc. ST/HR/1 (1973).

43. *See* Sharma, Wooldridge, *Some Legal Questions Arising from the Expulsion of the Uganda Asians,* 23 INT'L & COMP. L.Q. 397 (1974).

44. Zayas, *International Law and Mass Population Transfers,* 16 HARV. INT'L L. J. 207, 245 (1975).

tions vis-a-vis its component provinces and may not unilaterally evict them without regard for their future wellbeing or the effect of the new entity upon the international order, then a strong argument from mutuality may be made in support of the proposition that a component segment of a State may not unilaterally secede from its fellows without, at least, also satisfying certain conditions under international law. The argument in effect amounts to this: if the majority or dominant group is hindered by international law in its ability to cast out the minority, then the minority should be similarly fettered to the majority in its implementation of a secessionist demand.

The Specter of Secession

As a general principle, entities blessed with recognition as independent States by their sister States in the world community are reluctant to permit part of their population and territory to be removed from their boundaries. Secession will almost invariably result in a diminution of the unified State's wealth, resources, and power, thereby lowering its economic stamina, defensive capability, and potential international influence. Depending on their circumstances, some States will find the enormous societal trauma of a partition mortally disruptive to the life of the country or will fear the creation of a new, and possibly hostile, neighbor on its constricted borders. Nor can a State ignore the possibility that the seceding province will choose to annex itself to a traditionally antagonistic neighbor (as in the present Somalia/Ethiopia dispute) or cede part of its new territory to a hostile foreign Power (as the Huguenots were willing to cede the port of Le Havre to the English in return for assistance during their wars with Catholic France[45]). Thus, each member of the world community will experience some unique uneasiness with the mention of secession, for reasons related to its own peculiar situation, and no generalization of such individual concerns can be made.

On a more universal level, however, the political and emotional fears expressed in response to suggestions of secessionist self-determination tend to follow certain identifiable patterns. As a matter of argumentative form, most critics of the principle begin by pointing to the difficulties involved in limiting an international endorsement of this form of self-determination and then paint a rather apocalyptic portrait of a world so foolish as to recognize an unqualified right to secession. It might be helpful here to introduce the more fundamental apprehensions underlying this reaction.

45. *See generally* J. BLACK, THE REIGN OF ELIZABETH 1558–1603, at 57–58 (2d ed. 1959).

THE FEAR OF BALKANIZATION

By far the most frequent cry raised against the principle of secessionist self-determination is that it will result in a multiplicity of small, squabbling States, especially in areas where tribal or clannish divisions are still pervasive. It would, so the argument goes, give free rein to the parochial instincts of the countless insular groups around the world, resulting in an unhealthy fractionalization of previously unified States. Many of the resulting smaller units might then lack a viable economic base, strong political structure, and adequate military defense. It is assumed that this process, often termed Balkanization, would inevitably result in injury to both the internal social harmony of these territories and the general international order.

THE FEAR OF INDEFINITE DIVISIBILITY

What troubles both jurist and politician alike when discussing a right of secessionist self-determination is what might be called (to engage in a bit of pedantry) the threat of indefinite divisibility. That is, no State, no nation, has a population so homogeneous that it cannot be subdivided into smaller groups of greater homogeneity simply by altering the standards of what constitutes a "distinct" group. Once a right to secession is admitted, there are no clear limits to this process; it could conceivably be carried on until each clan or atomic family within a society constituted an entity entitled to self-determination. International jurists are understandably loath to acknowledge a "right" which could, for instance, justify the establishment of West Philadelphia as a member of the international community or entitle the Hatfields or McCoys to proclaim themselves an autonomous group. The present international legal system is based on the somewhat artificial institution of recognized States. In the absence of any invisible perforations along which the peoples of the world may be properly divided, a principle that would extend to any group regardless of size the right to participate in this system is obviously extremely dangerous. Additionally, a province that has itself just seceded is in an awkward political position to oppose a further secession by one of its own component groups.

THE FEAR OF THE EFFECT ON THE DEMOCRATIC SYSTEM

The first precept of any democratic system is that the will of the majority must prevail as long as all parties have been given the opportunity to express views and influence community decisions. An inter-

national recognition of secession, it is argued, would drastically undermine this system by allowing a disaffected minority to threaten
dismemberment if State policies do not reflect their wishes. It is con-
tended that a democracy can function only as long as a further remedy, like secession, is not available to those failing to persuade the majority on a course of conduct. Presumably, the existence of such a
further remedy might prove too great a temptation to the minority in
moments of heated dispute or political disappointment. In addition, it
might mandate a debilitating caution on the part of governments in
pursuing necessary, but partially unpopular, measures.[46]

THE FEAR OF INFIRM STATES

As a corollary to the fear of Balkanization, the international community may justifiably be concerned with the threat that some of the
numerous small entities resulting from the dismemberment of unified
States will be unable to maintain a viable economic posture and thus
become insupportable burdens on international charity.[47] The strain
upon development and foreign aid programs is already quite formidable and it may be assumed that many donor-States will react negatively to what they perceive as a self-inflicted wound by the donees. A
further burden will be placed upon the international community
should a significant percentage of these entities be unable to meet
their assessments for international organizations like the United Nations.[48]

THE FEAR OF "TRAPPED" MINORITIES

The secession of a national, racial, or religious group from a more
heterogeneous State may well result in some nonmembers of this dis-
tinctive group becoming trapped within the seceding province. Unwilling or unable to leave their homes and employment, such minority
pockets may lose the protection of civil rights legislation that mollified
the rivalry of groups in the more diverse, unified State. They remain

46. A recognized right of secession may also have a sobering effect on the majority's
policy decisions by chilling any temptation to exceed legal or constitutional limits on
their power. For a discussion of this phenomenon in Burma (which at one time constitutionally recognized a right of secession) see Silverstein, *Politics in the Shan State: The
Question of Secession from the Union of Burma*, 18 J. ASIAN STUDIES 43, 57 (1958).

47. *Cf.* Bowett, *Self-Determination and Political Rights in the Developing Countries*, 1966
AM. SOC. INT'L L. PROC. 129, 131 (1966).

48. These issues are discussed under the heading "The Disruption Factor" in chapter
4 *infra*.

behind as "aliens" in an area which is, *ex hypothesi,* the creation of strong parochial sentiment and are therefore exposed to a danger of discrimination, harassment, or worse. The treatment of Hindus remaining in Pakistan and Moslems in India after the partition is a convenient example of the serious risks facing trapped minorities after a geographical division.

A related concern might arise when a proposed secession would remove from the unified State a powerful ethnic minority predominately, but not exclusively, domiciled in the separating province. Where this group had successfully assured some protection of the ethnic minority as a whole in the unified State, and there is reason to expect that some mistreatment of the remaining members of the minority would follow after the removal of this protection, the secession might have the consequence of leaving those members of this minority living in other areas of the country without their traditional protectors and without the political influence they had enjoyed previously as part of a powerful minority.[49]

THE FEAR OF "STRANDED" MAJORITIES

The seceding province need not always be an impoverished region willing to suffer economic discomfort for the emotional satisfaction of self-government. On the contrary, one significant cause of secessionist feeling has historically been an awareness of the wealth of the province vis-à-vis the remaining State and a sense that the province could do much better on its own than by sharing its resources with the larger unified State. In these cases the concern is not with the secessionists' chances of survival but rather with the future of the remaining area when stripped of its economic base. The alternatives for a remaining population, whose most valuable resources may have been surgically removed by secession, are indeed grim. They must either become dependent upon international charity or be forced to annex themselves to a neighboring State or possibly to their own former province (both of which are arguably irreconcilable with the principle of self-determination). The secession of Katanga from the Congo, Biafra from Nigeria, and the recent separatist rumblings of Scotland all

49. Pierre Elliot Trudeau has advanced the following argument in the context of the Canadian situation: "As for French minorities in other provinces, they can only have a future if Quebec establishes itself as a strong, progressive force *within* Confederation; if Quebec withdraws into itself or secedes, these French minorities will have approximately the same rights and the same influence as cultural groups of German origin in Canada." P. TRUDEAU, FEDERALISM AND THE FRENCH CANADIANS 34 (1968).

evidence the temptation for a wealthy (or soon to be wealthy) province to abandon its less fortunate fellows.

SELF-DETERMINATION AS AN INTERNATIONAL NORM

Even a casual student of the discipline will quickly realize that international law embraces certain behavioral norms which, by virtue of their fundamental nature, are intended to be the first principles of civilized international conduct. Although occasionally subject to circumstantial exceptions, these principles are recognized as the starting points in the formulation of a State's external conduct and they operate as a touchstone against which the international community can measure the legal acceptability of the actions of its members.

Having said this much, one must resist the notion that even these few principles are universal in the sense that they enjoy a timeless existence similar to Plato's Forms or Newton's law of gravity—an existence that passively awaits discovery by the searching intellect of man. On the contrary, they are disturbingly mortal. Such principles are born when a significant number of States are willing publicly to announce the importance of the norms (and their correlative principles) in structuring their international policies or when they show an implicit acceptance of such principles as normative constraints on the States' freedom of action in the international sphere. Nor do such principles emerge full-grown from the loins of the world's decision-making elites. They have by necessity an evolutionary character, adaptable to the shifting exigencies of international life and capable of adjusting emphasis to meet the evasive ingenuities of international policy advisors. An unfortunate but inescapable corollary of this view is the conclusion that these peremptory norms can be extinguished if their consensual base is withdrawn.[50]

A convenient example of the process of the birth and maturation of international norms may be seen in the principle outlawing war as an instrument of national policy which was announced with a good deal of fanfare in 1928 in what has come to be called the Kellogg-Briand Pact. The circumstances left no doubt that the parties to the pact were

---

50. *Cf.* the definition of "peremptory norm" in article 53 of the Vienna *Convention on the Law of Treaties* as a "norm accepted and recognized by the international community of States as a whole as a norm from which no derogation is permitted and which can be modified only by a subsequent norm of general international law having the same character." 8 INT'L LEGAL MAT. 679, 699 (1969). *See generally* Onuf, Birney, *Peremptory Norms of International Law: Their Source, Function, and Future,* 4 DEN. J. INT'L L. & POL. 187 (1975).

in effect creating an international norm rather than "discovering" a preexisting one or even codifying the old and venerable doctrine of a "just" war.[51] From this proscription of war as an instrument of national policy has evolved article 2(4) of the United Nations Charter which prohibits the "threat or use of force." "Force," in the context of 2(4), has been widely seen as encompassing not simply the traditional strict definition of international war but also undeclared war, "indirect" aggression, arming of subversive groups within another State, war by proxy, and so on.[52] Most recently, a controversy has centered on the inclusion of even more subtle forms of force (such as economic or political coercion) either within the ambit of 2(4) [53] or as an aspect of a related norm.[54]

As the trend to outlaw aggressive war in this century demonstrates, however, a peremptory norm does not necessarily lose this character merely because it fails to command strict adherence in the behavior of States. That is, such norms were never intended to be a simple generalization of uniform State practice in a certain area; they represent some consensus concerning what *ought* to happen which must be regarded as more than a precatory suggestion. Because they typically seek to prevent or limit undesirable international conduct, the true effect of peremptory norms can never be measured with accuracy. One is asked to accept as a matter of faith that more of such undesirable conduct would have occurred in the absence of the promulgation of the international norm.

The 1970 U.N. General Assembly *Declaration on Friendly Relations* attempts a fairly explicit elaboration of seven primary norms of international conduct expressly stated or implicit in the United Nations Charter, including the principle prohibiting the use of force, the principle of nonintervention, and the principle of equal rights and self-determination of peoples.[55] A naive observer might well assume that, at

51. *See generally* J. SHOTWELL, WAR AS AN INSTRUMENT OF NATIONAL POLICY (1928); I. BROWNLIE, INTERNATIONAL LAW AND THE USE OF FORCE BY STATES 80–92 (1963).

52. *See* Int'l L. Comm'n, Report, 6 U.N. GAOR, Supp. 9, at 9, U.N. Doc. A/1858 (1951).

53. *See, e.g.,* Buchheit, *The Use of Nonviolent Coercion: A Study in Legality under Article 2(4) of the Charter of the United Nations,* in ECONOMIC COERCION AND THE NEW INTERNATIONAL ECONOMIC ORDER 41 (R. Lillich ed. 1976).

54. *See* Bowett, *Economic Coercion and Reprisals by States,* 13 VA. J. INT'L L. 1 (1972).

55. *Declaration on Principles of International Law concerning Friendly Relations and Co-operation among States in Accordance with the Charter of the United Nations,* G. A. Res. 2625, 25 U.N. GAOR, Supp. 28, at 121, U.N. Doc. A/8028 (1971). The portions of the Declaration dealing with the "principle of equal rights and self-determination of peoples" are reprinted in Appendix 1 of this book.

least on this highest level of normative discussion, the principles artic-ulated in this declaration form an harmonious whole, blessedly free of the occasional contradictions and dissonances that might plague the formulation of temporary, hastily considered regulations.[56] This is, of course, very far from the mark. In one sense, the universality of these principles virtually guarantees their conflict when translated into the gritty realm of State practice. The primary danger is that, without a hierarchical ordering of these principles, antagonists in the inter-national arena are left to justify their conflicting policies by reference to alternative "first principles" of international conduct. The prefer-ence of one norm over another by a given State at a given time can therefore often be dictated by simple political expediency with relative legal impunity. An additional uncertainty arises when one questions whether such broadly stated norms are, or ought to be, limited to the applications intended by their articulators at the time of pronounce-ment or whether they are expansive, evolutionary, and therefore, in part, perpetually vague as regards their marginal applicability.

The relationship between the principle of self-determination and the norms of nonintervention and proscription of the use of force provides an interesting example of this tension. The prohibition against the threat or use of force in international relations embodied in article 2(4) of the United Nations Charter has been called the "principal norm of international law of our time." [57] It is com-plemented by the principle of nonintervention by States in the inter-nal affairs of sister States which, although not mentioned per se in the charter,[58] has been recognized by the General Assembly in its 1965 *Declaration on the Inadmissibility of Intervention in the Domestic Affairs of States and the Protection of Their Independence and Sovereignty,*[59] and the 1970 *Declaration on Friendly Relations.*[60] These principles are meant to

---

56. The General Assembly itself apparently does not perceive any tension among these principles. In a previous (1966) resolution, *Strict Observance of the Prohibition of the Threat or Use of Force in International Relations and the Right of Peoples to Self-Determination,* the General Assembly strictly reaffirmed the principle contained in article 2(4) and also in the same document proclaimed that "peoples subjected to colonial oppression are en-titled to seek and receive *all* support in their struggle" (emphasis mine). G. A. Res. 2160, 21 U.N. GAOR, Supp. 16, at 4, U.N. Doc. A/6316 (1966).

57. Henkin, *The Reports of the Death of Article 2(4) Are Greatly Exaggerated,* 65 Am. J. Int'l L. 544 (1971).

58. Article 2(7) of the U.N. Charter provides that nothing in the charter "shall au-thorize the United Nations to intervene in matters which are essentially within the do-mestic jurisdiction of any State."

59. G. A. Res. 2131, 20 U.N. GAOR, Supp. 14, at 11, 12, U.N. Doc. A/6014 (1966).

60. *Supra* note 55, at 123–24.

have general applicability, and a deviation from them in a State's international conduct must be justified under a recognized doctrinal exception (such as self-defense, humanitarian intervention, or the like). They exist side by side with the principle of self-determination of peoples which is mentioned in article 1(2) of the Charter and reinforced by a veritable blizzard of General Assembly and Security Council resolutions over the years.[61] Self-determination, as appealingly characterized by Judge Fouad Ammoun in his Separate Opinion in the *Barcelona Traction* case, is one of those norms "profoundly imbued with the sense of natural justice, morality and humane ideals." [62]

Stated bluntly, the issue comes down to this: does a State that supports (politically, economically, or militarily) a movement for self-determination on the part of a people somewhere else in the world violate the norms against the use of force and nonintervention or can it legitimate its behavior by claiming that it responds to the demands of the alternative principle of self-determination of peoples, which transforms what would otherwise be admittedly delictual conduct into a legitimate, perhaps even laudatory, policy? A related question asks whether a State that aids a sister State in the suppression of a group under its control claiming a right to self-determination has violated the principle of self-determination and/or the principle of nonintervention despite any permission or request for intervention from the governing State.

A great deal of evidence can be marshalled either to support or to deny the right to intervene in furtherance of a self-determination struggle. Much of the problem turns on whether one gives a broad reading to statements that mention self-determination in a context suggesting its applicability to noncolonial circumstances and thus suggest a possible right of intervention in secessionist/separatist movements. The General Assembly, for example, has clearly expressed its conviction that in circumstances involving colonial *and* alien domination and racist regimes, peoples have an "inherent right to struggle by all necessary means at their disposal against colonial Powers and alien domination in exercise of their right of self-determination." [63]

In the colonial context at least, the General Assembly has gone fur-

61. *See* Sinha, *Is Self-Determination Passé?* 12 COLUM. J. TRANSNAT'L L. 260, 268 n. 37 (1973) for an extensive list of these resolutions.

62. [1970] I.C.J. 3, 310, 311.

63. *Basic Principles of the Legal Status of the Combatants Struggling against Colonial and Alien Domination and Racist Regimes,* G. A. Res. 3103, Dec. 12, 1973, reprinted in 68 AM. J. INT'L L. 379 (1974). *Cf.* the General Assembly's recent effort to define aggression

ther than merely bestowing its imprimatur on the struggle of peoples seeking self-determination; it has occasionally made direct requests that States provide aid for national liberation movements in colonial territories. Prior to the middle 1960s, the General Assembly satisfied itself with exhorting member States to use their influence with certain colonial Powers to reform the latter States' insensitivity regarding the demands of self-determination. Typical of this approach is the 1962 resolution *Territories under Portuguese Administration*,[64] paragraph 6 of which states that the Assembly

> *calls upon* Member States to use all their influence to induce the Portuguese Government to carry out the obligations incumbent upon it under Chapter XI of the Charter of the United Nations and the resolutions of the General Assembly relating to the Territories under its administration.[65]

By 1965, however, the General Assembly began wording its requests in the more aggressive form of calls upon States to lend moral and material aid to the national liberation movements themselves. This phraseology appears to authorize both intervention by third States in the affairs of a colonial Power and the extension of support, including military support, to a national liberation movement. On the theoretical level, the assembly apparently concluded both that the employment of interventionary force in such situations did not violate the principles against the use of force and intervention, and also that such claims for national liberation were not properly within the colonial Power's sphere of "domestic jurisdiction." By way of example, paragraph 3 of a 1965 resolution dealing with territories under Portuguese administration bluntly

> *appeals* to all States . . . to render the people of the Territories under Portuguese administration the moral and material support necessary for the restoration of their inalienable rights.[66]

---

which states that nothing in the definition could prejudice the right of self-determination, "particularly [of] peoples under colonial and racist regimes or other forms of alien domination." 13 INT'L LEGAL MAT. 710, 714 (1974).

64. G. A. Res. 1807, 17 U.N. GAOR, Supp. 17, at 39, 40, U.N. Doc. A/5217 (1963).

65. This was followed in paragraph 7 with a request that all States refrain from offering the Portuguese government any assistance which would enable it to continue its repression. *Id.* 40. For "influence" language in other resolutions see G. A. Res. 1699 para. 7, 16 U.N. GAOR, Supp. 17, at 38, U.N. Doc. A/5100 (1961); G. A. Res. 1889, 18 U.N. GAOR, Supp. 15, at 46, U.N. Doc. A/5515 (1964).

66. G.A. Res. 2107, *Question of Territories under Portuguese Administration*, 20 U.N. GAOR, Supp. 14, at 62, U.N. Doc. A/6014 (1966).

This form of resolution, which requests that States offer aid directly to the group struggling for self-determination, has now become quite common.[67] To the same effect is the 1970 *Declaration on Friendly Relations* provision which proclaims that, "in their actions against, and resistance to, such forcible action [which deprives peoples of their right to self-determination] in pursuit of the exercise of their right to self-determination, such peoples are entitled to seek and to receive support in accordance with the purposes and principles of the Charter."[68]

On the strength of such General Assembly pronouncements, a State wishing to relegate nonintervention and the prohibition against the use of force to a secondary normative status and to intervene, even forcibly, on behalf of a people struggling for self-determination would seem to have a colorable claim for the legality of its action.[69] This certainly seems to be the case in circumstances of a colonial struggle for self-determination, and some of the resolution language arguably supports a belief that the right to intervene extends beyond the colonial situation into cases of "alien" domination or control by a "racist" regime.[70] The contention that norms of nonintervention and nonuse of force can be overridden by the principle of self-determination has occasionally been explicitly voiced in the international forum. The No-

67. *See* G.A. Res. 2022 para. 10, 20 U.N. GAOR, Supp. 14, at 62, U.N. Doc. A/6014 (1966); G.A. Res. 2074 para. 12, *id.* at 60, 61; G.A. Res. 2151 para. 10, 21 U.N. GAOR, Supp. 16, at 68, 69, U.N. Doc. A/6316 (1967); G.A. Res. 2189 para. 7, *id.* at 5, 6; G.A. Res. 2184 para. 6, *id.* at 70; G.A. Res. 2383 para. 14, 23 U.N. GAOR, Supp. 18, at 58, U.N. Doc. A/7218 (1969); G.A. Res. 2395 para. 5, *id.* at 59; G.A. Res. 2918 para. 4, 27 U.N. GAOR, Supp. 30, at 75, 76, U.N. Doc. A/8730 (1973); G.A. Res. 2945 para. 7, *id.* at 77, 78; G.A. Res. 2983 para. 2, *id.* at 84; G.A. Res. 3031 para. 10(b), *id.* at 88, 89.

68. *Supra* note 55, U.N. Doc. A/8028 at 124. The relationship of self-determination to other international norms was extensively discussed by the Special Committee drafting the declaration. For a summary *see* Šuković, *supra* note 21, at 358–68. A similar statement in paragraph 6 of the *Declaration on Inadmissibility, supra* note 59, U.N. Doc. A/6014 at 12, exhorting "All states . . . [to] contribute to the complete elimination of racial discrimination in all its forms and manifestations" has been perceived as potentially being "radically interventionary." R. VINCENT, NONINTERVENTION IN INTERNATIONAL ORDER 239–240 (1974).

69. One writer acknowledges that a "realistic appraisal of current world values leads inevitably to the conclusion that self-determination is a co-equal prime value [i.e. co-equal with peace] to many states." Dugard, *Towards the Definition of International Terrorism*, 67 AM. SOC. INT'L L. PROC. 94, 97 (1973).

70. *See, e.g.,* text accompanying note 63 *supra*. For an opinion that the secessionists of Bangla Desh were legally entitled (1) not to have force used against them, and (2) to seek military support in pursuance of their right to self-determination, *see* Nawaz, *Bangla Desh and International Law*, 11 INDIAN J. INT'L L. 251, 256–57 (1971).

vember 13, 1974, speech of Yasir Arafat before the United Nations, for instance, expressed the opinion that the right of a people to self-determination justifies a right to wage war internationally in support of that right.[71] The Soviet doctrine of wars of national liberation uniformly supports and encourages the use of force by peoples struggling for self-determination and authorizes intervention by third parties on behalf of such peoples[72] (at least where the struggle takes place in a noncommunist country). It is equally vigorous in condemning, as unlawful, aid given to governments frustrating the right of a people to self-determination.[73] In the recent debate over controlling international terrorism, a number of governments have explicitly stated their view that certain activities undertaken to further the right of self-determination should not be considered international terrorism.[74]

Of course, no one seriously suggests that interventionary force may legally be used to aid a group illegitimately claiming a right to self-determination. Under the present legal order, however, there is no clear basis in law for criticizing an intervenor's subjective decision regarding the legitimacy of a group's claim to self-determination or for criticizing its judgment in giving priority in its normative hierarchy to the principle of self-determination over nonintervention and the prohibition of force. It is clear that at the present time, therefore, the effi-

71. N.Y. Times, Nov. 14, 1974, at 22–23. *See also* the views of the Ghanaian delegation summarized in the Summary Record of the 40th Meeting, 1966 Special Committee on Principles of International Law concerning Friendly Relations and Co-operation among States, U.N. Doc. A/AC.125/SR.40, at 8–9 (1966).

72. *See, e.g.*, Schmeltzer, *Soviet and American Attitudes toward Intervention: The Dominican Republic, Hungary and Czechoslovakia*, 11 VA. J. INT'L L. 97, 101 (1970). In the opinion of one Soviet writer:

> The principle of self-determination introduces new content in the principle of nonintervention in the domestic affairs of a state. . . . By virtue of the universal international recognition of the right of all people and nations to self-determination, assistance by foreign states to a nation fighting for its national liberation cannot be regarded as intervention in the domestic affairs of the state which oppresses the given nation and against which its struggle is directed.

Levin, *supra* note 31, at 48.

73. *See* Mitrovic, *The Principle of Non-Intervention in Contemporary International Law*, 1964 JUGOSLOVENSKA REVIJA ZA MEDUNARODNO PRAVO 29, 41.

74. *See, e.g.*, debates in the Sixth Committee on the *Draft Covenant on Measures to Prevent International Terrorism*, 27 U.N. GAOR, 6th Comm. 1355th–1370th meetings (1972). For explicit statements of this sentiment *see, e.g.*, comments of Mr. Tchankou, *id.*, 1359th meeting, para. 48, and Mr. Badawi, 1368th meeting, para. 9. *See also* Dugard, *International Terrorism: Problems of Definition*, 50 INT'L AFF. 67, 75–77 (1974).

cacy of these latter norms is seriously impaired in circumstances involving even a colorable claim to self-determination. The only exception to this disturbing conclusion arises in the rare cases where an international judgment regarding the legitimacy of a particular claim for self-determination (as in the Eritrean situation[75]) provides a basis for criticizing intervention on behalf of the "illegitimate" party.

It must be admitted, however, that Western juristic opinion runs strongly against the calculus outlined above for justifying third-party intervention on behalf of a people seeking self-determination. Nevertheless, there has been no clear consensus among jurists regarding the underlying rationale for this opinion. One response has been to advocate, on the normative level, an implicit hierarchy among the norms of nonintervention, the prohibition of force, and self-determination which would give preference to the former two principles, at least until more distinct boundaries of the principle of self-determination coalesce out of the present fog of State practice and General Assembly resolutions. R. J. Vincent, for example, has argued that within the framework of the United Nations Charter the principles of nonintervention and proscription of the use of force are of a qualitatively different nature from the principles of human rights and fundamental freedoms (among which, presumably, is the principle of self-determination). He writes: "The Charter . . . was primarily concerned with building an order between states not within them, with eliminating international war not civil conflict. Its concern with human rights and fundamental freedoms, values whose defense would require an intrusion into a traditionally domestic matter, was more aspiration than legislation." [76]

The extreme opinion advocates a right to intervene on behalf of a central government to help suppress an insurrection and a categorical denial of any corresponding right to aid the insurgents.[77] Such an attitude asks the international community to blind itself to the possibility of a legitimate claim to self-determination justifying intervention on

75. G.A. Res. 390, 5 U.N. GAOR, Supp. 20, at 20–22, U.N. Doc. A/1775 (1950).

76. VINCENT, *supra* note 68, at 236.

77. The possible motives for intervening on behalf of a central government challenged by an insurrection are obvious. They range from the understandable desire to support a sympathetic regime, to a fear of the so-called demonstration effect, i.e. the tendency of one successful insurrection to incite other attempts elsewhere, as witnessed, for example, by the infectious spread of revolutions in Europe in 1848. *See* Deutsch, *External Involvement in Internal War*, in INTERNAL WAR: PROBLEMS AND APPROACHES 100 (H. Eckstein ed. 1964).

the claimant's behalf (or, at a minimum, rendering impermissible intervention on behalf of those attempting to frustrate the claim), because of the serious threat to world order which might attend a system that allowed States to make subjective judgments regarding the legitimacy of such claims. Eugene Rostow, for instance, believes that the international community has accepted it as "the order of nature" that central governments can "legally obtain international assistance in putting down insurrection, while open or covert assistance to the rebels under such circumstances . . . [is] obviously and categorically illegal." [78]

Rostow's view is founded upon the venerable doctrinal teaching concerning situations where the insurgents have not succeeded in establishing effective political administration over a particular area. Where they have done so, international law perceives the insurgency as having been transformed into a state of belligerency, and "neutrality" will then demand that foreign States treat the two regimes as equals — each sovereign in its respective areas of control.[79] It seems questionable, however, whether an acceptance of this theory will avoid the problem of States making their subjective judgments the basis for intervention. A State may not, under this traditional view, make a decision regarding the legitimacy of a claim for self-determination, but it must make an often equally subjective decision as to who is the legal government and who is the rebel. In the frequently confused setting of a civil war, "a patron who wishes . . . to keep on the right side of the law has only to contend that the side he is assisting is the only true legal authority." [80]

A number of jurists utilize the distinction between colonial self-determination and separatist/secessionist self-determination as a part of their analysis of this problem. Although recognition of the latter, it is argued, would "drastically undermine the principle of nonintervention by extending the franchise of sovereignty to groups within states," [81] the concept of self-determination when limited to decoloni-

78. Rostow, Book Review, 82 YALE L. J. 829, 853 (1973). But see E. LUARD, PEACE AND OPINION 93 (1962).

79. See OPPENHEIM, supra note 38, vol. 2, § 298. But see Farer, Harnessing Rogue Elephants: A Short Discourse on Intervention in Civil Strife, reprinted in 2 THE VIETNAM WAR AND INTERNATIONAL LAW 1089, 1107–10 (R. Falk ed. 1969); and Farer, Intervention in Civil Wars: A Modest Proposal, 67 COLUM. L. REV. 266 (1967).

80. LUARD, supra note 78, at 93. For a related criticism see Bowett, The Interrelation of Theories of Intervention and Self-Defense 38, 41 n.9; Friedman, Comment, 574, 576 in LAW AND CIVIL WAR IN THE MODERN WORLD (J. Moore ed. 1974).

81. VINCENT, supra note 68, at 346.

zation at least "accepts the interstate order"[82] and is therefore less liable to be abused by intervening States in making a subjective judgment of legitimacy.

Even within the relatively limited scope of the relationship between principles of nonintervention and the proscription of force and a claim to secessionist self-determination, several different ways of striking the balance have been advanced. John Norton Moore has analyzed claims to intervention in the secessionist war context and concluded that the problems peculiar to this kind of self-determination strongly suggest "that unilateral assistance to either faction in a war of secession should be prohibited without a collective United Nations decision as to which faction should be aided."[83] His solution for "neutrality," however, in situations where a third State has been providing military aid to the federal government before the outbreak of the conflict is to suggest a continuation of such aid but only at the level being provided immediately prior to the secession attempt. The withdrawal of such aid, he reasons, could be equivalent to intervention in favor of the secessionists.[84] At the core of Moore's analysis is the fear that military aid to the secessionists or a diminution of previous levels of aid to the central government forces will only prolong the war [85]—a fear that might easily be seen as begging the question in favor of the central government. If, as the present legal order suggests, the proper model for secessionist conflicts is a gladiatorial one in which the rivals demonstrate their respective desire for separation or union by the intensity of their struggle, *any* external support for either side must constitute an artifical tampering with the supremely Darwinian character of the struggle. In an order that perceives legal legitimacy only in success,[86] such tampering destroys the clinical atmosphere the system relies on to reveal this legitimacy.

An alternative approach criticizes both the practice of a third party subjectively concluding that a "legitimate" claim to self-determination warrants intervention, and the equivalent judgment to intervene on

82. *Id.*
83. J. MOORE, LAW AND THE INDO-CHINA WAR 192 (1972).
84. *Id.* 193. This was precisely the argument employed by the United Kingdom to justify its continued supply of arms to the Nigerian Federal Government during the Biafran secession. *See* text accompanying note 102, chapter 3 *infra*. A similar justification was given by the United States for its continued supply of arms to Ethiopia despite the use of such arms to fight the Eritrean secessionists. *See* N.Y. Times, May 18, 1975, at 9, col. 1.
85. MOORE, *supra,* note 83, at 194.
86. *See* text accompanying note 4, chapter 2 *infra*.

behalf of an incumbent government which is "legitimately" resisting a claim to secessionist self-determination. When the argument from the danger of subjectivity is given mutual effect, the result seems to demand a strict neutrality on the part of outside States. It is essentially this view that allows Rosalyn Higgins to reach two conclusions, namely, that "if a people wishes strongly enough to form a separate political community, the matter is one to be resolved between them and the larger unit of which they form a part,"[87] but also that "nations are not free to encourage, let alone foment, a secession movement." [88]

In conclusion, it should be apparent that the relationship of the principle of self-determination to other crucial norms of international behavior is frighteningly obscure. Self-determination arguably can authorize the wholesale avoidance of the demands of nonintervention and the proscription of force in some of the very situations in which those principles are most necessary in maintaining international order. It is not surprising therefore that jurists have attempted to preserve the integrity of these principles either by questioning the juridical status of a "norm" of self-determination (Vincent), categorically denying the availability of the principle of self-determination as a legal basis for intervention (Rostow), or, in the secessionist context, denouncing the legitimacy of intervention on either side (Higgins). The fact remains, however, that a majority of the members of the General Assembly accept, at least in colonial settings, the preeminence of self-determination as an operative norm of international conduct. If, therefore, despite the lamentations of scholars, the General Assembly has decided that Birnum Wood has come to Dunsinane, a reevaluation of the problem would seem to be in order. Norms such as nonintervention and the proscription of force are of such a fundamental character that questions of their applicability cannot be left to the mercy of outside States interested in a civil conflict to decide when a legitimate assertion of a right to self-determination justifies forceful intervention. This clearly intolerable situation cannot adequately be remedied by blanket denials of the principle of self-determination, which will sound more and more hollow if the General Assembly per-

---

87. Higgins, *International Law and Civil Conflict*, in THE INTERNATIONAL REGULATION OF CIVIL WARS 169, 175 (E. Luard ed. 1972).

88. *Id.* Higgins's attitude toward nonsecessionist rebellions accords with orthodox doctrine that neutrality is demanded only when the rebels "have established themselves with a status tantamount to that traditionally regarded as meriting a recognition of belligerency." Higgins, *Internal War and International Law*, in 3 THE FUTURE OF THE INTERNATIONAL LEGAL ORDER 81, 103 (C. Black, R. Falk eds. 1971).

sists in its present pattern of thinking and resolving. In light of this trend, the more fruitful approach would seem to be an attempt at removing the open-ended subjectivity involved in unilateral determinations of "legitimacy." Thus, instead of artificially shoring up nonintervention and the proscription of force, we might profitably try to delimit the scope of "legitimate" self-determination, thereby reducing the number of instances of permissible deviation from the former two principles.

2.   The Search for a "Right" to Secede

Let us begin with the following scenario: A group of people living in a geographically distinct portion of a State governed by people with whom they share no significant ties of history, language, or culture make a demand for independence based upon a claimed right to self-determination. What sort of statement is this demand and what, if any, is its juridical status?

On the crudest level, the separatists' demand for self-determination may be seen as a simple rhetorical flourish with at best some moral appeal but wholly lacking in legal significance. Understandably, where the means are particularly violent or distasteful (terrorism, armed rebellion, and so on) it helps to be able to invoke an end with as much apparent nobility as self-determination. The belief that such claims are mere propaganda exercises seems to gain support from the frequent ability of both parties to a secessionist dispute to invoke self-determination as the legal justification for their conflicting actions.

A second interpretation of the demand is to view the group as having merely issued a challenge to the incumbent governors, saying in effect that the separatists' power (military or otherwise) warrants a recognition of their claim to independence. It would be unwise to dismiss this interpretation out of hand as a simple resurrection of the cynical "might makes right" idiom. Apart from its incorporation into philosophic speculation regarding a presocial state of nature,[1] that idiom is frequently based on a belief that those who win a struggle for political domination will enjoy the liberty of writing about who *ought* to have won it. It is plausible, however, to consider the separatists' demand as an instance of the Carlylean doctrine of "right makes might," [2] that is,

---

1. As a philosophic doctrine, the equation of "right" with "power" finds its most explicit defender in Benedict de Spinoza: "It follows that every individual has sovereign right to do all that he can; in other words, the rights of an individual extend to the utmost limits of his power." B. de Spinoza, *A Theologico-Political Treatise*, in 1 THE CHIEF WORKS OF BENEDICT DE SPINOZA 200 (R. Elwes trans. 1887). *See also* G. BELAIEF, SPINOZA'S PHILOSOPHY OF LAW 49–53 (1971).

2. An excellent summation of Carlyle's beliefs in this regard is given by his biographer, J. A. Froude: "Majorities, as such, had no more right to rule than kings, or nobles, or any other persons or groups of persons, to whom circumstances might have given temporary power. The right to rule lay with those who were right in mind and

the moral or legal righteousness of one's position will inevitably make it mighty,[3] or, with particular reference to this issue, the quantum of might in the form of public support that can be marshalled for a claim to self-determination is the best evidence of its right to succeed.

As a legal standard in the context of self-determination this approach may be seen as incorporating the theory that the legitimacy of a separatist claim finally rests not on juridical niceties of historical autonomy or ethnologic distinctness but rather on the extent and fervor of the people's desire for self-determination. The argument of proponents of this view can be reduced to the following form: if a claim to separatist self-determination is legitimate it will be popular; if it is popular it will finally succeed; therefore, if a claim to self-determination is successful it was (is) legitimate. The converse, they would argue, is also true; namely, that a lack of popular support for a separatist movement within a region is at once a sign that the movement lacks both the power, and the right, to succeed.

Upon closer analysis, both the major and minor premises of this argument are problematical, and as a litmus test for the legitimacy of secessionist claims this approach is unsatisfactory in a number of ways. First, it is overinclusive in the sense that a small but powerful group within a region may be able to accomplish the separation of that region from a governing State without the popular support normally associated with a legitimate exercise of self-determination (as in the Katanga); or the secession may owe its success to the timely intervention of a third party (as in Bangla Desh). On the other hand this approach is manifestly underinclusive in that it fails to recognize the claims of militarily weak groups located within States having large armies or police units (such as the Kurds or the Nagas). In both instances the success or failure of a claimant group can be attributed to essentially serendipitous factors (such as the military intervention of an outside

---

heart, whenever they chose to assert themselves. If they tried and failed, it proved only that they were not right *enough* at that particular time." J. FROUDE, 1 THOMAS CARLYLE: A HISTORY OF HIS LIFE IN LONDON 1834–1881, at 310 (1884).

3. An admirable expression of this faith was made by the Indian delegate to the Third Committee of the United Nations. He felt that the apprehension over an inclusion of a right of self-determination in the Draft International Covenants on Human Rights, as a possible encouragement to separatist movements or revolts by minorities, was exaggerated. "If an ethnic group which was claimed to be a minority was actually a people or a nation," he believed, "it would succeed in achieving its independence whether or not the covenant contained an article on the right of self-determination." 10 U.N. GAOR, 3d Comm., 651st meeting, at 135 para. 4, U.N. Doc. A/C.3/SR.651 (1955).

State) which are totally unrelated to the desire of a group for self-determination or the internal merits of their claim.

Moreover, the difficulty with this identification of right and power is that it has no predictive value: we can discern a "legitimate" separatist movement only by hindsight. It is this retrospective character that makes the equation of success and legitimacy useless as an aid to legal analysis of the right to self-determination. The international jurist can act only as an historian, chronicling instances of valid claims to self-determination after they succeed but unable to offer an opinion concerning their legitimacy before they reach, or fail to reach, fruition. This approach seems to preclude legal or rational analysis altogether, with the final judgment left to an often bloody trial by combat.

Despite its apparently alegal nature, the conviction that the legitimacy of a claim to self-determination can be tested by the degree of success that attends the claimants' undertaking is probably the prevailing view among most international jurists. Summarizing his opinion one commentator writes that "self-determination is not a right under international law, but by virtue of history and provided the act of self-determination is crowned with success. History, bestowing its 'grace' upon an attempt at self-determination, thereby recognizes the group's (historical) right *ex post*."[4] The appeal of this view can be explained only in terms of its ability to dispense with predictive (and therefore controversial) legal analysis entirely. Nevertheless, there is a certain obvious jurisprudential inadequacy in allowing the legitimacy of a claim to be determined by the fitness (in the Darwinian sense) of the claimant himself, rather than by the legal merits of his claim.

A final possible interpretation of the separatists' demand in our hypothetical case is that, by justifying their claim for independence in terms of a right of self-determination, these people are invoking what they consider to be an existing right under international law. The mere fact that some invocations of this right are transparently excr-

---

4. Bos, *Self-Determination by the Grace of History*, 15 NEDERLANDS TIJDSCHRIFT VOOR INTERNATIONAL RECHT 362, 372 (1968). *See also* H. JOHNSON, SELF-DETERMINATION WITHIN THE COMMUNITY OF NATIONS 50 (1967): "In cases of secession it is less a question of right than of success or failure." Kaur, *Self-Determination in International Law*, 10 INDIAN J. INT'L L. 479, 493 (1970): "The inevitable conclusion is that secession forms no part of the concept of self-determination and its revolutionary character derives legality only in success." Nayar, *Self-Determination beyond the Colonial Context: Biafra in Retrospect*, 10 TEX. INT'L L.J. 321, 342–43 (1975): "Once the demand for self-determination by a group within a state is left to be decided by a revolution, the claimed right of self-determination gets recognition only if the revolution is successful."

cises in propaganda need not discredit sincere and plausible appeals
to self-determination in all instances. If (as I will assume here) they intend this latter import for their demand, what is the basis and extent
of this "right" and what, if any, is its status within the doctrines of international law?

I will consider three putative "grounds" for the right of separatist
self-determination within international law. The right may be characterized as: (1) a precept of natural law, or a "natural right," (2) a tenet
of positive international law, or (3) a norm evidenced by the historical
behavior of States.

A clarification of the purported justification for a right of secessionist self-determination is a necessary propaedeutic to any suggestions
for a legal regulation of this issue. Without it, there can be no adequate response to secessionists' rejection of legal meddling with, and
qualification of, what they conceive as an "inalienable" right. Nor can
international law furnish an answer to incumbent governors who
maintain that secessionist self-determination lacks even the thinnest
shred of juridical legitimacy and who therefore resist any legal interference as a violation of domestic sovereignty. The purpose of this in-
vestigation is to ascertain whether either of these extreme views is accurate without qualification and, if not, then to illuminate the kinds of
qualifications imposed by the various theoretical bases of the right.

Is There a Natural Right to Secede?

At first sight it would appear that the most secure position available
to the apologist of a right of separatist self-determination is to cast it
as a species of the genus "fundamental" rights. Such fundamental or
natural rights may be seen either as deriving from and protected by
"natural law" in the medieval sense, or as an exercise of an in-
defeasible prerogative belonging to each person *qua* person and retained upon entrance to society. The legal effect of this classification is
to endow the right with an existence independent of recognition by
national States or the doctrines of international law. Self-determination is thus raised to the status of a panhuman legal principle which
cannot be abridged without incurring a violation of an unwritten, but
ubiquitous, natural law.

Upon closer examination, however, the traditional body of natural
law theory contains some serious obstacles to assertions of secessionist
rights by minority groups within a State and, at the very least, imposes
clear qualifications upon the right of groups to engage in such activi-

ties. The challenges to a natural right of secession are historical — arising from the actual historical development of natural law theory; philosophical — questioning the first principles of the natural law approach as a whole; and practical — stressing the implications of recognizing a natural right of secession in terms of political manageability and prudence. Although these formidable challenges do not entirely invalidate the natural right approach to this question, they do caution against any ill-considered reliance on it as a secure foundation for secessionist claims.

The Individualistic Character of Natural Law Doctrines

By its very nature a secessionist endeavor involves an attempt by a segment of a State's population to withdraw both itself and the territory it inhabits from the ambit of the governing State's political authority. To put the matter into the framework of a "rights" terminology, the secessionists seek to assert their right to an independent, self-governing existence against the State's right to exercise political control over its citizens. At a minimum, therefore, any theory of natural rights which purports to encompass claims of this kind must first recognize the State as a political entity with certain prerogatives and, second, acknowledge the right of component groups of citizens within the society to oppose the State's territorial sovereignty. In both these respects, the medieval development of natural law theory was deficient. In the first instance, the concept of the "State" as we now think of it did not really enter the framework of the medieval tradition until the absorption of Aristotelian doctrines concerning the State as the highest form of human association; that is, the State as a "natural" community composed of individual men in their role as citizens.[5] Prior to the infiltration of Aristotle's political thought in the thirteenth century, it was generally accepted that what governmental authority there was resided in the church or the King — neither of whom sought as the basis of authority what would now be called "the consent of the governed." The source of authority in both instances was a divine ordination; in no sense did they seek to portray themselves as "natural" or human political constructs, and their flock was composed of sub-

5. For a more complete development of this topic see "Juristic Obstacles to the Emergence of the Concept of the State in the Middle Ages," in W. ULLMANN, THE CHURCH AND THE LAW IN THE EARLIER MIDDLE AGES, ch. 12 (1975). On the character of the Aristotelian doctrine as it affected thirteenth-century thought see W. ULLMANN, PRINCIPLES OF GOVERNMENT AND POLITICS IN THE MIDDLE AGES 231–35 (1975).

jects, not citizens. It was thus only after the Aristotelian revival that
the proper relationship of State sovereignty to citizen rights became
an issue.

Even after it accustomed itself to the concepts of the State and the
citizen, the development of natural law theory did not easily adjust to
the further subtlety involved in structuring its juristic scheme to accommodate the claims of nonsovereign communities or corporations
to a personality under natural law. These difficulties arose from two
sources. First, as a simple matter of description, it had long been popular to analogize the relationship between the State and its individual
citizens to the organic relationship of a body to its component organs.[6]
The State, represented by the whole body or its directive faculty, the
head, exercised control or sovereignty over all the parts.[7] As a matter
of physiology, it was recognized that no separate organ or group of
organs can be withdrawn from most living organisms without endan-
gering both the organ and the life of the remaining body. Although
some later writers conceded that the State was formed by the association of all individuals and therefore the totality of individuals could,
theoretically, choose to disassociate themselves, few theorists applying
the analogy were willing to disregard the implications of the organic
model when it came to a secession of isolated groups from the remaining State. As far back as 494 B.C., for example, the Roman consul
Menenius Agrippa was reported to have utilized an "organic" parable
(which depicted the universally injurious result to the whole body
when, in a moment of pique, the limbs determined to stop feeding
the "idle" belly) to cure the famous "secession of the plebs."[8] Accordingly, the organic image of the social relationship did little to buttress
the claim of a group to quit its governing State.

Of much greater philosophical moment, however, was the tendency
of natural law thinking to consider the State, by virtue of its attribute
of sovereignty, as distinguishable from the nonsovereign smaller communities and associations that composed it. During the nineteenth
century, the German theorist Otto Gierke propounded this theme
forcefully in his attempt to trace the historical evolution of the con-

6. For references to early natural law theorists employing organic analogies *see* O.
GIERKE, NATURAL LAW AND THE THEORY OF SOCIETY 1500 to 1800, § 14 n. 92
(E. Barker trans. 1934). *See also* B. D. JOUVENAL, ON POWER: ITS NATURE AND THE HIS-
TORY OF ITS GROWTH 43–59 (J. Huntington trans. 1969).

7. *See* GIERKE, *supra* note 6, § 14 n. 93 for references. *See also* O. GIERKE, POLITICAL
THEORIES OF THE MIDDLE AGE 22–30 (F. Maitland trans. 1900).

8. For Livy's account see his HISTORY OF ROME, bk. 2, ch. 32.

cept of the State. He argued that these latter entities were largely ig-
nored in the scheme of natural rights and considered either as stages
in the evolution of the sovereign State or else as juristic fictions. While
such groups could not achieve a status in natural rights theory similar
to that of the State, they were equally unable to share in the position
of individuals (who possessed, according to the social contract theorists, certain natural rights in their presocial condition and surrendered all or some of these rights when entering society). Thus, on this
basis the ascription of rights to nonsovereign communities or associations opposable to the sovereign State, which lies at the heart of the
secessionists' claim, was widely denied. "Deprived . . . of the sanction
of Natural Law, associations were unable to vindicate an inviolable
right of existence against either the State or the Individual. With the
sacred and indestructible rights of the sovereign community confronting them on one side, and the no less sacred and indestructible
rights of the individual personality confronting them on the other, it
became a question of mere utility what measure of rights they ought
to be granted." [9]

It was only with the growth of a "federalist" theory of social structure in the sixteenth century, which postulated that the State was composed of smaller communities rather than being an aggregation of
discrete individuals, that the status of these associations was given a
secure place within natural law.[10] The most explicit proponent of this
view, Johannes Althusius (1557–1638), divided associations into five
main types (of increasing size): the family, the corporation, the local
community, the province, and the State. Althusius theorized that each
level is itself composed of the contractual union of smaller groups so
that, while individuals are the component atoms of the lower echelons
like the family, only local communities and provinces can conclude the
social contract forming the State. In addition, each level of association
acquires only the right to regulate activities necessary to its purposes,
the residual power remaining with the narrower associations. Thus,
each kind of association has a basis in natural law akin to that of the
State and each retains some of its natural rights when it enters into a
compact to form a larger unit. Among the rights not surrendered by
the provinces when they form the State, Althusius declares, is the

9. GIERKE, *supra* note 6, at 64; *cf.* Ullmann, *The Delictal Responsibility of Medieval Corporations*, 64 LAW Q. REV. 77, 95–96 (1948).

10. For a related discussion of the right of resistance by corporate bodies in earlier
Protestant thought *see* G. SABINE, A HISTORY OF POLITICAL THEORY 375–84 (3d ed.
1971).

right to secede from the State if necessary.[11] It is in this way that Althusius's analysis of society as a series of concentric associational levels,
each retaining certain natural rights despite participation in wider associations, allows him to admit explicitly a right of secession on the
part of local communities or provinces without condemning society to
a disintegration into perpetually warring individuals.

In a similar but much more circumspect fashion, Hugo Grotius concedes a right to minority secession under extreme circumstances. The
State, he argues, has no right to cede part of its territory without the
inhabitants' consent.[12] On the other side of the coin, however, he
maintains that a segment of the State's population cannot unilaterally withdraw from the State "unless it is evident that it cannot save itself in any other way."[13] Thus, Grotius accepts a right of secession
where the circumstances constitute a sufficient justification. Employing
the "organic" terminology, "the right which the part has to protect itself," he argues, is greater than "the right of the body over the
part."[14] Furthermore, he is clear in stating that when such a secession
occurs the seceding part "employs the right which it had before entering the association."[15]

It may be objected here that the search for a natural law acceptance
of the status of associations, and sanctions of group rights distinct
from both the individual and State, is an unnecessary academic exercise. The basis of a secessionist claim, it might be argued, accepts the
highly nominalistic character of traditional natural law theory in as-
cribing rights to individuals rather than groups or communities. Acts
of secessionist self-determination by such groups can therefore be explained simply as an exercise of the aggregate rights of participating
individuals.[16] If one explores this tempting hypothesis, which would

11. *See* O. GIERKE, THE DEVELOPMENT OF POLITICAL THEORY 46–47 (B. Freyd trans.
1939); GIERKE, *supra* note 6, at 70–76; J. GOUGH, THE SOCIAL CONTRACT 75–76 (1957);
SABINE, *supra* note 10, at 416–20.

12. H. GROTIUS, 2 DE JURE BELLIS AC PACIS LIBRI TRES, ch. 6, para. 4 (F. Kelsey
trans. 1964).

13. *Id.*, ch. 6, para. 5.

14. *Id.*, ch. 4, para. 6.

15. *Id.*

16. It is interesting to note, however, that when the individualism of the social contract is carried to its Rousseauian extreme, the individuals combine their forces into a
"general will" *(volonté générale)*. This general will is absolute and will not accept manifestations of diverging individual wills. It results, therefore, in a union which is "une et indivisible." *See* H. JOLOWICZ, LECTURES ON JURISPRUDENCE 88–92 (1963).

permit individuals to aggregate their separate "rights of resistance" (to use the later natural rights terminology) into a right of group secession, the threat of indefinite divisibility takes on an overwhelming significance. A federalist system such as that proposed by Althusius at least accepts a partition of society into levels and concedes a right of secession only to the larger associational groups. This may involve a confrontation of thorny problems concerning the definition of a province or community but it does not justify a dismemberment of society into clans, atomic families, or individuals. To suggest an analysis of secession as an aggregation of individual rights, however, is to run this very risk. If the inhabitants of a province can collectively "resist" by seceding from a larger union, there seems to be no reason why the inhabitants of a town or borough or house might not also engage in an aggregation of their rights for the same purpose. In this way the specter of indefinite divisibility is clothed with the protection of inalienable rights and this approach, in practical terms, is for this reason unlikely to win the support of even those favorably inclined to a legal recognition of secessionist self-determination. The individualistic tenor of traditional natural rights thinking cannot therefore be turned to the advantage of a separatist claim without incurring serious practical objections.

The Need for Requisite Oppression

When questioned closely, the advocate of a natural right of secession will probably wish to base his argument upon some variety of the "social contract" theme which preoccupied political theorists in the seventeenth and eighteenth centuries. These doctrines purport to reduce political associations to a basic (if fictional) agreement among their individual members by which these individuals surrender to the authority of the community certain of their natural rights in return for escaping the brutality of their nonsocial existence or in order to enjoy the positive benefits of life in a social grouping. The secessionist would argue that the act of separation by a minority of the society in effect constitutes a simple reassertion of these surrendered rights or, perhaps, an exercise of the residual rights retained by the people concerned. An examination of the historical development of these theories, however, makes it clear that they impose distinct limitations upon this sort of activity.

The various conceptions of the unpleasantness that presumably characterizes human life in a nonsocial condition determined the ease with which social contract theorists could accept the possibility of the contract being broken. Whether they regarded a presocial state as intolerably harsh (Hobbes) or envisioned a relatively peaceful existence of "natural" man (Rousseau), all were in agreement that the social condition can hold out some important benefits. Among the English thinkers in particular there was a willingness to accept the limitation that a right of resistance, or a right to break this beneficial contract, may be exercised only when the burdens of society (in the form of the sovereign's tyranny or oppression) outweigh its benefits. Of course, the threshold of the "intolerable" varied from thinker to thinker but each affirmed its place as a sine qua non of a legitimate act of resistance. Under this approach, therefore, a proponent of secessionist self-determination would seem to be required to demonstrate a requisite quantum of oppression before his claim could be recognized as legitimate.

A survey of some of the more influential natural rights theorists demonstrates the importance of both the individualistic and "requisite oppression" elements in an analysis of secession as a natural right. The most extreme position was propounded by Thomas Hobbes, who painted an unappealing picture of life in the presocial state as "solitary, poor, nasty, brutish and short."[17] With such a chilling alternative to social existence under a sovereign power, Hobbes argued that the sovereign's actions, regardless of how oppressive to individual men, do not supply a justification for a right of resistance.

> It is true, that a sovereign monarch, or the greater part of a sovereign assembly, may ordain the doing of many things in pursuit of their passions, contrary to their own consciences, which is a breach of trust, and of the law of nature; but this is not enough to authorize any subject, either to make war upon, or so much as to accuse of injustice or in any way to speak evil of the sovereign; because they have authorized all his actions, and in bestowing the sovereign power, made them their own.[18]

In Hobbes's view, a sovereign could be deposed only if he failed to provide adequate protection against the passions of his subjects directed against each other.[19] The sovereign's own extravagances had to be borne in silence.

17. T. HOBBES, LEVIATHAN 143 (J. Plamenatz ed. 1966).
18. *Id.* 233.
19. *Id.* 212.

Hugo Grotius, although ostensibly denying the inherent right of men to resist civil authority,[20] nevertheless admitted several exceptions to this general principle of nonresistance. Among them, in cases of severe oppression, is a right to self-defense, both for individuals and minorities: "I should hardly dare indiscriminately to condemn either individuals, or a minority which at length availed itself of the last resource of necessity in such a way as meanwhile not to abandon consideration of the common good."[21]

Emmerich de Vattel conceived of a subject's right to resist a tyrannical sovereign even more widely than Grotius. His writings nevertheless still evidence the need for some amount of oppression in order to legitimate an act of resistance. He states that an exercise of the right to resistance is legitimate only in "a case of clear and glaring wrongs, [such as] when a prince for no apparent reason attempts to take away our life, or deprive us of things without which life would be miserable."[22] Without this ingredient of oppression, however, Vattel argues that a body of citizens can dissolve their State only by a unanimous decision: "since compacts may be broken by the common consent of the parties, if the individuals who compose a Nation unanimously agree to break the bonds which unite them, they may do so and thereby destroy the State or Nation."[23] The usefulness and benefits of civil society, he continues, make it morally impossible that there should be such a unanimous consent without necessity.[24]

Vattel explicitly denies the right of a province or city to secede from the State of which it forms a part so long as the sovereign does not exceed the powers granted to him under the social compact. "The natural subjects of a prince are bound to him without other conditions than his observance of the fundamental laws."[25] It is an essential and

20. GROTIUS, *supra* note 12, bk. 1, ch. 4 § 2 *et seq. See also* P. REMEC, THE POSITION OF THE INDIVIDUAL IN INTERNATIONAL LAW ACCORDING TO GROTIUS AND VATTEL 213–20 (1960).

21. GROTIUS, *supra* note 12, bk. 1, ch. 4 § 7(4). Spinoza also couches his ideas about a right to rebellion in terms of self defense: "Since no one can so utterly abdicate his own power of self-defense as to cease to be a man, I conclude that no one can be deprived of his natural rights absolutely, but that subjects, either by tacit agreement, or by social contract, retain a certain number, which cannot be taken from them without great danger to the state." SPINOZA, *supra* note 1, *A Theologico-Political Treatise,* Preface, at 10.

22. E. VATTEL, THE LAW OF NATIONS OR THE PRINCIPLES OF NATURAL LAW, bk. 1, ch. 4 § 54 (C. Fenwick trans. 1916).

23. *Id.,* bk. 1, ch. 2 § 16. *See also* REMEC, *supra* note 20, at 173–78.

24. VATTEL, *supra* note 22, bk. 1, ch. 2 § 16.

25. *Id.,* bk. 1, ch. 17 § 200.

necessary condition of civil society, he argues, that "subjects remain united to their sovereign as long as it is in their power to do so."[26] This principle holds true even if the province is threatened or at-tacked by an outside power. As long as the State fulfills its duties to attempt a defense of its subjects, a province may not separate from the State in order to escape danger.[27]

Samuel Pufendorf is equally explicit in his rejection of a right of se-cession. He differs from Grotius in permitting large portions of a pop-ulation to emigrate, even though the State may be seriously weakened or entirely drained of its population by such a wholesale emigration of its citizens.[28] Nature, he says resignedly, never commanded that this or that State endure and flourish forever. This right to large-scale emigration, however, must not be confused with a right of secession: "if citizens wish to emigrate in large groups, they must leave the terri-tory of the state just as individuals must. For all governments would be thrown into confusion, if entire cities or districts could withdraw at their will from their allegiance, and either put themselves under an-other authority, or set up an independent state."[29]

Many of these same ideas were developed in the writings of John Locke, the single most influential thinker in terms of the American and French revolutions. Starting with a basic disagreement with Hob-bes over the harshness of the presocial state,[30] Locke concludes that individual men, upon their entrance into society, retain an inherent right to resist oppressive civil authority. The legislative power has cer-tain absolute limitations; it is "in the utmost Bounds of it . . . *limited to the publick good* of the Society. It is a Power, that hath no other end but preservation, and therefore can never have a right to destroy, en-slave, or designedly to impoverish the Subjects."[31] Where the legisla-

---

26. *Id.*

27. *Id.* § 201. For an example of the "failure to defend" argument as partial justifica-tion for a recent secessionist attempt, see the claim by East Pakistan (Bangla Desh) that it was left virtually undefended in the 1965 Indo-Pakistan War. *See* text accompanying note 167, chapter 3 *infra*.

28. S. PUFENDORF, DE JURE NATURAE ET GENTIUM LIBRI OCTO, bk. 8, ch. 11 § 4 (C., W. Oldfather trans. 1934).

29. *Id.* This was, in effect, the position of Kenya in response to the demands of So-mali nomads living within Kenyan territory. *See* text accompanying note 140, chapter 3 *infra*.

30. *See* H. CAIRNS, LEGAL PHILOSOPHY FROM PLATO TO HEGEL 337–51 (1967).

31. J. LOCKE, TWO TREATISES OF GOVERNMENT, *The Second Treatise* § 135 (P. Laslett ed. 1960). *See also id.* § 22.

tive power assumes this tyrannical character, then by virtue of "a Law antecedent and paramount to all positive Laws of men" the "Body of the People, or any single Man" has the liberty to "appeal to Heaven,"[32] that is, to exercise a natural right of resistance. Although Locke explicitly states that the ultimate decision of when the sovereign power has been unlawfully exceeded so as to justify resistance must rest with the people themselves, he believes that this step will not be taken lightly but only in the wake of "a long train of Abuses, Prevarications, and Artifices."[33]

It was predominantly the theories of Locke and Vattel that molded the thinking of Thomas Jefferson and, through his hand, set the tenor of the American Declaration of Independence. In what is undoubtedly the most famous formulation of the natural rights doctrine of resistance to civil authority, the assumption that these rights appertain to individual men and may not be exercised in the absence of some degree of oppression is clear.

> We hold these truths to be self-evident, that all men . . . are endowed by their Creator with certain inalienable Rights. . . . That whenever any Form of Government becomes destructive of these ends, it is the Right of the People to alter or abolish it, and to institute new Government. . . . Prudence, indeed, will dictate that Governments long established should not be changed for light and transient causes; . . . that mankind are more disposed to suffer, while evils are sufferable, than to right themselves by abolishing the forms to which they are accustomed. But when a long train of abuses and usurpations . . . evinces a design to reduce them under absolute Despotism, it is their right, it is their duty, to throw off such Government.[34]

In summary, at no point in the evolution of natural rights thinking has the doctrine of a right to resistance on the part of individuals or groups of individuals been affirmed in an unqualified manner. Nor has this inherent right of resistance generally been viewed as including a group right of secession except in isolated instances, such as the jurisprudence of Johannes Althusius. This suggests therefore, that the conscription of natural rights theory and terminology as support

32. *Id.* § 168.

33. *Id.* § 225. For a discussion of Locke's thinking on the right to rebellion *see generally* J. DUNN, THE POLITICAL THOUGHT OF JOHN LOCKE 165–86 (1969).

34. UNITED STATES DECLARATION OF INDEPENDENCE (1776).

for modern separatist movements, at least where the qualifications imposed by these doctrines are not met, is largely illegitimate.

In addition, the proponent of a "natural" right to secessionist self-determination must overcome more than the obstacles and limitations within natural rights doctrine itself. The natural law approach, with its entailment of natural-fundamental-inalienable rights, has been much maligned over the years by some very influential commentators. Jeremy Bentham's reaction, epitomized by his famous comment that "*natural rights* is simple nonsense: natural and imprescriptible rights, rhetorical nonsense,—nonsense upon stilts,"[35] has been shared by a significant number, perhaps a majority, of modern jurists. Thus, it seems fair to say that natural law, despite its perennial resurrections, is by itself an insecure jurisprudential foundation for a purported legal right of this kind in the twentieth century.[36]

These recurring, positivist criticisms have often been raised as a major objection to the first premises of fundamental rights theories. On the level of international law, J. L. Brierly has opined that all the objections to the natural rights view

> apply with even greater force when it is applied to the relations of states. It implies that men or states, as the case may be, bring with them into society certain primordial rights not derived from their membership of society, but inherent in their personality as individuals, and that out of these rights a legal system is formed; whereas the truth is that a legal right is a meaningless phrase unless we first assume the existence of a legal system from which it gets its validity.[37]

Aside from the philosophic uneasiness generated by suggestions of legal rights in the absence of a legal system, a secondary fear underlying much of the hostility to the fundamental rights approach is simply that such rights, once admitted, are by definition unassailable and therefore unqualifiable. Once having set one's foot upon the path leading to a natural right to secessionist self-determination, there

35. J. BENTHAM, *Anarchical Fallacies; being an Examination of the Declaration of Rights issued during the French Revolution*, reprinted in 2 THE WORKS OF JEREMY BENTHAM 489, 501 (J. Bowring ed. 1843).

36. *See, e.g.,* the statement of Sir Hersh Lauterpacht (who was quite sympathetic to the natural rights approach): "If the enthronement of the rights of man is to become a reality, then they must become part of the positive law of nations suitably guaranteed and enforced." H. LAUTERPACHT, INTERNATIONAL LAW AND HUMAN RIGHTS 126 (1950).

37. J. BRIERLY, THE LAW OF NATIONS 51 (5th ed. 1960).

seems no convenient stopping place until the right is granted to each atomistic group within a society, perhaps even each individual. The path is thus avoided because its final result is considered absurdly unmanageable in a political context.

A further problem arises from the traditional view of "inalienable" rights as rights that cannot be waived, conveyed, or voided.[38] They seem, therefore, to be of a qualitatively different order from, for example, our right to the return of borrowed property which can be assigned, waived, or voided. If this view is taken seriously, it leads to the inescapable conclusion that an inalienable right to secession, once recognized, resides in a people regardless of their previous political choices or present circumstances. The mucilage holding a society together is generally felt to be a "for better or worse" understanding among the component groups of its population. If, as this approach suggests, it is logically impossible for such groups to waive their right to secede or in any other way limit their freedom to exercise this right, then the bonds of the social compact are far more fragile than most would have imagined. In short, this interpretation of an inalienable right to secede makes the argument from the maxim *pacta sunt servanda* wholly inapplicable to the social condition. The social compact must be viewed as a continuing voluntary agreement of all component segments of the population who must bestow their blessing upon it virtually from one moment to the next.

Finally, the enthronement of separatist self-determination as a "natural" right leads to an unavoidable conflict with the equally "fundamental" rights of established States.[39] International law may be seen as offering support for the proposition that an existing State is justified in resisting any attempt at internal disintegration either under what Clyde Eagleton calls its "primordial right of self-preservation"[40] or as an aspect of self-defense.[41] Thus, the recognition of secessionist self-determination as a natural right merely allows a legal observer to bless

---

38. *See* Brown, *Inalienable Rights*, 64 PHILOSOPHICAL REV. 192 (1955). Brown argues that the seventeenth- and eighteenth-century conception of inalienable rights entailed a belief that it was both morally and logically impossible to transfer or void such rights.

39. *Cf.* Bisschop, *Sovereignty*, 2 BRIT. Y.B. INT'L L. 122, 131 (1921): "Sovereignty of a State involves the undisputed right and duty to maintain law and order: it does not involve an unlimited or undisputed right to grant or to refuse power of disposition to groups within its borders. The refusal may be a matter of self-preservation; it does not of itself exclude an appeal to a tribunal for a decision in the dispute."

40. C. EAGLETON, INTERNATIONAL GOVERNMENT 84 (1948).

41. *See generally* M. WHITEMAN, 5 DIGEST OF INTERNATIONAL LAW 87–88, 966–971 (1965); M. ST. KOROWICZ, INTRODUCTION TO INTERNATIONAL LAW 226–29 (1959).

both secessionist and unionist with the seal of "natural rights." He
can, however, do nothing to prevent their inevitable, but supremely
righteous, struggle. As a propaganda exercise for either side this approach may be fruitful, but to the legal cui bono there is no answer.

THE RIGHT UNDER POSITIVE INTERNATIONAL LAW

Since no indisputable basis for a natural right of separatist self-
determination can be established, the next logical step is to ask
whether positive international law provides any support for a claim of
this kind. Viewed from an historical perspective, the international
concern with the social conditions that give rise to demands for secession or some degree of political, economic, or cultural autonomy has
assumed different titles. In the years immediately prior to the formation of the League of Nations many influential figures assumed that
the employment of "national self-determination" as an operative political principle would allow an orderly geographical realignment of
populations on the basis of national affinities. It was thought that this
would have the effect of bringing the more artificial institution of
Statehood into line with the more natural phenomenon of nationhood
and would thereby satisfy the demands of nationalism, irredentism,
and the like which had blossomed so insistently in the nineteenth century.

The Paris Peace Conference of 1919 quickly showed the unwork-
able (not to mention unpopular) nature of self-determination as an
operative principle and therefore a shift of emphasis was seen to be in
order. Rather than speak about national self-determination as a touchstone for testing the legitimacy of any future rearrangement of the
political allegiances of national groups—which seemed to invite, by
implication, the interpretation of self-determination as a *remedy* for national groups within States not subject to the Great Powers' fiat after
World War I—a solution was sought in the expansion of an already
existing doctrine of "minority rights." Under this approach, the international concern for national or ethnic minorities contained within
multinational States could be demonstrated without seeming to authorize "self-determination" for all such groups, which still carried a dangerous implication of political independence. At the basis of this
trend, of course, was a consensus among the members of the world
community that a State's treatment of its minority groups was in fact
sometimes a matter for international concern and not a subject to be
left entirely to each State's discretion. Although the minority rights
approach has never fallen into disfavor, there appears to have been a

tacit agreement in the early years of the United Nations to concentrate upon individual human rights and, once some concrete international understanding had been achieved in this area, then to grapple with the more thorny problem of minority rights.[42]

The precise delimitation of the concepts of self-determination, minority rights, and human rights has never been clear. This in turn has led to a rather confused understanding of the interrelationship of these concepts; a confusion that has benefited from the historical tendency to use whatever term happens to be in vogue at a particular period to encompass all three concepts. Thus, among the questions raised by the interrelationship of these concepts are (1) whether a doctrine of self-determination that includes a recognition of minority separatist claims obviates the need for an additional protection of minority rights; (2) whether self-determination and minority rights are simply two species of the genus "human rights"; (3) whether human rights are solely concerned with individuals and therefore entirely distinguishable from minority (that is, group) rights; and (4) whether an effective guarantee of minority rights by a State vitiates any claim to self-determination by the groups enjoying such protection within the State. A further confusion arises from the equivocal nature of the phrase self-determination; it is sometimes used in a context which suggests that it is a *right* and therefore, like individual human rights, warrants continuing international protection, and at other times it seems to describe a self-help *remedy* which is available to certain groups and needs only a general international endorsement for its legitimacy.

The opposition to the inclusion of a right of self-determination in the various international declarations on human and political rights was very much a product of this confusion. As will be discussed below,[43] the desired effect of an international consensus on human rights was to marshal world opinion as an instrument for compelling States to recognize certain fundamental rights and liberties of each citizen. To include a right of self-determination (especially separatist self-determination) in these documents could be viewed as dangerously altering the character of this attempt by seeming to authorize a group right which—by the operation of the maxim "where there is a right, there is a remedy"—could ultimately be vindicated by self-help.

42. *See* J. KUNZ, THE CHANGING LAW OF NATIONS 298–306 (1968). *See also* Robinson, *From Protection of Minorities to Promotion of Human Rights*, 1948 JEWISH Y.B. INT'L L. 115, 132–51.

43. *See* text accompanying notes 125–71 *infra*.

The distinction between members of the international community using their collective authority to influence a sister State's policies, and an apparent international authorization of minority rights in opposition to traditional principles of State sovereignty and territorial integrity, remains a primary source of discord in this area.

The Juridical Status of the Right before 1945

The international concern for the plight of religious, national, or linguistic minorities contained within an "alien" State's boundaries long antedated the rise of any international machinery to deal with the problem. Realistically, however, this concern was generated far more by the tangible threat of intervention on behalf of such minorities by outside States sharing the same religious, national, or linguistic traits than by a felt need to minimize the theoretical justifications for possible secession by such groups. Nevertheless, such early attempts at securing certain fundamental rights for minorities are significant in that they provided precedents for the much more intensive effort at international protection undertaken during the League of Nations era.

The beginnings of this trend can be found in several seventeenth- and eighteenth-century treaties involving the cession of territory, which evidence a concern for the protection of religious liberty in the ceded province.[44] During the early nineteenth century this basis of concern broadened to include, in addition to religious toleration, a securing of fundamental civil rights in areas subject to a transfer of sovereignty. For example, the 1814 act by which the Prince of Orange accepted the assignment of Belgium to the Netherlands explicitly provided that no innovation would be made in those articles of the Constitution of Holland "which assure equal protection and favor to every sect, and guarantee the admission of all citizens, whatever their religious belief may be, to public employment" (article 2).[45] In addition, the act specified that the Belgic Provinces would be assured of representation at the Assembly of the States General (article 3);[46] and that all the provinces would enjoy the same commercial and other ad-

---

44. *See* C. MACARTNEY, NATION STATES AND NATIONAL MINORITIES 158 (1934) for examples of such treaties.

45. Act of Acceptance of the Sovereignty of the Belgic Provinces, signed July 21, 1814. E. HERTSLET, 1 THE MAP OF EUROPE BY TREATY 37, 38 (1875).

46. *Id.* 38.

vantages (article 4).[47] Similarly, the 1858 Convention of Paris, in recognizing the creation of an autonomous Roumanian principality, contained a provision that "Moldavians and Wallachians of all Christian confessions shall enjoy Political Rights. The enjoyment of those rights may be extended to other Religions by Legislative arrangements."[48] Articles relating to the guarantees of civil and political rights and the freedom of religious worship were also prominent in the Treaty of Berlin (1878).[49]

The first formal recognition of "national" rights occurred during the Congress of Vienna (1815) with reference to Poland. In an extraordinarily timorous fashion the parties agreed that "the Poles, who are respective subjects of Russia, Austria, and Prussia, shall obtain a Representation and National Institutions, regulated according to the degree of political consideration, that each of the Governments to which they belong shall judge expedient and proper to grant them."[50]

In these treaties, among others,[51] one can perceive a nascent concern for the protection of minority rights as a condition of world peace and, as a natural concomitant of the nineteenth century acceptance of nationalism as the basic political urge, a growing sensitivity to the sacredness of national character and consciousness. This sensitivity did not, of course, induce a self-imposed disintegration of multinational States. On the contrary, throughout this period the huge empires of Austria-Hungary, Russia, Germany, and Turkey remained inviolable. Indeed, the latter half of the century witnessed some notable setbacks in the protection of national rights within these empires.[52] Additionally, the thin line between nationalism and chauvinism was often crossed, resulting in the selective perception of "dominant" cul-

47. *Id.*

48. Convention respecting the United Principalities of Moldavia and Wallachia, signed Aug. 19, 1858, in 2 HERTSLET, *supra* note 45, at 1329, 1344.

49. Treaty for the Settlement of Affairs in the East, signed July 13, 1878, articles 5, 20, 27, 35, 44, 62. THE GREAT EUROPEAN TREATIES OF THE NINETEENTH CENTURY 332 (A. Oakes, R. Mowat eds. 1918).

50. General Treaty between Great Britain, Austria, France, Portugal, Prussia, Russia, Spain and Sweden, signed June 9, 1815, article 1, in 1 HERTSLET, *supra* note 45, at 208, 216.

51. For examples of treaties that provide for religious, cultural, or national protection prior to 1919 *see* MACARTNEY, *supra* note 44, at 157–75; Heyking, *The International Protection of Minorities: The Achilles' Heel of the League of Nations*, 13 TRANS. GROTIUS SOC. 31, 35 n. (c) (1927).

52. *See* A. COBBAN, THE NATION STATE AND NATIONAL SELF-DETERMINATION 46–49 (1970).

tures or nations which justified the frantic accumulation of overseas empires at the expense of indigenous nationalities. It was quite clear, however, that the seeds containing the concept of the nation as the legitimate political unit had been planted by the revolutionary fervor of the late eighteenth and early nineteenth centuries. In the face of the entrenched absolutism of the Ottoman Turks, Hapsburgs, Hohenzollerns, and Romanovs, of course, they appeared quite likely to remain seedlings—whatever their moral and philosophic appeal. It was in fact only the practical demands of the First World War that provided the manuring necessary for the rapid growth of the principle of nationality into a force commanding international attention.

Both the Allies and the Central Powers recognized the existence of disaffected minorities within the others' dominions and each sought to make whatever strategic use it could of this fact. Propaganda campaigns on both sides catered to the rights of small States and oppressed nationalities. The Allies spoke of "the liberation of Italians, of Slavs, of Roumanians and of Czecho-Slovaks from foreign domination; the enfranchisement of populations subject to the bloody tyranny of the Turks."[53] The Central Powers responded by focusing on the rather anomalous nature of their enemies' protestations regarding the rights of nationalities:

> If the adversaries demand above all the restoration of invaded rights and liberties, the recognition of the principle of nationalities and of the free existence of small States, it will suffice to call to mind the tragic fate of the Irish and Finnish peoples, the obliteration of the freedom and independence of the Boer Republics, the subjection of North Africa by Great Britain, France and Italy and, lastly, the violence brought to bear on Greece for which there is no precedent in history.[54]

The Central Powers also accused the Allies of using the "principle of nationality" as a pretense to disguise their real aims in the war,

53. Contained in Entente Reply to President Wilson, Jan. 10, 1917. OFFICIAL STATEMENTS OF WAR AIMS AND PEACE PROPOSALS, DECEMBER 1916 TO NOVEMBER 1918, at 35, 37 (J. Scott ed. 1921).

54. Contained in Austro-Hungarian Comment upon the Entente Reply to President Wilson, Jan. 12, 1917. Id. 42, 44 (quoted in COBBAN supra note 52, at 50). See also statement of Count Czernin for the Central Powers, Dec. 25, 1917: "The protection of the rights of minorities constitutes an essential component of the constitutional rights of peoples to self-determination." Id. 221, 222.

namely, "to dismember and dishonor Germany, Austria-Hungary, Turkey and Bulgaria."[55]

President Woodrow Wilson's articulation of the American war aims employed language later enlisted to advocate his doctrine of national self-determination. "We are fighting for the liberty, the self-government, and the undictated development of all peoples. ... No people must be forced under sovereignty under which it does not wish to live. No territory must change hands except for the purpose of securing those who inhabit it a fair chance of life and liberty."[56]

At the termination of the war, many minority groups understandably assumed that the use of bilateral or multilateral treaties for the protection of minority rights would be largely obsolescent in light of the rise of national self-determination as the guide for all future territorial rearrangements. President Wilson himself was sincere, if naive, in sharing this faith in the efficacy of self-determination, although he clearly stated that his principles were to be applied only to the territory of the defeated Powers and were not to be used to "inquire into ancient wrongs."[57] Wilson did not question the sheer number of ancient wrongs which had been incorporated into the map of Europe; his intention, however, was to avoid the potentially anarchical effect of self-determination universally applied, by limiting the doc-

55. Contained in German Note to the United States, Jan. 31, 1917. *Id.* 61, 62.

56. Contained in a message from President Wilson to Russia, June 9, 1917. *Id.* 104, 105.

57. Quoted in 4 A HISTORY OF THE PEACE CONFERENCE OF PARIS 433 (H. Temperley ed. 1921). Wilson's famous Fourteen Points were meant to show how the principle of national self-determination could be used as an operative standard for dividing up the large, polyglot empires of the Hapsburgs and the Ottoman Turks. The task did not seem one of overpowering difficulty. The accepted boundaries of the ethnographic map of Europe could be used, it was thought, as a basis for drawing a conforming political map after the war. Several examples from the Fourteen Points will serve to demonstrate how this was to be accomplished:

> 9. A readjustment of the frontiers of Italy should be effected along clearly recognizable lines of nationality. 10. The peoples of Austria-Hungary ... should be accorded the freest opportunity of autonomous development.... 12. The Turkish portions of the present Ottoman Empire should be assured a secure sovereignty, but the other nationalities which are now under Turkish rule should be assured an undoubted security of life and an absolutely unmolested opportunity of autonomous development.... 13. An independent Polish state should be erected which should include the territories inhabited by indisputably Polish populations.

W. WILSON, 1 THE MESSAGES AND PAPERS OF WOODROW WILSON 468–70 (A. Shaw ed. 1924).

trine to those areas subject to territorial rearrangement following the defeat of the Central Powers.

In practice, the subsumption of the concept of minority rights within the presumably broader protection offered by self-determination was to be very short-lived indeed. Despite the enormous prestige of Woodrow Wilson as *animateur* of the principle of self-determination at the Paris Peace Conference, the principle was not specifically included in the Covenant of the League of Nations. Article 3 of Wilson's original proposed draft of the Covenant would have made the contracting Powers agree that "territorial readjustments, if any, as may in the future become necessary by reason of changes in present social conditions and aspirations or present social and political relationships" would be made "pursuant to the principle of self-determination."[58] From the start, Wilson's proposals regarding the use of self-determination as an operative principle encountered severe difficulties, both practical and legal. On the practical side, the task of redrawing the demographic map of Europe in strict conformity with the principle of self-determination was found to be quite impossible.

> If Poland were to have that ethnographical frontier and access to the sea promised her in President Wilson's Fourteen Points, numbers of intensely patriotic Germans must be included within her borders; if Czechoslavakia were to have a frontier that corresponded with any intelligible reality, millions of Germans, Magyars, and Ruthenes must be left in the new state; the transfer of Transylvania to Roumania involved also the transfer of Magyars, Saxons, and Szecklers; throughout Eastern Europe were scattered groups of the ubiquitous Jews, secular objects of persecution. Briefly, the solution of one set of minority problems might involve the creation of another set, with the dismal prospect of the commencement of a fresh cycle of conflict, revolt, and war.[59]

58. Wilson's draft is reprinted in D. MILLER, 2 THE DRAFTING OF THE COVENANT 12 (1928). As a complementary provision designed to ensure the protection of minority rights in those areas that would become States after the commencement of the League, Wilson proposed a supplementary agreement (6) which read: "The League of Nations shall require all new States to bind themselves as a condition precedent to their recognition as independent or autonomous States, to accord to all racial or national minorities within their several jurisdictions exactly the same treatment and security, both in law and in fact, that is accorded the racial or national majority of their people." *Id.* 91.

59. C. WEBSTER, THE LEAGUE OF NATIONS IN THEORY AND PRACTICE 206 (1933).

The theoretical assaults on Wilson's faith in self-determination, which ranged from characterizations of the principle as hopelessly vague to explosively dangerous, came both from the other delegations at the conference and from Wilson's own staff.[60] Robert Lansing, Wilson's Secretary of State after W. J. Bryan and co-delegate at the Paris Conference, strongly opposed the inclusion of even the phrase in the treaty. In a serious attack on Wilson and his Paris strategy written after his resignation as Secretary of State, Lansing castigated the principle of self-determination as being politically unmanageable and utterly misleading to minority groups within established States. After attempting to show that a consistent application of the Wilsonian view would have required the Northern States to have recognized the Confederacy in 1860,[61] Lansing concluded that self-determination "is one of those declarations of principle which sounds true, which in the abstract may be true, and which appeals strongly to man's innate sense of moral right and to his conception of natural justice, but which, when the attempt is made to apply it in every case, becomes a source of political instability and domestic disorder and not infrequently a cause of rebellion."[62]

Wilson's legal adviser, David Hunter Miller, also fervently urged the omission of those parts of the proposed article 3 dealing with the significance of self-determination in future territorial readjustments. He

60. A British Foreign Office memorandum intended for the consideration of the British Delegation in preparation for the Conference reminded the reader that

efforts will doubtless be made to embody provisions in the treaty safeguarding the rights of racial, religious and other minorities and, further, to interpret the doctrine of 'national self-determination' as entitling such minorities, if they claim to be nations, to present their case to the Peace Conference and to subsequent Inter-State Conferences.... It would clearly be inadvisable to go even the smallest distance in the direction of admitting the claim of American negroes, or the Southern Irish, or the Flemings or Catalans, to appeal to an Inter-State Conference over the head of their own Government.

Reprinted in A. ZIMMERN, THE LEAGUE OF NATIONS AND THE RULE OF LAW 1918–1935, at 199–200 (1936).

61. R. LANSING, THE PEACE NEGOTIATIONS: A PERSONAL NARRATIVE 101 (1921).

62. Id. 102. Lansing quotes the following from notes he claims to have made during the conference itself. Presumably the substance of these sentiments was communicated, although perhaps in a more subdued tone, to President Wilson during the negotiations.

The more I think about the President's declaration as to the right of 'self-determination,' the more convinced I am of the danger of putting such ideas into the

argued instead for a return to the practice of securing protection for
minorities within States,[63] presumably through the vehicle of treaty
commitments.

In the face of such severe criticisms, the reference to self-determination in Wilson's proposal was deleted during the drafting of the
Covenant. The actual solution to the problem of minorities adopted at
the conference had two elements. First, those territorial readjustments
made by the conference — the dismemberment of some States and the
creation of others — were performed, where practicable, with an eye to
the demands of national self-determination and were aided by the extensive use of plebiscites to determine the political desires of the inhabitants.[64] This procedure was not without its tangible results; it has

---

minds of certain races. It is bound to be the basis of impossible demands on the
Peace Congress and create trouble in many lands.

What effect will it have on the Irish, the Indians, the Egyptians, and the nationalists among the Boers? Will it not breed discontent, disorder, and rebellion? Will
not the Mohammedans of Syria and Palestine and possibly of Morocco and Tripoli
rely on it? How can it be harmonized with Zionism, to which the President is prac-
tically committed?

The phrase is simply loaded with dynamite. It will raise hopes which can never
be realized. It will, I fear, cost thousands of lives. In the end it is bound to be discredited, to be called the dream of an idealist who failed to realize the danger until
too late to check those who attempt to put the principle in force. What a calamity
that the phrase was ever uttered! What misery it will cause!

Id. 97–8.

63. Miller submitted to the president the following comment on article 3 of Wilson's
draft:

That the territorial adjustments made by the Peace Conference will not satisfy all
claims, is the only thing now certain about them. Such general provisions as above
will make that dissatisfaction permanent, will compel every Power to engage in
propaganda and will legalize irredentist agitation in at least all of Eastern Europe.
It is submitted that the contrary principle should prevail; as the drawing of boundaries according to racial or social conditions is in many cases an impossibility, protection of the rights of minorities and *acceptance of such protection by the minorities*
constitute the only basis of enduring peace.

MILLER, *supra* note 58, at 71.

64. The historical development of the plebiscite before 1914 is traced in S. WAM-
BAUGH, A MONOGRAPH ON PLEBISCITES (1920), and the plebiscites conducted during the
early years of the League are exhaustively documented in S. WAMBAUGH, PLEBISCITES
SINCE THE WAR (1933). *See also* J. MATTERN, THE EMPLOYMENT OF THE PLEBISCITE IN THE
DETERMINATION OF SOVEREIGNTY (1920); H. JOHNSON, SELF-DETERMINATION WITHIN THE
COMMUNITY OF NATIONS (1967).

been estimated that even this limited application of the principle reduced the European minority problem by half.[65] Nevertheless, it was
manifestly unable to cope with the entire situation. Where territorial
realignment did not result in an adequate solution to minority problems (which was the case for roughly 25 to 30 million people left in
minority groups within European States[66]), the conference sought to
protect such groups through an elaborate system of treaty guarantees
of minority rights now known collectively as the "minority treaties,"
supplemented with unilateral declarations by certain States.[67] These
instruments were an obvious extension of the seventeenth-, eigh-
teenth-, and nineteenth-century efforts to secure religious and civil liberties by treaty provisions, with the important addition that the guarantee of the minority rights provision was undertaken by the League
of Nations[68] and under the supervision of the Council of the League.

Specific clauses defining the obligations toward minorities were included in the Treaty of Versailles[69] (June 28, 1919) between the Allies
and Associated Powers and Germany, and in the separate peace treaties with Austria[70] (signed at St. Germain-en-Laye, September 10,
1919); Hungary[71] (signed at Trianon, June 4, 1920); Bulgaria[72]

---

65. See I. CLAUDE, NATIONAL MINORITIES 13 (1955). A listing of the minorities put
under treaty protection is provided in MACARTNEY, supra note 44, at 510–34.

66. CLAUDE, supra note 65, at 13.

67. For a list of these declarations see Protection of Minorities: Special Protection Measures
of an International Character for Ethnic, Religious or Linguistic Groups, U.N. DOC.
E/CN.4/Sub.2/214/Rev. 1 (1967) at 8.

The literature on the minority treaties and their role during the League era is vast.
For more extended discussions see P. AZCARATE, LEAGUE OF NATIONS AND NATIONAL MI-
NORITIES (1945); D. ERDSTEIN, LE STATUT JURIDIQUE DES MINORITÉS EN EUROPE (1932);
O. JANOWSKY, NATIONALITIES AND NATIONAL MINORITIES 110–35 (1945); MACARTNEY,
supra note 44, at 212–369; T. MODEEN, THE INTERNATIONAL PROTECTION OF NATIONAL
MINORITIES IN EUROPE 49–65 (1964); R. REYDELLET, LA PROTECTION DES MINORITÉS
(1938); J. ROBINSON et al., WERE THE MINORITIES TREATIES A FAILURE? (1943); J. STONE,
INTERNATIONAL GUARANTEES OF MINORITY RIGHTS (1934); TEMPERLEY, supra note 57,
vol. 5, at 132–49.

68. See STONE, supra note 67, at 4–7.

69. Art. 86, 93. 112 BRITISH AND FOREIGN STATE PAPERS 1, 53, 60 (1919) [hereinafter
BRIT. ST. PAPERS]. This treaty, along with the following four treaties, is not reproduced
in the LEAGUE OF NATIONS TREATY SERIES but can be found in CARNEGIE ENDOWMENT
FOR PEACE, THE TREATIES OF PEACE 1919–1923, 2 vols. (1924).

70. Arts. 62–69. 112 BRIT. ST. PAPERS 317, 353–55 (1919).

71. Arts. 54–60. 113 BRIT. ST. PAPERS 486, 512–14 (1920).

72. Arts. 49–57. 112 BRIT. ST. PAPERS 781, 794–96 (1919).

(signed at Neuilly-sur-Seine, November 27, 1919); and Turkey[73] (signed at Sèvres, August 10, 1920). In addition, special minority treaties were concluded between the Great Powers and the newly created or enlarged States of Eastern and Central Europe. This group included treaties with Poland[74] (June 28, 1919), Czechoslovakia[75] (September 10, 1919), Yugoslavia[76] (September 10, 1919), Roumania[77] (December 9, 1919), and Greece[78] (August 10, 1920).

In general, the clauses in these treaties guaranteeing minority rights constitute a system securing (1) basic rights to life, liberty, and religious freedom for all inhabitants of the State;[79] (2) protections for the acquisition of nationality;[80] and (3) rights belonging to racial, religious, or national minorities. The last of these categories includes equality before the law[81] (with particular reference to civil and political rights, including equal access to public employment); the protection of national language in private or commercial intercourse, religious activity, the press, public meetings, and before law courts;[82] the right to establish charitable, religious, and social institutions (with particular reference to schools);[83] and the right to education in the mother-tongue in areas where the minority group constitutes a significant percentage of the population.[84] In addition, the treaties include special provisions designed to deal with local conditions. For example, the treaty with Poland[85] contains special clauses regarding the Jews;[86] the treaty with Czechoslovakia[87] provides for the autonomy of the Ruthene territory south of the Carpathians;[88] that with Roumania[89] secures local auton-

---

73. Arts. 140–51. *Id.*, vol. 113 at 652, 681–85 (1920). Minority provisions were also placed in the Treaty of Lausanne (arts. 37–45) which replaced the Treaty of Sèvres when it failed to be ratified by Turkey. *See* 28 L.N.T.S. 12, 31–37 (1924).

74. 112 BRIT. ST. PAPERS 232.

75. *Id.* 502.

76. *Id.* 514.

77. *Id.* 538.

78. 113 BRIT. ST. PAPERS 471.

79. *See, e.g.,* Treaty with Poland, art. 2, *supra* note 74, at 235.

80. *See, e.g.,* arts. 3, 6, *id.* 235–36.

81. *See, e.g.,* art. 7, *id.* 236.

82. *See, e.g., id.*

83. *See, e.g.,* art. 8, *id.*

84. *See, e.g.,* art. 9, *id.* 237.

85. *Supra* note 74.

86. Arts. 10, 11, *id.* 237.

87. *Supra* note 75.

88. Arts. 10–13, *id.* 507–08.

89. *Supra* note 77.

omy in scholastic and religious matters to the Saxons and Czecklers in Transylvania;[90] the treaty with Yugoslavia[91] has special safeguards for the rights of Moslems;[92] and that with Greece[93] specifically mentions the rights of Jews and Moslems.[94]

As a method of insuring respect for the rights of minority groups, the League's minority treaties had some severe limitations. Only those States signing the treaties were under any obligation to the League for the protection of racial, linguistic, or national minorities within their borders.[95] In addition, even the signatory States were bound only within the terms of the treaties.[96] What is important to note here, however, is the League's approach in attempting to safeguard minority rights and the racial, linguistic, or national identities of groups where the principle of self-determination could not, or did not, operate to grant national autonomy.[97] In many respects this was a profound disappointment to minorities that had staked their hopes on the principle of self-determination. Not only were they refused na-

90. Art. 11, *id.* 543.

91. *Supra* note 76.

92. Art. 10, *id.* 519.

93. *Supra* note 78.

94. Arts. 10, 14, *id.* 476.

95. *See* MACARTNEY, *supra* note 44, at 286–94. With regard to other States, the League was unable to do more than express its hopes for universal minority protection. The Assembly of the League did this, for example, by resolution in 1922: "The Assembly expresses the hope that the States which are not bound by any legal obligation to the League with respect to Minorities will nevertheless observe in the treatment of their own racial, religious or linguistic minorities at least as high a standard of justice and toleration as is required by any of the Treaties and by the regular action of the Council." LEAGUE OF NATIONS OFF. J., Spec. Supp. 9, at 35 (1922). There was a considerable amount of discussion regarding the wisdom of promulgating an international convention for the protection of minorities, or seeking the voluntary assumption of these obligations by other States. *See generally* Report of the Committee Instituted by Council Resolution of March 7th, 1929, LEAGUE OF NATIONS OFF. J., Spec. Supp. 73, at 66, 70, 74 (1929); LEAGUE Doc. C.C.M.1; Jones, *National Minorities in the British Empire*, 12 TRANS. GROTIUS SOC. 99 (1926).

96. The Permanent Court of International Justice interpreted the treaties as laying down "minimum guarantees" which the State concerned is required to accord. "The State is at liberty, either by means of domestic legislation or under a convention, to grant minorities rights over and above those assured by the Minorities Treaty." Treatment of Polish Nationals in Danzig [1932] P.C.I.J., ser. A/B, No. 44, at 40.

97. [T]he victors had declared that "peoples may now be domiciled and governed only by their own consent" and had consequently proclaimed the gospel of "self-determination". Thereupon they had been led, partly by irresistible external circumstances and partly by internal circumstance which they had not resisted, to violate the precepts of this gospel. They now offered as a palliative, and in lieu of self-

tional autonomy but, in return for the minimal protection offered by the treaties, they were required to act as loyal subjects of their alien governors.[98]

The League obviously hoped that this process would suppress in the future those special conditions which give rise to minority griev-ances and can arguably legitimate a claim to self-determination. Once this decision was made, of course, the League had to reject self-deter-mination and particularly secessionist self-determination as a further remedy for minority groups. In a conscious methodological choice, the League preferred to employ the external pressure of international commitments and world opinion as an inducement for States to mod-erate their minority policies rather than rely on whatever internal pressure would result from an international endorsement of self-help measures on the part of such minorities where a State's policies were manifestly immoderate.

One year after the Treaty of Versailles, the League was to make a formal statement of its understanding of the status of separatism within the framework of self-determination and minority rights. Rep-resentatives of the Aaland Islands, technically under the jurisdiction of Finland, had made a request for annexation to Sweden at the Paris Peace Conference based "on the ground of the right of peoples to self-determination as enunciated by President Wilson."[99] The Swedes proposed that the islanders be given a chance to express their choice by a plebiscite; the Finns maintained that such an action would be an

---

determination, a form of international protection by which they had hoped that the victims of these violations would "be more easily reconciled to their new position."

Rappard, *Minorities and the League,* 1926 INT'L CONC. 330, 333. *Cf.* letter from the Aus-trian Federal Government dated April 9, 1929: "Minority rights, as such, are simply part of and not inconsistent with the so-called right of self-determination of peoples; they constitute a form of compensation offered to the minority by reason of the fact that the latter could not or has not been granted the right of self-determination." LEAGUE OF NATIONS OFF. J., Spec. Supp. 73, at 65 (1929).

98. The Assembly of the League reaffirmed this obligation in 1922 saying: "While the Assembly recognizes the primary right of Minorities to be protected by the League from oppression, it also emphasizes the duty incumbent upon persons belonging to ra-cial, religious or linguistic minorities to co-operate as loyal fellow-citizens with the na-tions to which they now belong." LEAGUE OF NATIONS OFF. J., Spec. Supp. 9, at 35 (1922). *Cf.* the definition of a "minority" adopted by the United Nations Sub-Commis-sion on Prevention of Discrimination and Protection of Minorities which provides, *inter alia,* that such minorities "must be loyal to the State of which they are nationals." 16 U.N. ECOSOC, Supp. 8, at 73, para. 31, U.N. Doc. E/2447 (1953).

99. 4 FOREIGN RELATIONS OF THE UNITED STATES, THE PARIS PEACE CONFERENCE 172 (1943).

interference with their domestic jurisdiction.[100] An International Commission of Jurists was entrusted by the Council of the League with the task of giving an advisory opinion upon the legal aspects of the Aaland Islands question. That opinion began by pointing out that the principle of self-determination, despite its importance in modern political thought, was not mentioned in the Covenant of the League. Moreover, the commission opined that the principle had not yet attained the status of a positive rule of international law although it had been recognized in a number of international treaties.

> On the contrary, in the absence of express provisions in international treaties, the right of disposing of national territory is essentially an attribute of the sovereignty of every State. Positive International Law does not recognize the right of national groups, as such, to separate themselves from the State of which they form part by the simple expression of a wish, any more than it recognizes the right of other States to claim such a separation.[101]

In a subsequent report to the Council of the League of Nations on the Aaland Islands question, a Commission of Rapporteurs was even more explicit in its rejection of a legal right to separatist self-determination:

> To concede to minorities either of language or religion, or to any fractions of a population, the right of withdrawing from the community to which they belong, because it is their wish or their good pleasure, would be to destroy order and stability within States and to inaugurate anarchy in international life; it would be to uphold a theory incompatible with the very idea of the State as a territorial and political entity.[102]

100. A documentary history of the dispute can be found in LEAGUE OF NATIONS OFF. J., Spec. Supp. 1 (1920). The factors stressed by the Swedish representative to the Council which favored a recognition of the islanders' claim to secession included the following: (1) Aaland formed a geographical unit; (2) its frontiers could be traced without serious difficulty; (3) its economic value was comparatively small; (4) the economic needs of the inhabitants did not constitute a strong binding link with the governing State; (5) its history and the community of feelings and interests of the inhabitants supported the separation; and (6) the possession of the territory was in no way necessary for the defense of the country from which it desired to be separated. 2 LEAGUE OF NATIONS OFF. J. 703 (1921).

101. LEAGUE OF NATIONS OFF. J., Spec. Supp. 3, at 5 (1920).

102. The Aaland Islands Question; Report Submitted to the Council of the League of Nations by the Commission of Rapporteurs, LEAGUE Doc. B. 7. 21/68/106 (1921). For

The decision of the League to disavow a right of separatist self-determination on the part of the inhabitants of the Aaland Islands may be explained by a failure to find the element of what we have called requisite oppression. The Commission of Jurists, in remarkably cautious language, noted that it did not give an opinion "as to whether a manifest and continued abuse of sovereign power, to the detriment of a section of the population of a State, would ... give to an international dispute ... such a character that its object should be considered as one which is not confined to the domestic jurisdiction of the State concerned."[103] The Commission of Rapporteurs went so far as to say that the separation of a minority from a State and its attachment to another State could be considered as a "last resort when the State lacks either the will or the power to enact and apply just and effective guarantees" of religious, linguistic, and social freedom.[104] The Aaland Islands question was in fact resolved by the Council of the League in favor of Finland's sovereignty over the islands, but only when Finland gave guarantees to assure the population "the preservation of their language, of their culture, and of their local Swedish tradition."[105]

In conclusion, the League's decision to employ international guarantees of minority rights, which was a "strict and logical corollary" [106] of the inability of the Wilsonian principle of national self-determination to overcome obstacles of both a cartographic and a political nature, demonstrated the world community's reluctance to accept separatism as a method for vindicating minority rights. Perhaps a further corollary of this approach is an implicit recognition that a minority retains a right of reversion to self-determination where treaty protections and the pressure of international opinion fail to obtain the de-

---

an interesting discussion of personal factors that may have influenced the report see J. BARROS, THE ALAND ISLANDS QUESTION: ITS SETTLEMENT BY THE LEAGUE OF NATIONS 310–12 (1968).

103. *Supra* note 101.

104. Aaland Islands Report, *supra* note 102.

105. Resolution Adopted by the Council at Its Thirteenth Session, LEAGUE OF NATIONS OFF. J., Supp. 5, at 25 (1921). *See* Gregory, *The Neutralization of the Aaland Islands,* 17 AM. J. INT'L L. 63, 76 (1923) in which the author concludes: "The result of the determination as to the Aaland Archipelago it is believed is in the highest degree salutary on one point at least, namely, *the limitation of the right of free self-determination,* a toxic principle, which, unlimited and unrestrained, threatened the integrity and menaced the welfare of all nations, and thus all men."

106. Kunz, *The Present Status of the International Law for the Protection of Minorities,* 48 AM. J. INT'L L. 282 (1954).

sired results. This view of the status of self-determination as a remedy for a manifest, continued abuse of basic minority rights was suggested, but not authoritatively endorsed, during the League period.

The Charter of the United Nations

An increasing hostility to colonialism coupled with a renewed surge of nationalistic feeling during the interwar years thrust self-determination into the attention of the governments engaged in designing the organization now known as the United Nations. In its present form, the Charter of the United Nations contains two explicit references to the principle of self-determination. Article 1(2) establishes that one of the purposes of the organization is to "develop friendly relations among nations based on respect for the principle of equal rights and self-determination of peoples."[107] Article 55 states that the United Nations will promote certain objectives "with a view to the creation of conditions of stability and well-being which are necessary for peaceful and friendly relations among nations based on respect for the principle of equal rights and self-determination of peoples."[108]

An attempt to include a right of secession within the Charter's meaning of the phrase "self-determination" cannot be conclusively supported or discredited by reference to the *travaux préparatoires* of the San Francisco conference. The Dumbarton Oaks proposal made no reference to self-determination, and the proposal for the inclusion of the phrase within article 1(2)[109] was made at San Francisco by the four major powers at the behest of the Soviet Union.[110] Two viewpoints emerged in the debates of the Technical Committee (I/1) assigned to consider the matter. It was strongly emphasized on the one hand that the principle of self-determination "corresponded closely to the will and desires of peoples everywhere and should be clearly enunciated" in the Charter, and, on the other hand, "it was stated that the principle conformed to the purposes of the Charter only insofar

107. U.N. CHARTER, art. 1, para. 2.

108. *Id.*, art. 55.

109. The amendment to include the present language was prepared jointly by the representatives of the United Kingdom, United States, Soviet Union, and China. Doc. G/29, 3 U.N.C.I.O. Docs. 622 (1945). *See generally* L. GOODRICH, E. HAMBRO, A. SIMONS, CHARTER OF THE UNITED NATIONS 29–30 (3d ed. 1969). Clyde Eagleton believes that "[t]he term 'self-determination' was crowded into Article 1 of the Charter without relevance and without explanation." Eagleton, *Excesses of Self-Determination,* 31 FOREIGN AFF. 592 (1953).

110. See R. RUSSELL, A HISTORY OF THE UNITED NATIONS CHARTER: THE ROLE OF THE UNITED STATES 1940–1945, at 810–11 (1958).

as it implied the right of self-government of peoples and not the right of secession."[111]

The debates in the drafting subcommittee centered upon the significance of the words "States," "nations," and "peoples" which were clearly differentiated in the sponsors' proposal. The Belgian delegation criticized the wording of the joint proposal with two arguments, the first of which was summarized as follows:

> The amendment of the sponsoring governments mentions the equality of the rights of *peoples,* including that of self-determination. There seems to be some confusion in this: One speaks generally of the equality of *states;* surely one could use the word "peoples" as an equivalent for the word "states," but in the expression "the peoples' right of self-determination" the word *"peoples"* means the national groups which do not identify themselves with the population of a state.[112]

The Belgian delegation then offered the following proposed text: "To strengthen international order on the basis of respect for the essential rights and equality of the states, and of the peoples' right of self-determination."[113]

Read in conjunction with their criticism of the joint proposal, the Belgian text seems to advocate an extension of the right of self-determination to national groups which do not identify themselves with the population of their governing State. Assuming that this interpretation of the text was in fact the meaning intended by its authors, and given the position of Belgium as a colonial Power and a State having very distinct linguistic divisions, the delegation's sincerity in offering this amendment is open to a certain amount of skepticism. Whether this was a sincere attempt to clarify the meaning of the term[114] or was a manoeuver designed to force the other delegates to confront the expansive (and unacceptable) interpretation of the phrase self-determination, anticipating that this construction would be soundly rejected,[115] the committee acted predictably in rejecting the Belgian

111. Doc. 343, I/1/16, 6 U.N.C.I.O. Docs. 296 (1945).

112. Doc. 374, I/1/17, 6 U.N.C.I.O. Docs. 300 (1945).

113. *Id.*

114. *See* RUSSELL, *supra* note 110, at 812; Nawaz, *The Meaning and Range of the Principle of Self-Determination,* 1965 DUKE L. J. 82, 89.

115. *See* Rivlin, *Self-Determination and Colonial Areas,* 1955 INT'L CONC., No. 501, at 193, 206.

text.[116] Its reasons are significant if only for their immense obscurity. The relevant objection (for our purposes) to the Belgian text was explained by the rapporteur of the subcommittee in the following way: "what is intended by paragraph 2 is to proclaim the equal rights of peoples as such, consequently their right to self-determination. Equality of rights, therefore, extends in the Charter to states, nations, and peoples."[117]

When the proposed text of article 1(2) reached the Coordination Commmittee, the debate over the significance of the terms "nations," "peoples," and "States" was renewed. The French delegate objected to the use of the word "nations," especially when used in apparent differentiation from the word "peoples" in the same paragraph. This, he thought, seemed to imply a right of secession.[118] The delegate from Chile felt that if the word "nations" were used it "might be applied to any colony inhabited by a special and distinct race which could therefore ask that it be constituted a nation."[119] He doubted whether this was within the intention of the Technical Committee.

The French delegate suggested that the Technical Committee be requested to give an opinion whether "self-determination" meant the right of a State to have its own democratic institutions or the right of secession.[120] The Chinese delegate concurred with this suggestion but the British member was certain that there could be no agreement on this point and was reluctant to encourage a debate of many days.[121] The Coordination Committee finally agreed that the chairman and rapporteur of the Technical Committee (I/1) should be asked to give their opinion on points needing clarification. When the question of the exact meaning of the phrase "self-determination" was put to him, the Ukrainian chairman of committee I/1 replied that he thought that "the right of self-determination meant that a people may establish any regime which they favor."[122] Not surprisingly, this response did not remove all uncertainty in this area.

Although the proposed text of article 1(2) was approved by the Coordination Committee, the questions raised by the use of the words

116. Doc. 723, 1/1/A/19, 6 U.N.C.I.O. Docs. 704 (1945).
117. *Id.*
118. Doc. WD 410, 17 U.N.C.I.O. Docs. 142 (1945).
119. *Id.*
120. *Id.* 143.
121. *Id.*
122. Doc. WD 424, 17 U.N.C.I.O. Docs. 163 (1945).

"States," "nations," and "peoples" were not resolved and have now
passed into the hands of juristic commentators.[123] Apart from a continuing debate over the legal *significance* of the Charter's recognition
of self-determination (for example, whether it is a legal right in the
strict sense or merely a political principle), issues relating to the *meaning*
of the phrase as used in the Charter took second place to questions
concerning its status as a "human right" and were only recently re-
vived in the preparatory discussions of the General Assembly's *Declaration on Friendly Relations.*[124]

Self-Determination as a Human Right

During the early years of the United Nations the major arenas for
debates concerning the scope of the principle of self-determination
were the drafting committees of the various international documents
dealing with human rights. The first of these documents promulgated
under the auspices of the United Nations, *The Universal Declaration of
Human Rights* (1948), contained rather innocuous Wilsonian language
referring to the legitimacy of governmental regimes: "The will of the
people shall be the basis of the authority of government." [125] In 1950
however, the General Assembly decided to call upon the Economic
and Social Council and the Commission on Human Rights "to study
ways and means which would ensure the right of peoples and nations
to self-determination, and to prepare recommendations for its consideration by the General Assembly at its sixth session."[126] The Human

123. *See* text accompanying note 331 *infra.* Whether a particular group is styled as a
"nation" or a "State" can have some important practical consequences. Consider, for example, the appeal of the "Six Nations of the Iroquois" (living in Canada) to the League
of Nations in 1924. The Six Nations requested that they be considered a State within
the meaning of article 17 of the Covenant of the League and, in that capacity, be allowed to raise certain grievances against Canada. 5 LEAGUE OF NATIONS OFF. J. 829,
LEAGUE DOC. C.154.M.34. (1924). More recently, an organization representing the
world's Gypsies petitioned the United Nations Commission on Human Rights to recognize the Gypsies as a "nation." They specifically did not call for a Gypsy State. *See* Ti-
pler, *From Nomads to Nation,* 14 MIDSTREAM 61 (1968).
124. *See* text accompanying notes 184–204 *infra.*
125. Art. 21(3), G.A. Res. 217, U.N. Doc. A/810, at 71, 75 (1948). This same resolution noted that the fate of minorities was "a complex and delicate question" and that
rather than include a specific provision in the declaration on the question of minorities,
the Assembly requested the Economic and Social Council to ask the Commission on
Human Rights and Sub-Commission on the Prevention of Discrimination and the Protection of Minorities to make a thorough study of the problem. *Id.* 77–78.
126. G.A. Res. 421, 5 U.N. GAOR, Supp. 20, at 42–43, U.N. Doc. A/1775 (1952).

Rights Commission did not have time to consider the question, and at its next session the General Assembly renewed its request and declared its decision to include in the International Covenant or Covenants on Human Rights an article on "the right of all peoples and nations to self-determination."[127] The commission was also asked to prepare and submit to the General Assembly recommendations concerning international respect for the self-determination of peoples. The Assembly even specified that the article was to be drafted in the following terms: "All peoples shall have the right of self-determination";[128] and it should further "stipulate that all States, including those having responsibility for the administration of Non-Self Governing Territories, should promote the realization of that right."[129]

In response to this request, the Commission on Human Rights spent a great deal of time at its 1952 session discussing the inclusion of an article on self-determination in the proposed covenants on human rights, the terms in which the article should be drafted, and the recommendations concerning international respect for the principle. An enormous divergence of opinion regarding the scope of the concept of self-determination was already apparent at these meetings. Some delegates suggested that the right of self-determination encompassed the right of a people to decide its international status (direct access to independence, association, secession, union, and so on) and that the term "self-government" should be used to mean autonomy in the domestic administration of a country.[130] Others expressed the view that a "people" for the purposes of the principle should inhabit a compact territory and that its members should be related ethnically or in some other way.[131] Some representatives raised more mundane questions regarding the probable effect on ratifications of an article interpreting broadly the principle that all national aspirations should be fulfilled.[132] Despite these uncertainties, the commission did adopt a

127. G.A. Res. 545, 6 U.N. GAOR, Supp. 20, at 36, U.N. Doc. A/2119 (1952).

128. *Id.* 36–37. This language was introduced during the extensive debates in the Third Committee (1951–52) over the inclusion of an article on self-determination in the covenants, by a joint resolution (U.N. Doc. A/C.3/L.186) submitted by Afghanistan, Burma, Egypt, India, Indonesia, Iran, Iraq, Lebanon, Pakistan, the Philippines, Saudi Arabia, Syria, and Yemen. The draft resolution was then accepted by the committee, 6 U.N. GAOR, 3d Comm., 403d meeting at 345, para. 58, U.N. Doc. A/C.3/SR. 403 (1952).

129. *Supra* note 127, at 37.

130. 14 U.N. ECOSOC, Supp. 4, at 5, para. 36, U.N. Doc. E/2256 (1952).

131. *Id.* para. 42.

132. *Id.* 7, para. 56.

resolution to insert in the draft covenants on human rights the following article:

1. All peoples and all nations shall have the right of self-determination, namely, the right freely to determine their political, economic, social and cultural status.
2. All States, including those having responsibility for the administration of Non-Self-Governing and Trust Territories and those controlling in whatsoever manner the exercise of that right by another people, shall promote the realization of that right in all their territories, and shall respect the maintenance of that right in other States, in conformity with the provisions of the United Nations Charter.[133]

With regard to recommendations concerning international respect for the self-determination of peoples, the Human Rights Commission prepared two draft resolutions for the General Assembly, the first of which began by declaring in startling language that "it is as essential to abolish slavery of peoples and nations as of human beings" and that "such slavery exists where an alien people hold power over the destiny of a people."[134]

Not unexpectedly, the commission's provocative draft resolutions again touched off a bitter debate in the Third Committee (Social, Humanitarian, and Cultural).[135] One of the most volatile disagreements arose from an interpretation of the draft resolutions as legitimizing separatism. The Egyptian representative believed that this was "certainly the intention underlying the draft resolutions," but he hastened to add that this should not be a cause of fear. "The right of peoples to self-determination," he said, "was the right to free expression of the popular will. Whether that will was in favour of secession or association, it had to be respected."[136] The New Zealand delegate also con-

133. *Id.* 8, para. 69. A further resolution to insert the words "the right of peoples to self-determination shall also include permanent sovereignty over their natural resources" was adopted by 10 votes to 6 with 2 abstentions. *Id.* para. 70.

134. *Id.* 11, para. 91. The second draft resolution concerned the duties of those States responsible for non-self-governing territories. *Id.*

135. *See* 7 U.N. GAOR, 3d Comm., 443–64th meetings (1952).

136. *Id.* 454th meeting at 221, para. 36, U.N. Doc. A/C.3/SR.454 (1952). The Egyptian delegate went on to voice some rather surprising deductions which deserve to be quoted in full:

On the one hand there was the example of the British Commonwealth, which went so far as to allow the existence of a sort of royal republic, India, and its neutrality;

cluded that adoption of the resolutions might be interpreted as a recognition of an unlimited right of secession but he felt that a number
of delegations, including his own, had made it clear that this interpretation was unacceptable.[137]

When the Commission on Human Rights met for its ninth session,
the inclusion of an article in the covenants concerning self-determination was firmly established and the commission devoted its attention to
the problem of the implementation of the instruments. The salient
feature of the proposals for implementing the Draft Covenant on
Civil and Political Rights was the establishment of a Human Rights
Committee to deal with alleged violations of the covenant.[138] These
suggestions ran into considerable opposition when the question of the
competence of the committee to consider matters arising out of the
article on the right of self-determination was debated. Some members
of the commission insisted that the committee should not be empowered to consider matters relating to self-determination at all.[139] Others urged that a distinction should be drawn between rights of individuals concerning relations with their own government or another
government, and collective rights involving grave international political problems, such as the right of self-determination. With regard to
these latter issues, they argued, "it would hardly be possible for the
Committee to deal with such questions as the secession and reunion of
peoples."[140] In response, some members who felt that the committee
should be competent to consider matters arising out of the self-determination article demanded that those of their colleagues suggesting
exclusion come forward with alternative concrete measures for implementation; otherwise there might be no recourse in case of a violation
of the right.[141] In the end, a majority of the commission decided that

---

and, on the other hand, the French Constitution under which no territory could be
added to the Republic without a clear and definite expression of the people's will.
Consequently, two great free countries, the United Kingdom and France, in spite
of the attitude they sometimes took towards matters overseas, unreservedly admitted the possibility of secession.

Id.
137. *Id.* 460th meeting at 260, para. 24.
138. 16 U.N. ECOSOC, Supp. 8, at 10–25, U.N. Doc. E/2447 (1953). *See also*
Schwelb, *Civil and Political Rights: The International Measures of Implementation*, 62 AM. J.
INT'L L. 827, 835–68 (1968).
139. 16 U.N. ECOSOC, Supp. 8, at 17, para. 158, U.N. Doc. E/2447 (1953).
140. *Id.* para. 159.
141. *Id.* 18, para. 162.

violations of the article on the right of self-determination should not be excluded from the competence of the committee.[142]

The debate over the article on self-determination was renewed with similar vigor, and similar arguments, at the ninth,[143] tenth,[144] twelfth,[145] and thirteenth[146] sessions of the Third Committee. For our purposes, several themes can be identified in these discussions. First, a number of States felt very strongly that the inclusion of an article on self-determination in binding legal covenants was a serious mistake. The delegate from the United Kingdom preferred to see self-determination as a principle rather than a right—albeit a principle "with strong moral force."[147] He admonished his fellow delegates that the concept of self-determination could not be whittled down to exclude minorities or groups wishing to secede. He therefore asked "whether even States having no colonies were indeed prepared to face the consequences of assuming a legal obligation to promote the right of self-determination within their borders, and to consent to abide by the [Human Rights] Committee's decision on any claims that might be made."[148]

The Belgian representative supported this view, saying that the United Kingdom delegate had rightly drawn attention to the danger of basing a legal right on an ambiguous text. The Belgian believed that, as it stood, the article was "tantamount to an incitement to insurrection and separatism."[149] The Panamanian representative expressed the opposite view, namely, that the right should be fully recognized so that peoples could exercise it peacefully. If the right were not fully recognized and respected, he argued, those peoples who were not prepared to renounce it would be driven to resort to violence.[150]

142. *Id.* para. 164.
143. 9 U.N. GAOR, 3d Comm., 557–86th meetings (1954).
144. 10 U.N. GAOR, 3d Comm., 633–59th, 667–77th meetings (1955).
145. 12 U.N. GAOR, 3d Comm., 821–27th meetings (1957).
146. 13 U.N. GAOR, 3d Comm., 886–94th meetings (1958).
147. 10 U.N. GAOR, 3d Comm., 642d meeting at 90, para. 12, U.N. Doc. A/C.3/SR.642 (1955).
148. *Id.* 90–91, para. 15.
149. *Id.* 643d meeting at 94, para. 10, U.N. Doc. A/C.3/SR.643. *See also* comments of the representative of Iran: "the right of self-determination must never be confused with the right of secession. Secession was the outcome not of respect for the right of self-determination but of disregard for fundamental human rights and the absence of the free consent of peoples to the exercise of the right of self-determination." 13 U.N. GAOR, 3d Comm., 888th meeting at 257, para. 2, U.N. Doc. A/C.3/SR.88 (1958).
150. 12 U.N. GAOR, 3d Comm., 827th meeting at 322, para. 32, U.N. Doc. A/C.3/SR.827 (1957).

Second, there was a considerable debate over the inclusion of what seemed to be a collective right (self-determination) in a covenant otherwise devoted to individual rights such as the right to work or to be free from arbitrary arrest. The representative of Australia declared that self-determination was "a political principle applicable to peoples, not a legal right of individuals."[151] The significance of this distinction is apparent and raises many of the same considerations discussed above with regard to the individualistic character of the natural law doctrine of a right to resist civil authority.[152] To include self-determination within the body of rights appertaining to an individual clearly implies that each person may seek to vindicate that right either alone, or with anyone else he chooses; whereas an interpretation of self-determination as a collective right, although obviously not answering the question of the nature of the collectivity, at least avoids the danger of individual persons demanding to be treated as self-governing units. Thus, it could be argued that the recognition of an individual right to self-determination in a legally binding document authorizes self-help remedies by such individuals if, and when, the international mechanisms implementing the right prove ineffective.

It is interesting to note in this regard the fate of a Yugoslav proposal made at the eighth session of the Human Rights Commission. The representative of Yugoslavia proposed that "the right of peoples to self-determination should include the right of every person to participate in action to ensure or maintain the free exercise of the right by the people to which he belonged."[153] The commission then voted on the words "the right of self-determination shall include the right of every person to participate in action to assure or maintain the free exercise of that right." The proposal received 6 votes in favor, 6 against (with 6 abstentions) and was therefore considered to be rejected.[154] The even split of opinion on this proposal confirms that a significant segment of the commission desired to incorporate into self-determination as an individual right a doctrine legitimizing individual or group remedies for that right.

The opponents of the "individual versus collective" criticism of the article on self-determination pointed out that "so-called collective

151. 6 U.N. GAOR, 3d Comm., 400th meeting at 320, para. 19, U.N. Doc. A/C.3/SR.400 (1952).
152. See Text accompanying note 16 supra.
153. 14 U.N. ECOSOC, Supp. 4, at 7–8, para. 65, U.N. Doc. E/CN.4/669 (1952).
154. Id. 9, para. 72.

rights constituted the expression of individual will through collective methods."[155] They also felt that other articles of the draft covenants might be described as establishing collective rights. Among these, for example, are the right of assembly, the right of association, and trade-union rights.[156]

In addition, the draft article once again highlighted the problem of elucidating a difference between nations, States, and peoples. As a definitional matter, the concepts were seen as overlapping,[157] and in practical terms some delegates feared that an imprecise use of the words could intensify secessionist efforts by minorities[158] or other self-proclaimed "peoples."

Third, and last, the well-worn question of the nebulous relationship between self-determination and minority rights was discussed. Very little progress had been made in this area since the issue was confronted at the Paris Peace Conference in 1919.[159] Some of the delegates expressed what seems to have been the implicit view of the League of Nations, that is, that the concepts are separate, one operating only when the other is inapplicable or ineffective. The representative of Ireland, for instance, believed that "where political, economic, national or cultural rights were not secured, the principle of self-determination might be fairly invoked."[160]

The delegate from Greece, on the other hand, preferred to adopt a very limited interpretation of self-determination and consequently believed that the two concepts did not overlap in the slightest.

The fears of some representatives that the word "peoples" as used in article 1 would incite national minorities to separation

155. 10 U.N. GAOR, 3d Comm., 645th meeting at 105, para. 21, U.N. Doc. A/C.3/SR.645 (1955).

156. *Id.* para. 22.

157. *Id.* 642d meeting at 91, paras. 16, 17, U.N. Doc. A/C.3/SR.642.

158. *Id.* 641st meeting at 87, para. 18, U.N. Doc. A/C.3/SR.641.

159. A French proposal made at the eighth session of the Human Rights Commission would have urged the Economic and Social Council, should the occasion arise, to request the Sub-Commission on the Prevention of Discrimination and Protection of Minorities to study the subjects involved and the relation between the self-determination of peoples and the protection of minorities. 14 U.N. ECOSOC, Supp. 4, at 9, para. 82, U.N. Doc. E/2256 (1952). The draft resolution was, however, withdrawn before the commission voted on it. *Id.* 10, para. 88.

160. 13 U.N. GAOR, 3d Comm., 887th meeting at 253, para. 8, U.N. Doc. A/C.3/SR.887 (1958). She went on to say, interestingly, that "there were even cases where the removal of the grievances from which an independence movement had sprung did not satisfy the movement." *Id.*

were unfounded. Such minorities were within the jurisdiction of United Nations organs which saw to it that they received special protection from the State of which they formed a part; the issue of minorities should not be confused—indeed, the confusion at times seemed to be deliberate—with that of self-determination, which applied to national majorities living in their own territory but unable freely to determine their political status.[161]

Other representatives did not share this certainty about the relationship between self-determination and the protection of minorities, especially in view of the unclear status of secession as the ultimate remedy for a deprivation of minority rights. The Philippine representative opined that the right of secession is one part of the very important question of minorities. "If the right of self-determination was to be exercised without the right of secession, it was difficult to see where to draw the line between a policy of national integration, through the inculcation of a common language or the imposition of a centralized political and economic system, and a policy of respecting and preserving the language, culture and way of life of minority groups."[162]

As they were finally adopted by the General Assembly in 1966, both the International Covenant on Civil and Political Rights[163] and the International Covenant on Economic, Social, and Cultural Rights[164] contain the following language in article 1: "All peoples have the right of self-determination. By virtue of the right they freely determine their political status and freely pursue their economic, social and cultural development."

It would be a mistake to assume that the presence of this article in both covenants, representing as it does a victory for those States advocating recognition of a legal right of self-determination, can be interpreted as a general acceptance of the more radical views heard during the debates on the legitimacy of secession. On the contrary, the virulence of the debate over the inclusion of *any* reference to self-determination in these instruments, combined with the uneasiness aroused by the separatist implications of the article in many delegates who were generally in favor of inclusion, leads to the belief that article 1 of the

161. 10 U.N. GAOR, 3d Comm., 647th meeting at 113, para. 6, U.N. Doc. A/C.3/SR.647 (1955).
162. 12 U.N. GAOR, 3d Comm., 825th meeting at 309, para. 18, U.N. Doc. A/C.3/SR.825 (1957).
163. G.A. Res. 2200, 21 U.N. GAOR, Supp. 16, at 52–58, U.N. Doc. A/6316 (1966).
164. G.A. Res. 2200, 21 U.N. GAOR, Supp. 16, at 49–52, U.N. Doc. A/6319 (1966).

covenants appears in spite of its possible secessionist interpretation, rather than as a confirmation of that interpretation. The felt need for a strong, sweeping statement of the right to self-determination as a weapon against colonialism overcame the implorations of the Western powers for cautious draftsmanship. According to one commentator, who has followed the development of this matter closely, the debates "made it clear that the principle of self-determination would be invoked only for the liberation of colonial peoples and territories. It was not to be construed as implying the right of individuals within nations to express their special ethnic, cultural or religious characteristics or the exercise of the democratic method in internal affairs."[165]

In its final form, the International Covenant on Civil and Political Rights does offer some protection in article 27 to minority groups within the boundaries of established States but these protections do not imply a right of secession. Article 27 of the covenant reads: "In those States in which ethnic, religious or linguistic minorities exist, persons belonging to such minorities shall not be denied the right, in community with the other members of their group, to enjoy their own culture, to profess and practice their own religion, or to use their own language."[166]

The discussion in the Human Rights Commission generated by the proposed inclusion of this article in the covenant warrants some attention. At the ninth session of the commission several draft articles dealing with the protection of minorities were proposed by the Soviet Union,[167] Yugoslavia,[168] and the Sub-Commission on Prevention of Discrimination and Protection of Minorities.[169] These proposals reflected a marked divergence of opinion concerning the scope of the term "minorities." Some delegates believed that the term should cover "ethnic, religious or linguistic" groups, others favored an interpretation of "national minorities," and others suggested "national, ethnic, religious and linguistic minorities." Significantly, the reference to "national minorities" was defeated and the commission finally adopted the expression "ethnic, religious or linguistic minorities."[170] It seems clear that the commission did not intend by this reference to minority rights to suggest that such rights could be vindicated by self-help rem-

---

165. M. MOSKOWITZ, THE POLITICS AND DYNAMICS OF HUMAN RIGHTS 160–61 (1968).
166. *Supra* note 163, at 56.
167. 16 U.N. ECOSOC, Supp. 8, at 55, para. 13, U.N. Doc. E/2447 (1953).
168. *Id.* para. 14.
169. *Id.* para. 15.
170. *Id.* 56, para. 22. *See also id.* 7, para. 52.

edies on the part of such minorities. On the contrary, a majority of the commission did not even interpret this reference as entitling minority groups to form separate communities *within* a State where this would impair its national unity or security, and it may be assumed, a fortiori, that they would disavow any use of the article to justify a secession of such a community from a State.[171]

The Present Situation

The question of the legitimacy of secession as an aspect of self-determination has arisen in contexts other than those dealing with a "human right" of self-determination. These have tended to include discussions relating to the problematical status of secession within the wider United Nations campaign for decolonization and, more generally, a continuing speculation concerning its significance in the light of the Charter's expansive "self-determination" language in article 1(2). The former issue queries the extent to which an unqualified endorsement of self-determination in a United Nations document drafted under the impetus of the decolonization sentiment may legitimately be invoked to support a separatist claim (particularly where the separatists allege domination by an "alien" people). This uncertainty is clearly instanced by the General Assembly's 1960 *Declaration on the Granting of Independence to Colonial Countries and Peoples.*[172] The topic of this declaration was placed on the agenda of the fifteenth session of the General Assembly by Chairman Nikita Khrushchev of the Soviet Union,[173] who also included a short draft declaration.[174] A forty-three-Power draft of the declaration, submitted at the 926th meeting of the Assembly,[175] contained the language ultimately adopted by the Assem-

---

171. The discussion in the commission on this issue is summarized as follows:

> The majority of the members argued that the term "minorities" should be understood to cover well-defined and long established minorities; and that the rights of persons belonging to minorities should not be interpreted as entitling any group settled in the territory of a State, particularly under the terms of its immigration laws, to form within that State separate communities which might impair its national unity or its security.

Id. 7, para. 54. For the Third Committee debates on this article *see* 16 U.N. GAOR, 3d Comm., 1103–04th meetings (1961).

172. G.A. Res. 1514, 15 U.N. GAOR, Supp. 16, at 66, U.N. Doc. A/4684 (1960).

173. *See* 15 U.N. GAOR, Annexes, Agenda Item No. 84, at 1, U.N. Doc. A/4501 (1960).

174. *Id.* 6–7. This draft was ultimately rejected by the Assembly at its 947th meeting, 15 U.N. GAOR 1272–73, para. 29, 30 (1960).

175. 15 U.N. GAOR 989, para. 9 (1960).

bly including an article (2) which specified: "All peoples have the right to self-determination; by virtue of that right they freely determine their political status and freely pursue their economic, social and cultural development."[176]

This forceful statement of the right to self-determination was followed closely in article 6 by the following provision: "Any attempt aimed at the partial or total disruption of the national unity and the territorial integrity of a country is incompatible with the Purposes and Principles of the Charter of the United Nations."[177]

The interrelationship of these articles was never made clear during the discussion of the draft. The representative from Sweden wondered whether the practical implication of the general principle articulated in article 2 would justify, for example, the Congo (Leopoldville) in claiming a right to separate from other parts of the republic, or would the "territorial integrity" provision (article 6) be applied to such cases?[178] The delegate from Libya expressed an opinion that article 6 was "essential in order to counter the consequences of the policy of 'divide and rule', which often is the sad legacy of colonialism and carries its evil effects further into the future."[179] The representative of Somalia said that his delegation supported the content of articles 6 and 7 (which adjured States to observe strictly the provisions of the Charter and the Universal Declaration of Human Rights, including "non-interference in the internal affairs of all States"). He continued, however, by saying,

> We should like to emphasize that phrases such as "territorial integrity" and "non-interference in the internal affairs of States" should not be used as a disguise for the continued domination of dependent peoples and the denial to them of the right of self-determination. When we speak of dependent peoples, we do not mean merely those who live under the domination of overseas metropolitan Powers but also peoples who live under the domination of overland colonial Powers.[180]

176. *Supra* note 172.
177. *Id.*
178. 15 U.N. GAOR 1266, para. 14 (1960).
179. *Id.* 1255, para. 93. *See also* the remarks of the Indonesian representative, who said that his delegation had been one of the sponsors of paragraph 6 and that "we had in mind the continuation of Dutch colonialism in West Irian as a partial disruption of the national unity and territorial integrity of our country." *Id.* 1271, para. 9.
180. *Id.* 1249, para. 20.

Despite this rift of opinion regarding the significance of article 6, the forty-three-Power draft was adopted by the Assembly by 89 votes to 0, with 9 abstentions.[181] Realistically, however, both the context of the declaration ("Granting of Independence to *Colonial* Countries and Peoples") and the plain terms of article 6 outweigh any speculation regarding a possible separatist interpretation of "the right to self-determination" in article 2. It seems inescapable that the use of the phrase "self-determination" in the declaration means "colonial self-determination."

The history of United Nations practice lends substantial support to the thesis that the principle of self-determination, as interpreted by that body, is primarily a vehicle for decolonization, not an authorization of secession. The reactions of the organization to the situations in (among others) the Congo, Tibet, Biafra, and Bangla Desh, as will be discussed below, evidence a lack of sympathy for separatist demands that conflict with the principle of the territorial integrity of established States. This sentiment was twice given voice by Secretary General U Thant, although in dogmatic terms which are belied by the persistent arguments over this issue found throughout the history of the United Nations. At a press conference in Dakar (January 9, 1970), the secretary general replied in the following manner when asked whether there was a deep contradiction between a people's right to self-determination and the attitude of the Federal Government of Nigeria toward Biafra:

> You will recall that the United Nations spent over $500 million in the Congo primarily to prevent the secession of Katanga from the Congo. So, as far as the question of secession of a particular section of a Member State is concerned, the United Nations' attitude is unequivocable [sic]. As an international organization, the United Nations has never accepted and does not accept and I do not believe it will ever accept the principle of secession of a part of its Member State.[182]

Shortly thereafter, at a January 9, 1970, press conference in Accra, U Thant reiterated his view on the scope of self-determination:

> Regarding the . . . question of self-determination, I think this concept is not properly understood in many parts of the world.

181. *Id.* 1273–74, para. 34.
182. 7 U.N. MONTHLY CHRONICLE, Feb. 1970, at 36.

> Self-determination of the peoples does not imply self-determina-
> tion of a section of a population of a particular Member State. . . .
>   What is relevant for the consideration of the United Nations is
> the simple basic principles of the Charter.
>   When a State applies to be a Member of the United Nations,
> and when the United Nations accepts that Member, then the im-
> plication is that the rest of the membership of the United Nations
> recognizes the territorial integrity, independence and sovereignty
> of this particular Member State.[183]

Of crucial importance to an understanding of the present status of
secessionist self-determination within the law of the United Nations is
the General Assembly's 1970 *Declaration on Friendly Relations*.[184] The
declaration finds its origins in a 1962 resolution of the Assembly to
undertake a study of the fundamental principles of the Charter and
the duties deriving therefrom, including "the principle of equal rights
and self-determination of peoples." [185] A Special Committee was established by the General Assembly in 1963 to study these principles and
member States were invited to submit in writing to the secretary general any views or suggestions they might have regarding these principles.[186] In the written comments submitted in response to this
request one can see the battle lines already being drawn in the traditional way over the extension of the principle of self-determination to
include secessionist claims. Both Poland and the United Kingdom chose
to fire early salvos for their respective positions in their written comments, presaging a long and bitter contest during the coming years
and the actual drafting of the declaration. The Polish government
commented:

> From the principle of sovereignty of each nation comes the
> right to establish an independent State organization and con-
> sequently the right to secession, i.e. separation from a given State,
> the right to associate with other States, the right to determine

183. *Id.* 39.
184. *Declaration on Principles of International Law concerning Friendly Relations and Co-operation among States in accordance with the Charter of the United Nations,* G.A. Res. 2625, Annex, 25 U.N. GAOR, Supp. 28, at 121, U.N. Doc. A/5217 (1970).
185. G.A. Res. 1815, 17 U.N. GAOR, Supp. 17, at 66–67, U.N. Doc. A/5217 (1962).
The principle of self-determination was put on the provisional agenda of the nineteenth session of the General Assembly by G.A. Res. 1966, 18 U.N. GAOR, Supp. 15, at
70–71, U.N. Doc. A/5515 (1963).
186. G.A. Res. 1966, *id.* 70.

freely its State constitutional system. Secession, as an essential element of the principle of self-determination, must, however, result from the desire of the population concerned to detach itself from the former State. In such cases, third States are bound to abstain from any interference.[187]

The United Kingdom devoted the whole of its comments to self-determination and did not choose to remark on the other principles to be included in the declaration. The statement reaffirms the United Kingdom's oft-repeated belief that self-determination is a political principle, not a legal right. Article 1(2) of the Charter, it was argued, "was not intended to form any basis on which a province, or other part, of a sovereign independent State could claim to secede from that State." [188] Furthermore, the United Kingdom was convinced that recognition of a *right* of self-determination would be in conflict with other concepts enshrined in the Charter. It could be held to authorize the secession of a province such as, they noted revealingly, the secession of Wales from the United Kingdom.[189]

During the next several years, the Special Committee discussed the content of the principle of equal rights and self-determination of peoples with frequent reference to secessionist self-determination. The usual positions, pro and con, were adopted by the delegates. Some members, notably the communist bloc, favored explicit recognition of a right to secession.[190] Others took a more cautious approach, like France, which argued that "it was at least doubtful whether the right of secession existed as part of the *lex lata*."[191] One member of the Special Committee solved the problem by saying that the principle, as set out in the United Nations Charter, did not sanction an "unjustifiable" claim to secession by a minority group which had traditionally formed

187. 20 U.N. GAOR, Annexes, Agenda Items No. 90 and 94, at 69–70, U.N. Doc. A/5725/Add.1 (1964).

188. *Id.* 73, 74, U.N. Doc. A/5725/Add.4 (1964).

189. *Id.* 74. The United Kingdom argued this view throughout the Special Committee debates. *See, e.g.,* 1966 Special Committee on Principles of Int'l Law concerning Friendly Relations and Cooperation among States [hereinafter Spec. Comm.], Summary Record of 44th Meeting [hereinafter Record __th Mtg.] at 9, U.N. Doc. A/AC.125/SR.44 (1966); 1967 Spec. Comm., Record 69th Mtg. at 19, U.N. Doc. A/AC.125/SR.69 (1967).

190. *See, e.g.,* the comments of the representative of Yugoslavia, 1966 Spec. Comm., Record 40th Mtg. at 10, U.N. Doc. A/AC.125/SR.40 (1966).

191. 1966 Spec. Comm., Record 41st Mtg. at 8, U.N. Doc. A/AC.125/SR.41 (1966).

part of an independent sovereign State.[192] The majority of the members said that they did not recognize secession as a legitimate form of self-determination and cited a variety of reasons for this belief. Some delegates felt that self-determination was limited to the traditional colonial context or instances of alien subjugation and did not include the partial disruption of an independent State.[193] The representative of Algeria opposed recognition of a right of secession because "the rights of peoples within States were a matter to be dealt with entirely by the constitutions and municipal laws of the States concerned." [194] Others attributed their opposition to a fear that a widening of the principle to include secessionist movements would open the door to subversion and intervention.[195]

The declaration that emerged out of the debates in the Special Committee on Friendly Relations and the Sixth Committee (Legal) of the General Assembly,[196] although a product of extensive compromise, is a forceful and significant document. That portion of the declaration dealing with the principle of equal rights and self-determination at-

192. *See* comments of the representative of Kenya, 1967 Spec. Comm., Record 69th Mtg. at 22–23, U.N. Doc. A/AC.125/SR.69 (1967).

193. *See, e.g.,* comments of the Indian representative, 1966 Spec. Comm., Record 43d Mtg. at 15, U.N. Doc. A/AC.125/SR.43 (1966); comments of the representative of Burma, 1967 Spec. Comm., Record 68th Mtg. at 6, U.N. Doc. A/AC.125/SR.68: "The sum total of the experience gained by the United Nations in the implementation of the principle had clearly and incontrovertibly established its meaning and its purpose, namely that it was relevant only to colonialism and was to be specifically applied in the promotion of the independence of peoples under colonial domination." *Cf.* the comments of the representative of Ghana, *id.,* Record 68th Mtg. at 19: "The people to whom the right of self-determination would be accorded would have to be those which, in an area which was geographically distinct from the ruling area, were subjugated by the Government in a manner repugnant to modern notions of government by consent of the governed."

194. 1966 Spec. Comm., Record 43d Mtg. at 6, U.N. Doc. A/AC.125/SR.43 (1966).

195. *See, e.g.,* comments of the Nigerian representative, 1968 Spec. Comm., Record 91st Mtg. at 8, U.N. Doc. A/AC.125/SR.91 (1968).

196. A summary of these debates can be found in Report of the 1966 Spec. Comm. on Friendly Relations [hereinafter Report of the Spec. Comm.], 21 U.N. GAOR, Annexes, Agenda Item No. 87, at 91–99, U.N. Doc. A/6230 (1966); Report of the Spec. Comm., 22 U.N. GAOR, Annexes, Agenda Item No. 87, at 29–37, U.N. Doc. A/6799 (1967); Report of the 6th Comm., 23 U.N. GAOR, Annexes, Agenda Item No. 87, at 8–9, U.N. Doc. A/7429 (1968); Report of the Spec. Comm., 23 U.N. GAOR, Annexes, Agenda Item No. 87, at 52–66, U.N. Doc. A/7326 (1968); Report of the 6th Comm., 24 U.N. GAOR, Annexes, Agenda Item No. 89, at 5–7, U.N. Doc. A/7809 (1969); Report of the Spec. Comm., 24 U.N. GAOR, Supp. 19, at 48–68, U.N. Doc. A/7619 (1969); Report of the Spec. Comm., 25 U.N. GAOR, Supp. 18, at 18–19, U.N. Doc. A/8018 (1970).

tempts to reconcile many of the conflicting viewpoints over the status of self-determination, its scope, and means for implementation.[197] The preliminary question of whether self-determination is a legal right or a political principle was highlighted by the draft texts placed before the committee. The United States[198] and United Kingdom[199] recommended terminology stressing the "principle of equal rights and self-determination of peoples" which was countered by a joint draft submitted by ten Third World nations which spoke of "the inalienable right to self-determination." [200] The phraseology adopted in the declaration in parargraph 1 clearly favors the view that self-determination is in fact a right and not merely a political principle.

The scope of the right to self-determination was also clarified if only by a rejection of extreme opinions advanced during the debates. One suggested draft proposed by Third World Powers would have limited the principle, by implication, to cases of colonialism.[201] On the other extreme, a proposal submitted by Czechoslovakia, Poland, Roumania, and the Soviet Union broadened the principle to encompass a right of secession: "Each people has the right to determine freely their political status, including the right to establish an independent national State." [202] The declaration rejects both of these polar views in favor of a description which states that, by virtue of the principle, "all peoples have the right freely to determine, without external interference, their political status and to pursue their economic, social and cultural development. . . ." [203]

The declaration also attempts a clarification of the relationship between human rights and self-determination. Paragraph 2 implies that the concepts are separable by saying that the subjection of peoples to alien subjugation, domination, and exploitation constitutes a violation of the principle of equal rights and self-determination of peoples *as*

197. This was the seventh principle discussed by the declaration. See *supra* note 184, at 123–24. For the relevant text see Appendix 1 to this book.

198. U.N. Doc. A/AC.125/L.32 (1967); Report of the Spec. Comm. 24 U.N. GAOR, Supp. 19, at 50, para. 140, U.N. Doc. A/7619 (1969).

199. U.N. Doc. A/AC.125/L.44, pt. 6 (1967); Report of the Spec. Comm., *supra* note 198, at 51, para. 142.

200. U.N. Doc. A/AC.125/L.48 (1967); Report of the Spec. Comm., *supra* note 198, at 52, para. 143.

201. *Id.* "The subjection of peoples to alien subjugation, dominion and exploitation as well as *any other* forms of colonialism . . ." (emphasis mine).

202. U.N. Doc. A/AC.125/L.74 (1969); Report of the Spec. Comm., *supra* note 198, at 53, para. 145.

203. Para. 1.

well as a denial of human rights. Paragraph 3 reaffirms the duty of every State to promote the respect for, and observance of, human rights and fundamental freedoms.

The provision of the declaration dealing with the means of implementing the principle of self-determination warrants special attention. The United States proposal[204] drew on the General Assembly's Resolution 1541[205] to suggest that the achievement of self-government may take the form of (1) emergence as a sovereign and independent State; (2) free association with an independent State; or (3) integration with an independent State. As adopted, paragraph 4 of the declaration's self-determination principle contains a provocative, but vague, addition to this list by appending the language "or the emergence into any other political status freely determined by a people." Of equal significance here is the fact that the implementing provision is addressed to the peoples themselves, rather than to States, thus implying a right of self-implementation.[206]

Finally, and most importantly, paragraph 7 of the principle seems to recognize, for the first time in an international document of this kind, the legitimacy of secession under certain circumstances. Like Gaul, paragraph 7 is divisible into three parts. The first warns that nothing in the foregoing text should be construed as authorizing or encouraging the dismemberment or impairment of the territorial integrity or political unity of sovereign and independent States. This clause was to be expected, for it reaffirms paragraph 6 of the *Declaration on the Granting of Independence to Colonial Peoples.*[207] A similar warning that States should refrain from disrupting the unity and territorial integrity of sister States is given in paragraph 8 of the self-determination principle—after appearing in the draft proposals of the United States,[208] the United Kingdom,[209] and the ten nonaligned nations.[210] Paragraph 7, however, implies that not *all* States will enjoy this inviolability of their territorial integrity but only those States "conducting themselves in compliance with the principle of equal rights

204. *Supra* note 198.
205. Principles which should guide Members in determining whether or not an obligation exists to transmit the information called for under article 73e of the Charter, annex, principle VI; 15 U.N. GAOR, Supp. 16, at 29, U.N. Doc. A/4684 (1960).
206. *See* Note, *Toward Self-Determination: A Reappraisal as Reflected in the Declaration on Friendly Relations,* 3 GA. J. INT'L & COMP. L. 145, 149 (1973).
207. *See* text accompanying note 177 *supra.*
208. *Supra* note 198.
209. *Supra* note 199.
210. *Supra* note 200.

and self-determination of peoples as described above." Here again, had paragraph 7 ended on this note, the general nature of the duties prescribed in the declaration, calling upon States to "promote" and to "respect," would have made it very difficult to indict with certainty any more than a few States for not conducting themselves in compliance with the principle. In a telling final clause, however, the paragraph offers a partial definition of what it means to act in compliance with the principle of equal rights and self-determination of peoples. The final clause expands on the meaning of the "compliance" provision by stating: "and thus possessed of a government representing the whole people belonging to the territory without distinction as to race, creed or colour."

The notion embodied in this final clause is clearly a direct descendant of the belief repeatedly expressed in the writings of Locke, Jefferson, and Wilson that the legitimacy of government derives from the consent of the governed, and furthermore that consent cannot be forthcoming without the enfranchisement of all segments of the population (although, interestingly, the declaration does not say "without distinction as to sex").[211] By placing the language at the end of the paragraph in the form of a saving clause, the drafters have apparently affirmed a corollary to the "consent of the governed" concept: if a government does not represent the whole people it is illegitimate and thus in violation of the principle of self-determination, and this illegitimate character serves in turn to legitimate "action which would dismember or impair, totally or in part, the territorial integrity or political unity" of the sovereign and independent State. Finally, it does not seem that the drafters intended by the "and thus possessed" clause to offer a complete statement of the requirements for conducting oneself in compliance with the principle. Rather, the need for a representative government should be seen as a continuation of the demands of the principle "as described above" or, alternatively, as a necessary condition underlying their complete satisfaction.[212]

211. Given the United Nations position on Rhodesia (condemning minority rule as incompatible with self-determination) the "consent of the governed" principle here could scarcely be defined in any other way. *See* G.A. Res. 2012, *Question of Southern Rhodesia*, 20 U.N. GAOR, Supp. 14, at 53–54, U.N. Doc. A/6014 (1965).

212. Note, for example, the rejection of paragraphs in both the United States and United Kingdom proposals that would have considered a State possessing a representative government effectively functioning as to all distinct peoples within its territory as *presumptively* satisfying the principle of equal rights and self-determination as regards those peoples. *Supra* note 198, at 51 (United States); *supra* note 199, at 52 (United Kingdom).

Having noted this much, it is necessary to point out what the declaration does *not* say. It does not give an unlimited recognition to separatism; on the contrary, the opening lines of paragraph 7 reaffirming the territorial integrity and political unity of independent and sovereign States suggest that the drafters elected to start from the conservative position of giving prima facie respect to the present State-centered order. The innovation of the declaration rests in its implicit acceptance of limitations upon the deference to be accorded to the territorial integrity of States—limitations arising from the States' duty to provide a democratic government and protection for basic human rights.

Second, the question concerning whether the presence of a representative democracy vitiates any claims to separatist self-determination on the part of those groups participating seems to be answered by the declaration. It is crucial to note that the terms of this document offer very little comfort to groups demanding political autonomy simply for the sake of parochialism. What seems to be required is a denial of political freedom and/or human rights as a sine qua non for a legitimate separatist claim. This does not of course totally invalidate the claims of, for instance, the French Canadians, American Blacks, Welsh, or Bretons, but it does suggest that their respective States are under no obligation imposed by international law to recognize their demands beyond providing protection for human rights, a representative government that does not discriminate on the basis of race, creed, or color, and the other requirements set forth in the declaration. If these conditions are satisfied, the instrument apparently consigns discussions regarding the political status of such groups within their States to the level of internal constitutional law.

It is not yet entirely clear how the provisions of the *Declaration on Friendly Relations* dealing with self-determination will affect the actual practice of States and international organizations confronted with separatist claims. Certainly the commentators on the declaration have recognized its wide and significant applicability.[213] The first suggestion of the legal impact of the declaration on claims of this nature was

213. *See, e.g.,* Rosenstock, *The Declaration of International Law concerning Friendly Relations: A Survey,* 65 AM. J. INT'L L. 713, 732 (1971):

Although paragraph 7 [of the declaration] is drafted in a somewhat remote manner in the form of a saving clause, a close examination of its text will reward the reader with an affirmation of the applicability of the principle to peoples within existing states and the necessity for governments to represent the governed. The fact that these aspects of the principle must be extracted by an *a contrario* reading of the

given by the International Commission of Jurists in its 1972 study entitled *The Events in East Pakistan, 1971*.[214] The jurists' report characterized the 1970 *Declaration on Friendly Relations* as "the most authoritative statement of the principles of international law relevant to the questions of self-determination and territorial integrity." [215] The commission perceived the principle of self-determination as essentially conflicting with that of territorial integrity. In the declaration's "extremely wide" statement of the right of peoples to self-determination, the report noted,

> the free determination by a people of the form of their political status . . . constitutes the exercise of their right to self-determination; a decision freely taken automatically leads to the acquisition of a status, and it becomes an infringement of international law for any state to attempt to deprive them of that status by forcible action, and if any state does so, other states should give support to the people asserting their right of self-determination.[216]

Nevertheless, the commission felt that the conflicting principle of territorial integrity had to be given full weight when considering the principle of self-determination. Referring to paragraph 7 of the declaration, which they called a "courageous attempt" to reconcile these principles, the commission chose to interpret it in the light of what they felt was a "widely held view" among international lawyers, namely, that self-determination is a right that can be exercised only once.[217] "According to this view," they said, "if a people or their representatives have once chosen to join with others within either a unitary or a federal state, that choice is a final exercise of their right to self-determination; they cannot afterwards claim the right to secede

---

paragraph should not be misunderstood to limit the sweep and liberality of the paragraph.

Nayar, *supra* note 4, at 337, writes: "This provision of the Declaration [paragraph 7] constitutes an unambiguous affirmation of the applicability of the right of self-determination to peoples inside the political boundaries of existing sovereign and independent states in situations where the government does not represent the governed." *See also* Note, *supra* note 206, at 152–53.

214. SECRETARIAT OF THE INT'L COMM'N OF JURISTS, THE EVENTS IN EAST PAKISTAN, 1971 (1972).

215. *Id.* 67.

216. *Id.* 68.

217. Despite the commission's optimism, the notion that self-determination can be exercised only once is very questionable indeed. *See* text accompanying notes 30–31, chapter 1 *supra*.

under the principle of the right to self-determination." [218] It was on this principle, the jurists believed, that the claims of the American Confederacy in 1860 and more recently those of the Biafran secessionists had been resisted. In a crucial passage, the report goes on to state: "It is submitted, however, that this principle is subject to the requirement that the government does comply with the principle of equal rights and does represent the whole people without distinction. If one of the constituent peoples of a state is denied equal rights and is discriminated against, it is submitted that their full right of self-determination will revive." [219]

Thus, an historical survey, from the League of Nations period through the developing law of the United Nations, of the status of secessionist self-determination within the confines of positive international law confirms the evolution of a limited acceptance of its legitimacy. Curiously, the greatest threat to a recognition of the legal legitimacy of this aspect of self-determination came not from those who remorselessly opposed it in every forum, but rather from the movement to undermine its utility by removing the oppressive social conditions for which secession is the ultimate method of redress. Had this attempt to secure an international guarantee of human rights (including minority rights within independent States) been completely successful, it is doubtful whether the world community would have seen a need to legitimate self-help remedies such as secession. As it turned out, even in the heyday of this approach, secessionist self-determination lingered quietly in the background as the logical alternative should international pressure fail to achieve its goal.

By way of historical comparison, the human/minority rights solution to the problem was found to be patchy and inadequate; the "self-determination as a human right" attempt offered an apparent compromise but was severely limited by the overriding consideration of territorial integrity; and an international legitimation of remedial secession promised to be effective where the minority group was sufficiently powerful but even then raised enormous practical and legal difficulties in its wake. It is obvious, therefore, that some reconciliation of the various approaches to the problem was inevitable. To the extent that the 1970 *Declaration on Friendly Relations* constitutes such a reconciliation it (1) borrows from the League of Nation's approach the primacy of seeking an improvement of the condition of individuals

---

218. *Supra* note 214, at 69.
219. *Id.*

and minority groups within heterogeneous States by subjecting those States to external international pressure; (2) inverts the movement to establish self-determination as a human right by demanding a protection of human rights as one element (along with others such as the establishment of a representative government) to be observed when acting in compliance with the principle of self-determination; and (3) reinforces the external pressure to respect the principle by brandishing a legitimization of secession where the coercive force of international opinion is insufficient to moderate a State's internal policies. From this viewpoint the evolution of an international legal recognition of secessionist self-determination, although cautious and uniformly conservative, is nevertheless perceptible. It seems fair to assume that this development may be of enormous significance in a world regularly importuned by separatist demands.

THE PRACTICE OF STATES

An inquiry into the legal content of a right of secessionist self-determination gains little by an analysis of the practices of independent States, except perhaps in a negative fashion. For obvious reasons, in the absence of *force majeure* most States are understandably loath to recognize a right which some or all of its component racial, linguistic, or religious groups may invoke in justifying a separation from the original country. However, although the majority of secessionist attempts, and certainly the publicized ones; are of the "contentious" variety, this is not to say that the historical practice of States taken as a whole stands in unflinching opposition to the legitimacy of all secessionist claims. On the contrary, there are notable instances of sovereign independent States that have accepted an internal division of their territory in a gracious manner. Perhaps even more surprisingly, several States have gone so far as to recognize, in explicit terms, a right of secession in their constitutional framework. Even among those States that disavow any legitimacy for this form of self-determination one can perceive a certain defensive attitude which suggests that in the current international atmosphere those favoring arbitrary limitations on the principle of self-determination must support their positions with principled (and not just practical) arguments.

There is a tendency to rely on a vague historical sense for the belief that the announcement of a secession by a group within a State will be followed by opposition from the central government in much the same way, and with much the same regularity, as thunder follows lightning. In fact, there are historical precedents for a State accepting a separation of part of its territory amicably and without an automatic resort to forceful measures to preserve the union. It is significant, however, that the cases in which this has been accomplished with the least opposition are those involving a previous voluntary union or federation of territories having some degree of autonomy, made within comparatively recent history.[220] Where the original unification was accomplished through other means, such as conquest or cession, or where it occurred in the dimly remembered past, the central State has historically been more likely to feel a proprietary interest in the seceding province and to react accordingly. Even in those instances where the legal status of a union and the extent of its volitional character are in doubt (as, for example, the relationship of the individual states of the United States was debated prior to the Civil War in 1860), the central government's presumption is more likely to remain in favor of union.[221]

There are, however, several examples of pacific secession in the category of States which were formed by a relatively recent, voluntary union. The union of Norway and Sweden, which was accomplished by an Act of Union on August 6, 1815, was amicably dissolved in 1905. The Act of Union in this case had specified that the relationship was a voluntary union of two separate and equal kingdoms under one sovereign.[222] After a plebiscite in Norway resulted in an overwhelming

---

220. In discussing the question of secession within the framework of the Indian constitution, and in particular the significance of the constitution's description of India as a "Union of States," M. C. Setalvad has remarked:

> The real distinction may lie not in the use of the word "Union" but in the antecedent, historical background which establishes that the constituent states were at no time independent or autonomous states which entered into a voluntary compact to surrender some of their powers to the general government. The States constituting the Indian Union were thus at no time "indestructible states." Having no existence as states anterior to the Constitution they could never claim a right to secede.

M. Setalvad, Union and State Relations under the Indian Constitution 29 (1974).

221. It is for this reason that the Drafting Committee of the Indian constitution wanted to make it clear at the outset that "though India was to be a federation the Federation was not the result of an agreement by the States to join in a Federation and that the Federation not being the result of an agreement no State has the right to secede from it." Quoted in Setalvad, id. 28–29.

222. Article 1 of the act declared, "Le royaume de Norwège formera un royaume libre, indépendant, indivisible et inaliénable, réuni avec la Suède sous un même Roi." 65 Consolidated Treaty Series 114, 115 (C. Parry ed. 1969).

approval of the separation by the Norwegian people, the Swedish government acquiesced in the dissolution of the union.[223]

When the government of Senegal chose to secede from the Mali Federation in 1960,[224] its justification for the legality of its action included, among others, the argument that the federation was composed of sovereign States and therefore each retained an implied right to secede from it at will.

In a similar fashion, the State of Singapore's secession from the Malaysian Federation was accomplished in a wholly amicable atmosphere in August of 1965. In fact, so amicable was the separation that the prime minister of Singapore is reported to have broken down in tears at a press conference shortly after announcing the secession—an outburst that resulted in a twenty-minute suspension of the conference.[225] Although President Gamal Nasser Abdal cannot be accused of showing these same effusive emotions when a successful coup resulted in the separation of Syria from the United Arab Republic in November 1961, nevertheless he also eventually acquiesced in the separation. It is noteworthy, however, that his first reaction was to oppose with armed force this "deadly blow" to the union, and only later did he agree to accept the result of what he termed a "reactionary separatist movement serving the interests of the imperialists." [226]

There have also been several hesitant attempts to incorporate a right of secession within the constitutional framework of an independent State. For obvious reasons, this has never been a popular practice with constitutional draftsmen, and even where operative provisions regarding secession have been included as constitutional rights, they have typically been surrounded with heavy limitations. The 1947 Constitution of the Union of Burma, for example, contained in chapter 10 an express recognition that every state shall have the right to

223. See WAMBAUGH, A MONOGRAPH ON PLEBISCITES supra note 64, at 1051 72 for documents concerning the dissolution.

224. The Mali Federation was composed of the Republic of Senegal and the Soudanese Republic, both of which had been French colonies. For a general discussion of the formation and dissolution of the federation see W. FOLTZ, FROM FRENCH WEST AFRICA TO THE MALI FEDERATION (1965). For a discussion of the legal aspects of the dissolution see Cohen, Legal Problems Arising from the Dissolution of the Mali Federation, 36 BRIT. Y. B. INT'L L. 375 (1960).

225. See 15 KEESING'S CONTEMPORARY ARCHIVES (1965-66) at 20891 (Aug. 7-14, 1965). For a discussion of the previous history of the region see P. BOYCE, MALAYSIA AND SINGAPORE IN INTERNATIONAL DIPLOMACY (1968).

226. 13 KEESING'S CONTEMPORARY ARCHIVES (1961-62) at 18437 (Nov. 18-25, 1961).

secede from the union "in accordance with conditions hereinafter prescribed." [227] Among these conditions are the following: (1) the right of
secession shall not be exercised within ten years from the date on
which the constitution comes into operation; (2) a state wishing to exercise the right must have a resolution to that effect passed by two-
thirds of the total number of members in its State Council; and (3) a
plebiscite will then be taken to ascertain the will of the people of the
state concerned, supervised by a Plebiscite Commission consisting of
an equal number of members representing the union and the particular state. In addition to these procedural hurdles, chapter 10, when
read in the light of other provisions in the 1947 constitution, limits
the number of states that can exercise the right to two: the Shan State
and the Kayah State.[228] It should be noted that this unique attempt to
define a substantive right of secession and the procedural rules for exercising the right in the 1947 constitution was deleted from the 1974
Constitution of the Socialist Republic of the Union of Burma.[229] It has
been replaced, significantly, with the declaration that "local autonomy
under central leadership is the system of the State," and with a provision that every citizen shall, in the exercise of his rights and freedom,
abstain from undermining the "unity and solidarity of the national
races." [230]

The Constitution of the Union of Soviet Socialist Republics also
provides, in article 17, that "the right freely to secede from the
U.S.S.R. is reserved to every Union Republic." [231] Unlike the authors
of the 1947 Burmese constitution, however, the Soviet draftsmen did
not find it prudent to articulate the procedural steps to be followed in
exercising this right.

The development of the doctrine of a right of secession in Soviet
theory, and its severe limitation by Soviet practice, will be discussed in
more detail below.[232] It is sufficient to note here, however, that im-

227. The 1947 constitution is reprinted in M. MAUNG, BURMA'S CONSTITUTION
258–301 (1961).

228. *See id.* 192. *See also* Silverstein, *Politics in the Shan State: The Question of Secession
from the Union of Burma,* 18 J. ASIAN STUDIES 43, 49 (1958).

229. The 1974 constitution is reprinted in 3 CONSTITUTIONS OF THE COUNTRIES OF
THE MODERN WORLD, Burma (A. Blaustein, G. Flanz eds. 1974).

230. *Id.* art. 166(c). These exhortations have not relieved the continuing insurgency
of Burmese minority groups. *See, e.g.,* "Burmese minorities call for arms to equip an
army of 100,000," The Times (London), June 2, 1976, at 5, cols. 3–5.

231. 13 CONSTITUTIONS OF THE COUNTRIES OF THE MODERN WORLD, *supra* note 229,
U.S.S.R. (1972).

232. *See* text accompanying notes 299–318 *infra.*

plicit limitations were placed on this constitutional provision even while it was being drafted. Joseph Stalin, in his *Report on the Draft of the U.S.S.R. Constitution* (1936), outlined three requirements before what were called "autonomous republics" could be transferred into the category of "union republics" and thus, according to the constitution, acquire the right to secede from the union.[233] These conditions for the existence of a union republic also show, by implication, the nature of the limitations on the right of secession envisioned by the draftsmen of the Soviet constitution. The first criterion for transfer into the category of a union republic, Stalin argued, was that the area be a borderland, not encircled by Soviet territories. No republic physically contained within the union could, "logically and in fact," [234] raise the question of withdrawal from the USSR. Second, it is necessary that the nationality from which the Soviet republic in question derives its name represent therein a more or less compact majority. The final requirement was that the territory have a substantial population (more than one million) because with an independent State of smaller size "there can hardly be any doubt that the imperialist beasts of prey would soon grab it." [235] Thus, even without the enlightenment provided by the history of Soviet reactions to secessionist movements within their sphere of influence, it can be seen that the intended beneficiary of the expansive Soviet constitutional guarantee of a right of secession must be a relatively large borderland with a compact, well-defined national majority.[236]

Before the Communist Chinese had assumed control of the whole of mainland China, they too found it useful to guarantee a right of

233. For a general discussion of the echelons of governmental organization within the U.S.S.R. *see* L. GRIGORYAN, Y. DOLGOPOLOV, FUNDAMENTALS OF SOVIET STATE LAW 204–28 (1971). *See also* 1 ENCYCLOPEDIA OF SOVIET LAW 69–72 (F. Feldbrugge ed. 1973).

234. J. STALIN, ON THE DRAFT CONSTITUTION OF THE U.S.S.R. 36 (1936). *See also* A. VYSHINSKY, THE LAW OF THE SOVIET STATE 272–73 (1948).

235. STALIN, *id.* 37.

236. *Cf.* the remarks of a modern Soviet jurist in disputing the validity of these limitations:

> According to the meaning and spirit of Leninist nationality policy, the right of nations to self-determination is unconditional. It cannot be qualified by any conditions, nor can it be governed by the quantitative makeup of the population or by its geographic position. . . . [T]he arguments of scholars who consider it essential even today that a republic be on the external border of the USSR in order to qualify for the governmental-legal status of union republic appear to us unpersuasive.

Korkmascova, *The Criterion for Forms of National Statehood in the USSR*, 10 SOVIET LAW AND GOVERNMENT 22, 29 (1971).

secession to the component nationalities of China and, in some cases (like the Tibetans), to nationalities not yet part of China. The First All-China Soviet Congress proclaimed in its November 7, 1931, Constitution of the Soviet Republic:

> The Soviet government of China recognizes the right of self-determination of the national minorities in China, their right to complete separation from China, and to the formation of an independent state for each national minority. All Mongolians, Tibetans, Miao, Yao, Koreans, and others living on the territory of China shall enjoy the full right to self-determination, i.e. they may either join the Union of Chinese Soviets or secede from it and form their own state as they may prefer.[237]

After the Communist Chinese succeeded in assuming control over the mainland, and after the subjugation of neighboring territories like Tibet, the perception of the right to secession underwent a marked change. The 1975 Constitution of the People's Republic of China (adopted January 17, 1975) contains in article 4 the provision that the "People's Republic of China is a unitary multi-national State. The areas where regional national autonomy is exercised are all inalienable parts of the People's Republic of China."[238]

These rare attempts to minimize the actual danger of overt secession by providing an internal constitutional safety-valve which can be regulated to avoid hasty or frivolous claims to separation should not mislead the reader into concluding that there is widespread or growing recognition of secession by independent States. Indeed, a candid appraisal of the current trend in the international responses to these phenomena suggests that the opposite conclusion is probably more accurate.

The most unyielding opposition to secessionist self-determination has come, not from the erstwhile imperial Western powers, but from those nations that have themselves only recently emerged from the process of colonial self-determination. The newly acquired national independence of these States has often been jealously preserved against internal disintegration resulting from separatist claims. The argument supporting this inflexible stand against secession is quite plausible.

---

237. For the text of this constitution *see* C. BRANDT, B. SCHWARTZ, J. FAIRBANK, A DOCUMENTARY HISTORY OF CHINESE COMMUNISM 220, 223 (1952).

238. *See* 3 CONSTITUTIONS, *supra* note 229, People's Democratic Republic of China 14–15 (1975).

Where the new State's boundaries are not the result of any communal sentiment of the populaton but rather were determined simply by the limits of the energy of a colonial Power in some past century, and then bequeathed to the independent State at the end of the colonial period, any slight genuflection in the direction of separatist legitimacy could result in a disastrous reassertion of ancient tribal, linguistic, or religious divisions. Furthermore, the unifying desire for independence from the colonial Power will often be dissipated by the actual achievement of that independence, leaving the new State suddenly vulnerable to the demands of the rival groups within its borders.[239] In view of these circumstances, the argument goes, even the slightest recognition of secession by these States would be as unwise as showing blood in the lion's cage.[240]

It has largely been fears of this kind which have dictated the Third World, and especially the African, reaction to secessionist self-determination. This has been reflected in both internal State structure and in policies advocated before international forums. The Charter of the Organization of African Unity, for example, expresses the determination of the signatories to "safeguard and consolidate the hard-won independence as well as the sovereignty and territorial integrity of our States." [241] In addition, each member proclaims its adherence in article 3 to the principle of respect for the sovereignty and territorial integrity of each State.[242] These sentiments have been reaffirmed in subsequent OAU resolutions such as the *Resolution on Border Disputes* (1964) which stated that the borders of African States, on the day of their independence, constitute a "tangible reality" and declared that member States were pledged to respect those frontiers.[243] The implications of this emphasis on respecting territorial integrity became

239. *See* D. ROTHCHILD, TOWARD UNITY IN AFRICA: A STUDY OF FEDERALISM IN BRITISH AFRICA 2 (1960): "The integrative energies generated by the struggle for independence cannot be depended upon to survive after independence is won."

240. Despite its apparent plausibility, the central thesis of this argument—that there exists a relatively high conflict potential within boundaries of States which were formerly colonial possessions—has been seriously questioned in the African context. *See, e.g.,* Kapil, *On the Conflict Potential of Inherited Boundaries in Africa,* 18 WORLD POLITICS 656 (1966).

241. 479 U.N.T.S. 39, 70 (1963).

242. *Id.* 74.

243. The resolution is reprinted in I. BROWNLIE, BASIC DOCUMENTS ON AFRICAN AFFAIRS 360–61 (1971). Brownlie calls the OAU policy on frontiers "a qualification of the principle of self-determination." *Id.* 360. Significantly, both Somalia and Morocco (for their own good reasons) objected to this resolution. *See generally* A. MCEWEN, INTER-

quite clear in 1967, when the OAU passed its *Resolution on the Situation in Nigeria* in which the members began by bluntly "*reiterating* their condemnation of secession in Member States." [244]

The articulated justifications for the Third World's desire to limit the doctrine of self-determination to "classic" instances of Western colonialism (or, at least, to remove from it any secessionist implications) encompass more than an appeal to the probable disruptive consequences of any endorsement of secession in view of the unstable, heterogeneous character of these States. An alternative justification has been advanced which seeks to categorize any movement toward "Balkanization" as a species of neocolonialism. One of the manifestations of neocolonialism, according to a *Resolution on Neo-colonialism* adopted by the All-African Peoples Conference held in Cairo, March 23–31, 1961, is "Balkanization as a deliberate political fragmentation of States by creation of artificial entities such as, for example, the case of Katanga, Mauritania, Buganda, etc." [245]

Balkanization, when used in this context, is not limited to the process of the disintegration of an independent State into smaller, autonomous entities. It includes any constitutional or political scheme such as federalism or local self-government which in any way impairs the political authority of the central government. [246] A suggestion of such political decentralization, through which many developed States have managed to preserve their national unity in the teeth of strong parochial sentiment, is viewed not as advice for the strengthening of the new State but rather as a sinister attempt to perpetuate the evils of colonialism by inducing crippling divisions in the newly independent

---

NATIONAL BOUNDARIES OF EAST AFRICA 21–35 (1971); S. TOUVAL, THE BOUNDARY POLITICS OF INDEPENDENT AFRICA (1972); Touval, *The Organization of African Unity and African Borders,* 21 INT'L ORGANIZ. 102 (1967).

244. Reprinted in BROWNLIE, *supra* note 243, at 364. *See also* Mayall, *African Unity and the OAU: The Place of a Political Myth in African Diplomacy,* 1973 Y.B. WORLD AFF. 110, 129–33.

245. The resolution is reprinted in C. LEGUM, PAN-AFRICANISM: A SHORT POLITICAL GUIDE 254–55 (1962).

246. Now that Africa has asserted itself and has been achieving its independence, the irreconcilable and scheming former colonists are viewed as seeking through constitutional and political devices, such as federalism, . . . multiparty political systems, local self-government, and entrenched bills of rights, to prevent the development of strong, unified and economically as well as politically independent African States. Thus federalism is seen as a refined neocolonialist extension of the colonial balkanization practice, designed to enfeeble or split up independent African states.

A. RIVKIN, NATION BUILDING IN AFRICA: PROBLEMS AND PROSPECTS 87 (1969).

States. If one can so easily commit the sin of neocolonialism by recommending a federalist political structure, it is clear that by suggesting a limited international recognition of secession one is, a fortiori, irrecoverably damned.

It therefore seems probable that an accurate survey of international opinion would reveal less support for the legitimacy of secessionist self-determination, both in terms of the number of States willing to countenance the suggestion of such legitimacy and in the intensity of feeling over the issue, than would have been the case fifty years ago. The developed nations have generally accorded some measure of legitimacy to a "right of revolution" [247] as a remedy for intolerable governmental oppression. Many have found that a devolution of political power to the component regions of the State is an adequate safeguard against the growth of overreaching governments or simply a convenient way of defusing regional separatist feelings. By rejecting this type of political structure out of hand, some developing States clearly dispute the legitimacy of a "revolutionary" remedy while increasing the risk that their citizens will find such a remedy necessary. Whatever the deficiencies of this approach in terms of political prudence, this trend toward disapproving any decentralization of power (much less the ultimate decentralization—secession) must be accounted strong evidence against the case for a "State practice" recognition of separatist rights.

Perhaps the only certain lesson to be derived from a study of State practice with reference to secessionist self-determination is that, given the present absence of any indisputable rule of international law, a State's response to a particular situation will most often be determined solely by its own political interests. Thus, the articulated reaction of most States to a secessionist attempt in an area of the globe which does not directly concern them will tend to be critical of the secession because of its possible use as a precedent for disaffected groups within their own borders. If the State is the victim of the secessionist attempt, of course, there is likely to be an even more noticeable lack of good fellowship all around. In cases where a State is apt to benefit from a secession, either by gaining an ally in the new nation or by weakening an old enemy, it may well adopt a somewhat more latitudinarian view of the scope of self-determination.

This relativistic tendency can occasionally result in inconsistent, even embarrassingly inconsistent, pronouncements by the same State.

247. *See* Emerson, *Self-Determination*, 1966 AM. Soc. INT'L L. PROC. 135 (1966).

Consider, for example, the positions adopted by India and Pakistan during their long-standing dispute over the fate of Kashmir. Pakistan argued that the principle of self-determination should be applied to the people of Kashmir, thereby allowing them to decide for themselves their future political affiliation.[248] For its part, India vehemently denied that the principle of self-determination had any relevance when the putative "self" was a constituent part of a country. The Indian representative at the Security Council in 1964 unreservedly declared that "the principle of self-determination cannot and must not be applied to bring about the fragmentation of a country or its people." [249] The Indian spokesman went on to point out the dangers of a wide interpretation of the principle for the "innumerable countries in Africa and Asia with dissident minorities." [250]

By 1971, the positions of the parties had been effectively reversed under the stimulus of Bangla Desh's secession from Pakistan. Pakistan inveighed against the Indian support for the secession, and the language used by the Pakistan representative to the Security Council bore a distinctly minatory aspect: "There will not be a Bangla Desh only in Pakistan. There will be a Bangla Desh everywhere. We will see to it that it is not only in Pakistan. There will be Bangla Desh everywhere." [251]

For his part, the Indian representative expressed in these debates the belief that, where a mother State has irrevocably lost the allegiance of such a large section of its people as represented by Bangla Desh and cannot bring them under its sway, international law recognizes that conditions are suitable for that section to come into being as a separate State.[252]

Before leaving the realm of State practice, it is worthwhile to consider in more detail the reactions of both the United States and the Soviet Union toward the problem of secession. These two States warrant special attention for a number of reasons: (1) each was the offspring of a revolutionary parenthood in relatively recent history; (2) each contains a large, heterogeneous population; and (3) each State

248. *See, e.g.,* 19 U.N. SCOR, 1089th meeting at 2, para. 7 (1964). Pakistan noted, however, that it was not seeking support for the right of a minority to secede from the Indian Union. *Id.* 29, para. 95.
249. 19 U.N. SCOR, 1088th meeting at 27, para. 70 (1964).
250. *Id.* para. 71.
251. 27 U.N. SCOR, 1611th meeting at 21, para. 192 (1971).
252. *Id.* 13, para. 124.

occupies a central position within its international "camp" and strongly influences the attitudes of its ideological compatriots toward international issues.

The American Response to Secession

An historian attempting to extrapolate a right to self-determination from the history of the United States must confront what can only be called the "inauspicious" character of the early Puritan New England colonists' attitude toward such notions. The victims of religious persecution themselves, the American colonists lost little time in embracing intolerance and ostracism as mainstays of their own society. In the 1630s, for example, both Roger Williams and Anne Hutchinson were invited to leave the Massachusetts colony and practise a kind of forced self-determination elsewhere because of religious differences with their fellow colonists.[253] The American ideals of liberty and tolerance were not always evident in the germ of the nation; their acceptance, when and to the extent it came, was to be a gradual and painful process.[254]

The importance of the doctrine of natural rights to the American revolutionaries has been noted earlier.[255] With the incorporation of this view into the documents establishing the existence of the new republic, it might have been anticipated that the United States would support the claims of other peoples for independence and, more importantly, that the republic would respect the self-determining wishes of groups within itself. A gradual cooling of revolutionary ardor, however, coupled with a growing appreciation of the complexities of setting consistent foreign and domestic policies, did much to dampen

---

253. *See* C. A. BEARD, M. R. BEARD, THE BEARDS' NEW BASIC HISTORY OF THE UNITED STATES 34–35 (1968).

254. The colonies were remarkable merely for the consistency with which they were able to enforce uniformity and suppress dissent within their boundaries at a time when larger empires were finding themselves physically unable to reduce all citizens to complete conformity. So successful were Massachusetts and Connecticut in vindicating the rules of intolerance and coercion that they were extremely reluctant to abandon them, even after English nonconformists during the Restoration turned to toleration as a *modus vivendi*.

P. MILLER, THE NEW ENGLAND MIND: THE SEVENTEENTH CENTURY 457–58 (1963). *See also* H. OSGOOD, 1 THE AMERICAN COLONIES IN THE SEVENTEENTH CENTURY 219–23 (1904).

255. *See* text accompanying note 34 *supra*.

early expectations. In one sense, the practice of the United States has reflected what may well be an a priori political truth: that no country, however well intentioned, can recognize an unlimited right to self-determination and expect to survive as a unified nation. The lesson learned by the United States during the first hundred years of its history has been summarized (in a different context): "That government should rest on the consent of the governed is a fundamental principle to which we all subscribe. To translate it into a popular right of self-determination is a singularly difficult and hazardous task."[256]

The symptoms of the American loss of innocence in the face of this difficult and hazardous task are epitomized by the reactions of Thomas Jefferson, the principal draftsman of the American Declaration of Independence and a man whose motto proclaimed, "Rebellion to tyrants is obedience to God."[257] The basic Jeffersonian beliefs are well known: an unshakable faith in the dignity and wisdom of the average man coupled with a healthy respect for the inherent right of such men to resist overreaching sovereigns. "Every man," Jefferson wrote, "and every body of men on earth, possesses the right to self-government. They receive it with their being from the hand of nature."[258]

Despite his espousal of this broad view of man's inherent right to self-government, he was not unaware of the difficulties involved in governing large and heterogeneous populations. Jefferson's solution was a kind of loose federalism composed of relatively small political units retaining a significant amount of local autonomy. He felt that any attempt at creating artificially large areas of regional government, beyond what community and economic affinities will bear, risks the secession of these communities. It is significant that during the entire Jeffersonian period the threat of secession was never very far from the public mind.[259] Jefferson's administration inherited this problem despite George Washington's exhortation in his farewell address that his fellow citizens ought properly to estimate the immense value of their national union and discountenance "whatever may even suggest a

---

256. Emerson, *supra* note 247, at 140–41.
257. D. MALONE, JEFFERSON AND THE RIGHTS OF MAN, xviii (1951).
258. T. JEFFERSON, 3 THE WRITINGS OF THOMAS JEFFERSON 60 (A. Bergh ed. 1905).
259. "There seems never to have been a time in the early decades of American history under the Constitution when the secession of one section or another was not considered a real possibility." C. SWISHER, AMERICAN CONSTITUTIONAL DEVELOPMENT 127 (2d ed. 1954).

suspicion that it can in any event be abandoned and indignantly frown upon the first dawning of every attempt to alienate any portion of our Country from the rest."[260] In a 1786 letter to James Madison, Jefferson discussed a proposed division of the western territory into states:

> I find Congress have reversed their division of the western States, and proposed to make them fewer and larger. This is reversing the natural order of things. A tractable people may be governed in large bodies; but, in proportion as they depart from this character, the extent of their government must be less. . . . [T]he moment we sacrifice their [the western States'] interests to our own, they will see it better to govern themselves. The moment they resolve to do this, the point is settled. *A forced connection is neither our interest, nor within our power.*[261]

At about this same time, Jefferson found himself defending Shays' Rebellion in Massachusetts (1786–87) and approving the therapeutic effect of such movements on entrenched governments. "The tree of liberty," he wrote, "must be refreshed from time to time with the blood of patriots and tyrants. It is its natural manure."[262] In the same vein, he was even willing to contemplate a disruption of the union in 1816 under the influence of commercial differences: "If any State in the Union will declare that it prefers separation . . . to a continuance in union . . . I have no hesitation in saying, 'let us separate.' "[263] But the real danger was to come from the issue of slavery and, in a despairing tone, Jefferson foresaw in 1820 the disaster that would overtake the nation four decades later:

> I regret that I am now to die in the belief, that the useless sacrifice of themselves by the generation of 1776, to acquire self-government and happiness to their country, is to be thrown away by the unwise and unworthy passions of their sons, and that my only consolation is to be, that I live not to weep over it. If they would but dispassionately weigh the blessings they will throw away, against an abstract principle more likely to be effected by union

260. 35 THE WRITINGS OF GEORGE WASHINGTON 1745–1799, at 219 (J. Fitzpatrick ed. 1940).
261. 6 JEFFERSON, *supra* note 258, at 9–10 (emphasis mine).
262. *Id.* 373.
263. Letter to W. Crawford, June 20, 1816, 15 JEFFERSON 29.

than by scission, they would pause before they would perpetrate this act of suicide on themselves, and of treason against the hopes of the world.[264]

The reaction of the United States in 1860 to its first and only serious instance of a forceful claim of secessionist self-determination by a large segment of its population is too well known to be worth documenting. There was, of course, no unanimity of opinion in the years before the outbreak of the Civil War over the status of secession as a right inhering in the separate states of the union. Both the Federalists of New England and the western states had argued for a right of secession earlier in the century. The "right" to secede had in fact "been accepted both as truth and as treason by each section of the country in turn, depending on whether its interests were temporarily served by affirming or by denying the sovereignty of the central government."[265]

These precedents did not, however, impede the trend of Northern opinion in denying the right of secession for their Southern brethren.[266] Depending on one's viewpoint, the metamorphosis that took place between the era of Jefferson and that of Lincoln may be seen as either a growth in social maturity or an increase in political ossification. The general movement away from the Jeffersonian approval of occasional rebellion and belief in the salutary effect of secessionist rumblings was not confined to the national level. Many individuals underwent a similar transition as the stark reality of disunion came near. Thus, a dozen years before assuming the burdens of the presidency, the young politician Abraham Lincoln was willing to concede that:

---

264. *Id.* 250. He was not without hope, however, for the eventual reunification of the nation. His prediction, which was never given the opportunity to prove itself, was that, should

> the schism be pushed to separation, it will be for a short term only; two or three years' trial will bring them back, like quarrelling lovers to renewed embraces, and increased affections. The experiment of separation would soon prove to both that they had mutually miscalculated their best interests. And even were the parties in Congress to secede in a passion, the soberer people would call a convention and cement again the severance attempted by the insanity of their functionaires.

Letter to R. Rush, Oct. 20, 1820, *id.* 283–84.

265. H. AGAR, THE PRICE OF UNION 405 (1950).

266. The South was itself not unanimous in affirming a right of secession. For examples of criticism of the doctrine in the South before the war *see* A. CRAVEN, 4 A HISTORY OF THE SOUTH: THE GROWTH OF SOUTHERN NATIONALISM 1848–1861, at 122–26 (1953).

Any people anywhere, being inclined and having the power, have the *right* to rise up, and shake off the existing government, and form a new one that suits them better. This is a most valuable, — a most sacred right — a right, which we hope and believe, is to liberate the world. Nor is this right confined to cases in which the whole people of an existing government, may choose to exercise it. Any portion of such people that *can, may* revolutionize, and make their *own*, of so much of the territory as they inhabit. More than this, a *majority* of any portion of such people may revolutionize, putting down a *minority*, intermingled with, or near about them, who may oppose their movement.[267]

By the date of his inauguration, Lincoln expressed a somewhat different opinion on this subject. Secession was no longer seen as a "sacred right," but rather as the "essence of anarchy."[268] His argument for the perpetual nature of the union[269] invoked two of the traditional themes of those opposing 'secession: the need for governmental oppression as a precondition of a legitimate secession and the prospect of indefinite divisibility. Granting that the nature of a democracy is rule by the majority and that this fact will sometimes be the cause of a disaffection in the minority, Lincoln nevertheless reiterated that the United States Constitution guarantees protection for both minority groups and individuals against an undue tyranny of the majority.[270] By implication, in the absence of such tyranny and in the light of those protections, Lincoln felt that there was no "right" to secede. Furthermore, Lincoln took the occasion of his inaugural address to remind the secessionists that there was no logical stopping place for the principle of secession. "If a minority, in such case, will secede rather than acquiesce, they make a precedent which, in turn, will divide and ruin them; for a minority of their own will secede from them, whenever a majority refuses to be controlled by such a minority."[271]

The issue decided upon the battlefields of the American Civil War — that the union was indivisible and component states could not

267. Speech in the U.S. House of Representatives: The War with Mexico, Jan. 12, 1848, 1 THE COLLECTED WORKS OF ABRAHAM LINCOLN 431, 438 (R. Basler ed. 1953).
268. First Inaugural Address, 4 COLLECTED WORKS OF LINCOLN, *id.* 262, 268.
269. "Perpetuity," Lincoln said, "is implied, if not expressed, in the fundamental law of all national governments. It is safe to assert that no government proper ever had a provision in its organic law for its own termination." *Id.* 264.
270. *Id.* 267.
271. *Id.*

unilaterally secede from it—was given judicial recognition at the war's end. The answer in terms of constitutional law was, of course, a reaffirmation of the legality of the unionist wartime cause. In the case of *Texas* v. *White,* decided in April 1869, Chief Justice Salmon P. Chase, speaking for a majority of the United States Supreme Court, did not consider it necessary to discuss at length the question whether the right of a state to withdraw from the union for any cause regarded by itself as sufficient was consistent with the Constitution of the United States. The union of the states, he believed, was never a purely artificial and arbitrary relation. Beginning with the original colonies, the relation grew out of common origin, mutual sympathies, kindred principles, similar interests, and geographical relations.

> It was confirmed and strengthened by the necessities of war, and received definite form, and character, and sanction from the Articles of Confederation. By these the Union was solemly declared to "be perpetual." And when these articles were found to be inadequate to the exigencies of the country, the Constitution was ordained "to form a more perfect Union." It is difficult to convey the idea of indissoluble unity more clearly than by these words. What can be indissoluble if a perpetual Union, made more perfect, is not?[272]

If the Civil War demonstrated with the utmost clarity the hostility of the United States to acts of secessionist self-determination within its borders, the policies pursued between the death of Lincoln and the beginning of the Wilsonian era evidenced an equivalent insensitivity to claims of self-determination by other national groups. This was the age of "manifest destiny," with its remorseless subjugation of native American Indians; of economic imperialism; the Spanish War; the annexation of Puerto Rico, the Philippines, Guam, and Hawaii; the "Boxer" Rebellion in China; and a much criticized policy toward the Latin American States.[273] It was a time during which the nation consolidated its territory on the North American continent and began to test its youthful muscles abroad—both of which were accomplished at the expense of what we would now call a reasonable respect for the demands of self-determination.

---

272. 7 Wall. 700, 725 (1869). For a defense of the legality of the South's secession *see* B. SAMUEL, SECESSION AND CONSTITUTIONAL LIBERTY, 2 vols. (1920).

273. For a general summary of the events during the period *see* BEARDS, *supra* note 253, at 318–33; L. SEARS, A HISTORY OF AMERICAN FOREIGN RELATIONS 433–510 (3d ed. 1936).

Although the United States did not emerge as the paladin of peoples seeking self-government, it was nevertheless not entirely blind to
such wishes when they coincided with its own interests. In 1903, for
example, the United States prevented Colombia from landing troops
to suppress the secession of Panama. Shortly thereafter the United
States received from the new Panamanian government a grant, in perpetuity, of the land known as the Panama Canal Zone.[274]

The election of Woodrow Wilson in 1912 offered hope for a significant change in American foreign policy. Wilson the theorist, Wilson
the internationalist, Wilson the humanitarian — all of these suggested
that the face of American foreign policy would gain a new com-
plexion unblemished by the "big stick" or "dollar diplomacy." It would
be Wilson, after all, who would enthrone the phrase "self-determination" as a shibboleth in the vocabulary of American statesmanship.
From the outset, two aspects of Wilson's administration must be kept
separate: his handling of the foreign policy of the United States during the years of his presidency, and his hopes for self-determination
as a principle governing the post–World War I period. It is far too
facile merely to cite the former as the basis for a healthy cynicism
about the latter. The apparent inconsistency between these two elements of Wilson's presidency may be explained by his desire to limit
the principle of self-determination to areas ready to assume the burdens of democratic self-government. In politically immature States, a
certain amount of external guidance did not, in Wilson's mind, violate
any precepts of self-determination. Once the process of political maturation had succeeded, however, Wilson would insist on the use of the
principle of self-determination to legitimate any resulting government.

In point of fact, Wilson became deeply embroiled, with more or less
justification, in the internal affairs of Mexico, Haiti, Santo Domingo,
and Nicaragua during the term of his presidency.[275] One noted biographer of the president has concluded, "In contrast to Wilson's fair
promises stands the record of American interference in Mexico, Central America, and the Caribbean region from 1913 to 1917, unparal-
leled before or since in the history of the western hemisphere." [276]

274. *See* G. CONNELL-SMITH, THE UNITED STATES AND LATIN AMERICA: AN HIS-
TORICAL ANALYSIS OF INTER-AMERICAN RELATIONS 104–05 (1974).

275. For a discussion of these interventions *see* T. BURLEY, A DIPLOMATIC HISTORY OF
THE AMERICAN PEOPLE 592–609 (3d ed. 1947); L. CANFIELD, THE PRESIDENCY OF WOOD-
ROW WILSON 39–57 (1966); A. LINK, WOODROW WILSON AND THE PROGRESSIVE ERA
81–144 (1954); A. LINK, WILSON, THE NEW FREEDOM 319–416 (1965); H. NOTTER, THE
ORIGINS OF THE FOREIGN POLICY OF WOODROW WILSON 221–314 (1937).

276. LINK, WILSON, THE NEW FREEDOM 327.

Wilson's response to these situations, however, is more akin to a professorial annoyance with a disorderly classroom and squabbling students than to the territorial acquisitiveness of his predecessors. Wilson and his Secretary of State, William Jennings Bryan, "were both fundamentally missionaries, evangelists, confident that they comprehended the peace and well-being of other countries better than the leaders of those countries themselves. This urge to do good, to render disinterested service, was so compelling that it motivated interference in the internal affairs of other nations on such a scale as the United States had not heretofore attempted." [277] Although not politically exculpatory, this view of Wilson's hemispheric policy is at least personally explanatory. The historian need not dismiss, on the strength of this interventionist record, the sincerity of Wilson's crusade for a recognition of the principle of self-determination as one of the war aims of the Allied Powers.

As the end of World War I came into sight, Wilson began to proselytize for his image of a world order that would regulate the peacetime conduct of nations and prevent the outbreak of future wars. The first step in this process he understood to be the establishment of a just peace, a peace without retribution and founded on a universal respect for the principle of self-determination. "Self-determination," he told Congress on February 11, 1918, "is not a mere phrase. It is an imperative principle of action, which statesmen will henceforth ignore at their peril." [278] Wilson's own view of self-determination was essentially that of a devout believer in democracy, and he would have agreed with J. S. Mill that, "Where the sentiment of nationality exists in any force, there is a prima facie case for uniting all the members of the nationality under the same government, and a government to themselves apart. This is merely saying that the question of government ought to be decided by the governed." [279] The proponent of such a view must be prepared to accept the possibility that a multiplicity of small States will be generated. Under these circumstances, Wilson argued, it is clear that the principle of national self-determination requires an international organization to insure the integrity of such small States against aggression. Without it, the Wilsonian reasoning runs, conquest or simply the strategic realities of an armed continent

277. LINK, WILSON AND THE PROGRESSIVE ERA 81–82.

278. W. WILSON, 1 THE MESSAGES AND PAPERS OF WOODROW WILSON 475 (A. Shaw ed. 1924) (hereinafter MESSAGES).

279. J. S. MILL, UTILITARIANISM, LIBERTY AND REPRESENTATIVE GOVERNMENT 486 (1951).

would again force the amalgamation of small States into larger group-ings.

Once again, it would be a serious error to use the tarnished record of the Paris Peace Conference with regard to the principle of self-determination, and Wilson's acquiescence in the results of the confer-ence, as a basis for a healthy skepticism about the sincerity of Wilson's motives at the opening of the talks. By acknowledging the criticism of Wilson as overly ingenuous in assuming that moral righteousness would conquer political venality at Paris, we can acquit him of the charge of disingenuousness based upon his espousal of principles that had the effect of furthering the Allied war effort during the bellig-erency, and his apparent abandonment of them afterwards. Wilson himself explained the circumstances of this inconsistency in an almost pathetic tone in the 1919 hearings before the United States Senate Committee on Foreign Relations:

> When I gave utterance to those words ["that all nations had a right to self-determination"], I said them without the knowledge that nationalities existed, which are coming to us day after day. . . . You do not know and cannot appreciate the anxieties that I have experienced as the result of many millions of people having their hopes raised by what I have said. For instance, time after time I raise a question here in accordance with these prin-ciples and I am met with the statement that Great Britain or France or some of the other countries have entered into a solemn treaty obligation. I tell them, but it was not in accord with justice and humanity; and they tell me that the breaking of treaties is what has brought on the greater part of the wars that have been waged in the world.[280]

Through the haze of his obsessive concern with self-determination as a political principle, Wilson's beliefs regarding separatist or seces-sionist movements within recognized States are difficult to pinpoint. Sarah Wambaugh has interpreted Wilson's repeated refusals to favor the petitions from subject nationalities which flooded him toward the end of the war as evidence that the president's words did not endorse a right of secession.[281] He referred to the problem obliquely during his railroad tour of the United States undertaken to marshall the sup-port of the American people for the League of Nations. Wilson,

---

280. *Quoted in* 4 TEMPERLY, *supra* note 57, at 429.
281. S. WAMBAUGH, 1 PLEBISCITES SINCE THE WAR 4 (1933).

speaking in defense of article 10 of the Covenant of the League at Salt Lake City on September 23, 1919,[282] stressed that this clause would never require the United States to help another member of the League to put down a rebellion of its own citizens. He did *not* say that America would be legally or morally bound to aid the insurrectionists; rather, that nothing in the Covenant would compel the United States to abandon a neutral position between the two forces. Wilson clearly felt that any American denial of a people's right to revolution in such a case would, in effect, be a denial of its own parentage. He said: "The glory of the United States is that when we were a little body of 3,000,000 people strung along the Atlantic coast we threw off the power of a great empire because it was not a power chosen by or consented to by ourselves. We hold to that principle. We never will guarantee any Government against the exercise of that right, and no suggestion was made at the conference that we should." [283]

The debate between President Wilson and those like his Secretary of State Robert Lansing, who were unalterably opposed to self-determination as an operative principle, has had a lasting effect on American foreign policy. In the final analysis, perhaps both Wilson and Lansing were right. Wilson can be commended for his singleminded determination that the legitimacy of any government depends ultimately upon the consent of those governed, and that the transformation of this principle into a political reality is as much a matter of self-discipline as of diplomatic art. For his part, Lansing was justified in admonishing that disillusionment must surely follow in the wake of so much "principled" talk,[284] and for his reminder that kings were not yet philosophers, and that citizens corresponded at least as much to Hobbes's model as to that of Jefferson. The practice of American diplomacy in the area of self-determination since the First World War may be seen as an attempt to reconcile these conflicting viewpoints and amalgamate them, sometimes with little success, into a recognizable foreign policy.

282. Article 10 reads: "The High Contracting Parties undertake to respect and preserve as against external aggression the territorial integrity and existing political independence of all states members of the League. In case of any such aggression or in case of any threat or danger of such aggression the Executive Council shall advise upon the means by which this obligation shall be fulfilled." 2 MESSAGES 626.

283. *Id.* 1081.

284. *See, e.g.,* J. GARRATY, WOODROW WILSON 130 (1970): "Fine-sounding slogans like 'self-determination' . . . led inevitably to misunderstanding, distortion, and frustration. Hopes raised heavenward by well-meaning idealism then crashed to sinful earth." To the same effect is CLAUDE, *supra* note 65, at 13.

In the decades following Wilson's presidency, self-determination gained a considerable amount of currency in the vocabulary of American foreign policy. The nation was gradually weaned from the more flagrant temptations of imperialism and the American position against colonialism became firmer. In the Declaration of Principles of August 14, 1941, known as the Atlantic Charter, Franklin Delano Roosevelt and Winston Churchill agreed that "they [would] respect the right of all people to choose the form of government under which they will live; and they wish to see sovereign rights and self-government restored to those who have been forcibly deprived of them." [285] It is significant that exclusion of colonial territories from the meaning of the Atlantic Charter was a British demand secured over Roosevelt's protest.[286]

Within international forums, American pronouncements on the principle of self-determination have sought to convey several themes. First, although the United States has consistently reiterated its disapproval of colonialism, it has never agreed to an arbitrary limitation of the principle as encompassing only cases of Western colonial occupation. Instead, the American approach has sought to muster a general recognition of the principle of self-determination as applicable to those countries, such as the nations of Eastern Europe and Tibet, which were forcibly subjected to communist control.[287] Of course, rather than use just these terms — which would, after all, sound suspiciously like a case of selective myopia in the perception of the scope of the principle for political ends — the delegates of the United States attempted to formulate a more abstract statement which would include colonial territories and the communist satellites but little else. Thus, it became common to hear American representatives argue that the principle was "applicable to peoples which had formerly enjoyed independence but who were deprived of the possibility of governing themselves." [288]

285. Quoted in M. WHITEMAN, 5 DIGEST OF INTERNATIONAL LAW 44 (1965).

286. *See* Venkataramani, *The United States, The Colonial Issue, and the Atlantic Charter Hoax,* 13 INT'L STUDIES 1 (1974).

287. *See* Kohn, *Nationalism in the United Nations,* in THE UNITED STATES AND THE UNITED NATIONS 42–64 (F. Gross ed. 1965); Jacobson, *Decolonization,* in SOVIET AND AMERICAN POLICIES IN THE UNITED NATIONS 73–93 (A. Rubinstein & G. Ginsburgs eds. 1971).

288. 6 U.N. GAOR, 3d. Comm., 364th meeting at 105, para. 19, U.N. Doc. A/C.3/SR.364 (1951). *See generally* Barbour, *The Concept of Self-Determination in American Thought,* 31 DEP'T STATE BULL. 576 (1954).

Second, the American view of self-determination has never recognized a general legitimacy of secessionist self-determination by groups within unified, independent States. This was made clear in 1952 by Eleanor Roosevelt, then American representative to the United Nations General Assembly. In an article entitled, interestingly, "The Universal Validity of Man's Right to Self-Determination," Mrs. Roosevelt claimed that the universal validity of the principle does not include secession.

> Does self-determination mean the right of secession? Does self-determination constitute a right of fragmentation or a justification for the fragmentation of nations? Does self-determination mean the right of people to sever association with another power regardless of the economic effect upon both parties, regardless of the effect upon their internal stability and their external security, regardless of the effect upon their neighbors or the international community? Obviously not.[289]

The refusal of the United States to accord any measure of legitimacy to secessionist movements within independent States has on several occasions been invoked as the theoretical justification for American behavior in the world arena. After the United States supported the action to suppress the secession of Katanga from the Congo, for instance, a State Department spokesman, asked whether this violated "traditional United States support for the principle of self-determinaton," replied in the negative. His explanation began with a denial of any "absolute" principle of self-determination: "We fought a civil war to deny it. We have recognized both at home and abroad the danger of Balkanization." [290] Similarly, the United States has shown disfavor to the attempted separation of Biafra from Nigeria and the secession

---

289. 27 DEP'T STATE BULL. 917, 919 (1952). This view has been consistently repeated by State Department spokesmen. Deputy Under-Secretary Robert Murphy, speaking on "The Principle of Self-Determination in International Relations" in 1955, for example, cited historical reasons for the American disapproval of both secessionism and colonization. The two decisive facts of American history, according to Murphy, are that "we struggled to free ourselves from alien rule, and we struggled to remain a united people by rejecting the principle of secession carried to the point where we as a nation would have ceased to exist." Murphy, *The Principle of Self-Determination in International Relations,* 32 DEP'T STATE BULL. 889 (1955). *See also* Lent, *American Foreign Policy and the Principle of Self-Determination,* 133 WORLD AFF. 293 (1971).

290. Gardner, *The United Nations in Crisis: Cuba and the Congo,* 48 DEP'T STATE BULL. 477, 479 (1963). The theoretical basis for the American position is also explained in E. GROSS, THE UNITED NATIONS: STRUCTURE FOR PEACE 111 (1962). For a discussion of the more mundane motivations *see* S. WEISSMAN, AMERICAN FOREIGN POLICY IN THE CONGO 1960–1964 (1974).

of Bangla Desh from Pakistan. In the latter case, in fact, accusations have been made that the United States continued to supply arms to the Pakistani government which were then used to further the unsuccessful attempt to suppress the secession.[291]

Even in those instances in which the United States is reputed to have covertly supported a separatist movement, as reports indicate was true in Tibet[292] and more recently in the Kurdish revolt against Iraq, the actions appear to have been motivated by political self-interest rather than a perceived obligation arising from the demands of self-determination. In the Kurdish situation at least, recent reports suggest that the American offer of covert support and its subsequent abrupt withdrawal because of a change in political circumstances showed a cynical disregard for the fate of the Kurdish people.[293] The reported circumstances of these actions, if true, certainly indicate that the American government believed them to be outside of, rather than in vindication of, the doctrines of international law, and they do not portend any general movement toward an American acceptance of separatist legitimacy.

The search for an American recognition of some degree of legitimacy for claims based on a right to secessionist self-determination finds its high-water mark in a 1966 proposal to the Special Committee on Principles of International Law concerning Friendly Relations and Co-operation among States. The proposal begins by securing within the ambit of the principle both territories under colonial domination and areas unwillingly subjected to communist control. This is done by affirming in paragraph 2 (A) (1) that the principle is applicable to situations involving (i) a colony or other non-self-governing territory, (ii) a zone of occupation ensuing upon the termination of military hostilities, and (iii) a trust territory. The text then goes on to say, however, that "(2) The principle is *prima facie* applicable in the case of the exercise of sovereignty by a State over a territory geographically distinct and ethnically or culturally diverse from the remainder of that State's territory, even though not as a colony or other Non-Self-Governing Territory."[294]

291. For a refutation of these charges *see* Choudhury, *The Emergence of Bangla Desh and the South Asian Triangle*, 1973 Y.B. WORLD AFF. 62.

292. *See, e.g.,* V. MARCHETTI, J. MARKS, THE CIA AND THE CULT OF INTELLIGENCE 143, 146 (1974).

293. *See* Shawcross, *Banned Report Says America Left Kurds in the Lurch*, The Sunday Times (London), Feb. 15, 1976, at 6.

294. U.N. Doc. A/AC.125/L.32 (1966). The text of the United States proposal is contained in 1966 Special Committee on Principles of International Law concerning Friendly Relations and Co-operation among States, Report, 21 U.N. GAOR, Annex, Agenda Item No. 87, at 91, U.N. Doc. A/6230 (1966).

The use of the phrase *"prima facie* applicable" in this provision suggests an extension of the principle to encompass separatist claims in certain circumstances — such claims to be investigated on a case by case basis. This was, moreover, the apparent intention of the United States when it introduced the proposal. The American representative in the Special Committee explained the text by saying that the applicability of the principle to the situations covered by this paragraph was prima facie only and could be rebutted by a further examination of the characteristics of the situation. "It rested," he said, ". . . on the fundamental premise that when a territory over which a State exercised sovereignty exhibited certain basic divergencies from the bulk of that State's territory, there was at least a legitimate question whether [the principle] was being satisfied."[295]

The American delegate continued by drawing the committee's attention to paragraph 2(B) of the United States proposal which read: "The existence of a sovereign and independent State possessing a representative Government, effectively functioning as such to all distinct peoples within its territory, is presumed to satisfy the principle of equal rights and self-determination as regards those peoples." [296] This paragraph, he noted, served a dual function. "First, no rational international legal order could exist if the Charter were taken to sanction an unlimited right of secession by indigenous peoples from sovereign and independent States, nor could such a right be found in the Charter." [297] Second, the Charter's inclusion of the concept of self-determination of "peoples," he explained, provided a certain standard by which to judge the legitimacy of the modes of political organization which were imposed on peoples. The requirement of an effectively functioning representative government was intended by the United States to express that standard.[298]

To the student of the development of the United States attitude toward secession, what is significant about this explanation is not that it fails to recognize a general right of secession but rather that it disavows only an *unlimited* right to secede. Although the proposal does not give an indication of what criteria, beyond geographic and ethnic distinctness and subjection to a nonrepresentative regime, are necessary to invoke the application of the principle, the fact remains that secession is clearly available as a remedy in *some* situations and, more-

295. Report Spec. Comm., 44th Mtg. at 7, para. 10, U.N. Doc. A/AC.125/SR.44 (1966).
296. *Supra* note 294.
297. *Supra* note 295, para. 12.
298. *Id.* 8, para. 12.

over, that a group separating from its governing State under such circumstances is acting under the aegis of the principle of self-determination.

Secession in Soviet Theory and Practice

Even extending every benefit of the doubt, one is forced to summa-
rize the development of the doctrine of secessionist self-determination
in Soviet history by saying that theory has once again failed significantly to influence practice. In one sense, of course, the very existence of a constitutionally acknowledged right of secession within such
a large, multinational State as the Soviet Union is quite extraordinary,
and certainly there is presently no counterpart to this explicit recognition in the so-called free societies of the Western bloc. As we have
seen, much propaganda mileage has been squeezed out of this fact by
Soviet spokesmen in international forums. The Soviets have enjoyed
the rare pleasure of being able to denounce the classic varieties of
Western colonialism[299] while confirming their own virtue in this regard by stressing the theoretical availability of the right of secession to
every republic within the USSR.[300] Even the former colonial territories
have not been able to share in the full righteousness of this apparent
acceptance of the totality of the principle of self-determination. The
growth of this doctrine, and the actual extent, in practice, of the
"right" to secede, therefore merit close attention.

The early Soviet theorists were remarkably explicit in admitting a
right to secessionist self-determination, probably as a result of, rather
than in spite of, the numerous national groups contained within the
Soviet borders. It was primarily Lenin's thesis that some expansive
talk about secessionist rights was necessary to insure the acceptance of
the early revolutionary movement by the many nationalities contained
within tsarist Russia. By offering a protection of national rights, up to
and including the right to secede, Lenin hoped to assuage the fears of
the disparate populations within the Russian empire and woo them to
the revolutionary cause. Thus, in 1914, Lenin wrote, "if we want to

299. For discussions of the Soviet disapproval of colonialism *see* Ginsburgs, *"Wars of
National Liberation" and the Modern Law of Nations—The Soviet Thesis,* in H. BAADE, THE
SOVIET IMPACT ON INTERNATIONAL LAW 66 (1965); Goodman, *The Cry of National Libera-
tion: Recent Soviet Attitudes toward National Self-Determination,* 14 INT'L ORGANIZ. 92
(1960); Levin, *The Principle of Self-Determination of Nations in International Law,* 1962 So-
VIET Y.B. INT'L L. 45.

300. One Soviet jurist has recently touted the significance of the right of secession in
the Soviet constitution by saying, "The Soviet state gave the world a shining example of
resolving the national question on the basis of the principle of self-determination." G.
TUNKIN, THEORY OF INTERNATIONAL LAW (W. Butler trans. 1974).

grasp the meaning of self-determination of nations . . . we must inevitably reach the conclusion that the self-determination of nations means the political separation of these nations from alien national bodies, and the formation of an independent national state."[301] This expansive theory of self-determination did not meet with universal approval from Lenin's colleagues, some of whom felt it to be a declaration of political suicide to recognize such a right in light of the multinational character of the country.

Lenin responded with a series of arguments to the criticism that an identification of the right to self-determination with the right of secession would inevitably lead to the propagation of small, disunited States. First, he noted that to support freedom of secession is *not* to encourage separatism any more than an advocate of liberal divorce necessarily wishes to encourage the destruction of family ties.[302] In addition, the benefits of belonging to a large State will induce minority nationalities to exercise their right of secession only in the most intolerable of circumstances. Lenin clearly believed that the right would be a remedy of last resort and not, as his critics suggested, an attractive panacea casually exercisable by any small group.[303] Indeed, in Lenin's view, an acknowledged freedom to secede occupied an important place in convincing component nationalities that the State was bent upon preventing conditions from becoming intolerable.

Finally, any short-term separations from the mother State would certainly be made good when the centripetal effects of large-State economies were recognized by the separatists. The result of freedom of secession, Lenin argued, would therefore be an even larger, voluntary amalgamation of nationalities: "To defend this right [to secession] does in no way mean encouraging the formation of small states, but to the contrary, it leads to a freer, . . . wider formation of larger states— a phenomenon more advantageous for the masses and more in accord with economic development."[304]

Even as he formulated it, however, Lenin's rhetoric on self-determi-

---

301. V. I. LENIN, ON THE NATIONAL QUESTION AND PROLETARIAN INTERNATIONALISM 9–10 (1969) [hereinafter NATIONAL QUESTION]. For general discussions of Lenin's theory of self-determination *see* R. PIPES, THE FORMATION OF THE SOVIET UNION: COMMUNISM AND NATIONALISM 1917–1923, at 41–49 (1964); Peeters, *The Right of Nations to Autodetermination*, 3 WORLD JUSTICE 147, 153–64 (1961).

302. NATIONAL QUESTION 41. *See also* A. LOW, LENIN ON THE QUESTION OF NATIONALITY 36 (1958).

303. NATIONAL QUESTION 42.

304. *Quoted in* Low, *supra* note 302, at 68. *See also* Groshev, BOOK REVIEW, 13 SOVIET LAW AND GOVERNMENT 100, 107 (1975):

nation was never allowed to interfere with the dictates of political expediency. The limitations on the doctrine were already suggested in 1917 when he wrote, "The right of nations freely to secede must not be confused with the advisability of secession by a given nation at a given moment." [305] This latter question, he urged, must be decided by the party of the proletariat "having regard to the interests of social development as a whole and the interests of the class struggle of the proletariat for socialism." [306] As a tactical weapon against the capitalistic empires, Lenin's declarations on self-determination were of undoubted efficacy. As a constitutional principle for dealing with national groups within the Soviet Union and along its borders, the absolute right to secession was found to be a politically unmanageable policy.[307] As it happened, the doctrine used to draw the teeth of self-determination was ready at hand in the theory of proletarian internationalism. The tension between the Soviet rhetoric of secessionist rights and the goal of proletarian (socialist) internationalism had always been evident to the sensitive observer. Lenin had suggested that the formation of small States was simply a transitional phase between

---

[Lenin] pointed out that the convergence and merger of nations are defined primarily by the operation of the economic laws of social development that inevitably lead to breaking down the barriers between nations, to the end of national self-containment and exclusiveness, and to mutual influencing of peoples on the basis of the internationalization of production, science, technology, the achievement of culture, and so forth.

305. Resolution on the National Question, V.I. LENIN, 2 SELECTED WORKS 139 (1970).
306. *Id.* The confusion that can result from an attempted application of the Leninist doctrine on secession to particular cases is instanced by the various communist responses to the Biafran situation. The Soviet Union chose to support the Nigerian Federal Government against the Biafran secessionists because, as a spokesman in the Soviet press agency Tass phrased it, "Never has tribalism been identified with self-determination." Quoted in S. CRONJE, THE WORLD AND NIGERIA 258 (1972). A British Communist Party statement quoted Lenin to support the opposite conclusion—that communists have an obligation to fight for the right of the Biafrans to decide the question of secession by a free and democratic method. The Biafrans themselves also enlisted Lenin's writings in support of their separation. *See id.* 259–60.
307. *See generally* E. CARR, 1 THE BOLSHEVIK REVOLUTION 1917–1923, at 292–383, 414–35 (1973); W. CHAMBERLIN, 2 THE RUSSIAN REVOLUTION 1917–1921, at 370–71 (1965); O. JANOWSKY, NATIONALITIES AND NATIONAL MINORITIES 86–104 (1945); Low, *supra* note 302, at 129–39; R. SCHLESINGER, FEDERALISM IN CENTRAL AND EASTERN EUROPE 319–414 (1945); S. SHAHEEN, THE COMMUNIST (BOLSHEVIK) THEORY OF NATIONAL SELF-DETERMINATION (1956); J. TRISKA, R. SLUSSER, THE THEORY, LAW, AND POLICY OF SOVIET TREATIES 198–202 (1962); A. COBBAN, *supra* note 52, at 187–218 (1970). Cobban writes: "The Communist government, in other words, was forced to recognize that as a practical policy national self-determination, or the right of secession, was incompatible with the military and economic interests of Soviet Russia." *Id.* 197.

the artificiality of the capitalist multinational State and a voluntary union of socialist communities. Moreover, the tactical value of a Soviet recognition of a right to secessionist self-determination, Lenin reasoned, outweighed any temporary hindrance of an international proletarian culture.[308]

In practice, however, the claims of internationalism were to operate as an effective qualification on the national right of secession. The welfare of the general proletarian revolution, it was argued,[309] must be considered in balancing whether a particular nation should exercise its right of secession. Where the territory in question was closely tied to the military or economic well-being of Greater Russia, an exercise of the right to secession could only mean a retrograde, counter-revolutionary movement, and the demands of the socialist community as a whole must prevail in discouraging the exercise of the right.[310] In 1916 Lenin wrote, "The various demands of democracy, including self-determination, are not absolute, but a *small part* of the general democratic; now general socialist, *world* movement. In individual concrete cases, the part may contradict the whole; if so it must be rejected." [311] In a similar vein, Joseph Stalin warned that the question of the rights of nations is not an isolated, self-sufficient question; "it is part of the general problem of the proletarian revolution, subordinate to the whole, and must be considered from the point of view of the whole." [312] In 1923, when he was holding the post of People's Commissar of Nationalities, Stalin expounded his belief that the right of peoples to self-determination must be subordinated to the right of the working class to strengthen its power. This latter right, described by Stalin as a "higher" right, occasionally conflicts with that of self-determination. When this happens, he said, "the right of self-determination cannot and must not serve as an obstacle to the working class in exercising its right to dictatorship. The former must yield to the latter." [313]

308. "If, in our political agitation, we fail to advance and advocate the slogan of the *right* to secession, we shall play into the hands, not only of the bourgeoisie, but also of the feudal landlords and the absolutism of the *oppressor* nation." NATIONAL QUESTION, *supra* note 302, at 28.

309. *See* SHAHEEN, *supra* note 307, at 128–29.

310. CARR, *supra* note 307, at 388, quotes Stalin as saying that "the interests of the masses of the people say that the demand for the separation of the borderlands at the present stage of the revolution is profoundly counter-revolutionary."

311. Quoted in SHAHEEN, *supra* note 307, at 128.

312. The Foundations of Leninism, J.V. STALIN, 6 WORKS 147 (1953).

313. Reply to the Discussion on National Factors in Party and State Affairs, *id.* vol. 5, at 270.

Historically, the preference for the interests of the general socialist movement over the secessionist wishes of a particular nationality has embodied the typical Soviet response to claims of self-determination arising within its borders. Thus, the Ukraine, Georgia, and Turkestan each learned that its nationalistic sentiment was incompatible with the good of the general socialist order. As the borders of Russia were expanded by the envelopment of such areas as Latvia, Estonia, and Lithuania, and (after World War II) by the assertion of Soviet influence in the satellite countries of Eastern Europe, the requirements of Soviet internationalism broadened accordingly to prevent any manifestations of divergent self-determination in the new additions. The logic seems to be simply one of disbelief; any movement toward leaving the Soviet fold is unimaginable and could not represent the true wishes of the proletarian masses involved. Therefore, the other socialist republics are justified in stifling what could only be a counterrevolutionary minority and restoring the socialist regime both for the good of the masses of workers within the maverick country and for the good of the international socialist order. The movement of USSR and Warsaw Pact military forces into Czechoslovakia in 1968 was justified on precisely these paternalistic grounds. An apologist for the Soviet action, writing in the Soviet Communist Party newspaper *Pravda*, criticized the withdrawal of Czechoslovakia from the socialist community by saying that "the sovereignty of individual socialist countries cannot be counterposed to the interests of world socialism and the world revolutionary movement." [314] The justification for such a move by reference to the principle of self-determination was, in his view, dangerously mistaken.

The implementation of such "self-determination," in other words, Czechoslovakia's detachment from the socialist community, would have come into conflict with its own vital interests and would have been detrimental to the other socialist states.

Such "self-determination," as a result of which NATO troops would have been able to come up to the Soviet border, while the community of European socialist countries would have been split, in effect encroaches upon the vital interests of the peoples of these countries and conflicts, as the very root of it, with the right of these people to socialist self-determination.

Discharging their internationalist duty toward the fraternal

314. Kovalev, *Sovereignty and International Duties of Socialist Countries*, reprinted in 7 INT'L LEGAL MAT. 1323 (1968).

peoples of Czechoslovakia and defending their own socialist gains, the U.S.S.R. and other socialist states had to act decisively and they did act against the antisocialist forces in Czechoslovakia.[315]

The article goes on to suggest that the legality of the invasion, even if in apparent disharmony with some traditional norms of international law, was nevertheless justified by a higher principle of socialist internationalism. "Laws and legal norms," the author continues, "are subject to the laws of the class struggle, the laws of social development. These laws are clearly formulated in Marxist-Leninist teaching, in the documents jointly adopted by the Communist and Workers' parties." [316] By thus adopting a dual structure of legal norms,[317] the Soviet Union has been able to argue with impunity for the right of peoples to self-determination, including the right of secession. The only qualification to this principle in Soviet thinking arises from its subsidiary position to the higher demands of socialist internationalism, a status which has the incidental effect of circumscribing the operative sphere of the principle to the noncommunist areas of the world.

In summary, despite a singularly explicit rhetoric, the practice of the Soviet Union will not comfort the jurist searching for a clear recognition of a right to secessionist self-determination by an influential member of the world community. On the commonsense level, a multinational State as large and as disparate as the USSR could not have hoped to survive even as a loose federation if it had permitted an absolute right to secession. On the theoretical plane, the gap between Soviet rhetoric and Soviet practice, and in particular the resulting need for a reference to conflicting normative levels as a justification for limiting the right of self-determination, can be explained in terms of a misjudgment concerning the unifying appeal of the socialist international doctrine. In the final analysis, if the intrinsic appeal of this doctrine has not resulted in a mass migration into the Soviet camp, its

315. *Id.* 1323–24.

316. *Id.* 1324–25. *See generally* Lapenna, *The Soviet Concept of "Socialist" International Law,* 29 Y.B. WORLD AFF. 242 (1975).

317. Selyaninov, *Internationalism of Soviet Foreign Policy,* 1971 INT'L AFF. (Moscow), No. 7, at 11, 16: "It is rightly pointed out in the works of a number of Soviet authors that democratic principles and the rules of general international law are applied in relations between socialist countries only in conformity with the basic principle of proletarian internationalism, thus acquiring a consistently democratic socialist content." *See also* Ginsburgs, *Socialist Internationalism and State Sovereignty,* 25 Y.B. WORLD AFF. 39 (1971); Selyaninov, *The International and the National in the Policy of the Socialist States,* 1970 INT'L AFF. (Moscow), No. 8, at 14.

conscription as a basis for the Soviet limitation of self-determination has at least insured that no one can easily leave the camp.

Within the international arena, the Soviet response to demands for secessionist self-determination has closely followed the interests of Soviet diplomacy in the area concerned. For example, the Soviet publicists were vehement in their disapproval of the dissolution of the Mali Federation, where Russian influence had been waxing.[318] The USSR offered military support to crush the secessions of Katanga and Biafra but strongly backed the demand of the people of Bangla Desh for self-determination. In each instance, the Soviet attitude was apparently dictated by political expediency and not a principled judgment regarding the legitimacy of the particular claim.

JURISTIC OPINION

"The right of secessionist self-determination" has endured an inconsistent treatment at the hands of juristic commentators. At the outset, one must be careful not to confuse the debate over the status of a general right of self-determination with the arguably quite distinguishable question of the place of secessionist self-determination. Those writers who deny self-determination the position of a legal right may confidently be assumed also to deny any legal right of secession. On the other hand, those commentators who affirm a general right of self-determination may not always intend thereby to express themselves in favor of the legitimacy of secession. It therefore seems wise to approach this latter category of writers in a cautious manner and, as was suggested earlier with reference to statements emanating from international organizations, to swing the benefit of the doubt against a secessionist interpretation where this is not specifically mentioned. Finally, even among the commentators who affirm a right of secessionist self-determination, care must be taken to represent fairly the limitations such juristic opinion places upon an exercise of that right.

Aside from its possible relevance to a scheme for the protection of human rights (including a right to self-determination) which involves a procedure for submitting grievances to some supranational body, it is difficult to see the operative difference between characterizing self-determination as a legal right or as a political principle. At the present state of affairs, after all, it is scarcely a justiciable issue likely to go before an international tribunal. Perhaps the most significant difference

---

318. *See* R. LEGVOLD, SOVIET POLICY IN WEST AFRICA 91 (1970).

lies in the remedial import of each expression. To say that self-determination is a political principle implies that individual States ought to recognize it within their internal management and, at most, that the international community can use the pressure of its opinion to move States in this direction. To say that peoples have a legal right to self-determination, however, seems to invest them with a right independent of their governing States, which can indeed be exercised in opposition to those States. The present task of the international community, under this latter view, is to be more specific regarding the kind of "peoples" who can legitimately invoke this right.

The trend of self-determination talk in the United Nations from the San Francisco Conference well into the 1950s developed a very useful terminological shorthand for expressing rather cumbersome legal doctrines. When someone spoke about "the principle of self-determination" he often meant thereby to express his belief that the concept was a political principle—not a legal right—and therefore not to be included in the body of rights protected by international law. Similarly, when the expression "the right of self-determination" was used, this was often intended as a statement of the speaker's opinion that the concept was a legal right under international law. Thus, for more than a decade, delegates could categorize the ideological affiliation of a colleague within the first sentence of his address; votes were cast for and against resolutions on the basis of their use of one or the other variant of the expression; and much ink was saved in not printing lengthy, repetitive explanations of the two views. Had this convention been consistently followed, it would now be possible graphically to illustrate the growth of the acceptance of self-determination as a legal "right" by noting the increased use of this word in preference to "principle" in the debates and resolutions arising out of the organs of the United Nations. Unfortunately, this is not really feasible. Some statements, either as a deliberate equivocation or in ignorance of the customary ideological baggage each expression carried, showed an indiscriminate use of the words or an amalgamation of them. Eleanor Roosevelt, for example, was fond of speaking about "the principle of the right of peoples to self-determination." [319] More recently, Ian Brownlie has combined the phrases "political principle" and "legal right" to give his opinion that self-determination is at present a "legal principle." [320] Nevertheless, it is possible to perceive in this history a

319. *See, e.g.*, 6 U.N. GAOR, 3d Comm., 364th meeting at 105, para. 19, U.N. Doc. A/C.3/SR.364 (1951).
320. I. BROWNLIE, PRINCIPLES OF PUBLIC INTERNATIONAL LAW 577 (2d ed. 1973).

more frequent affirmation of a *right* to self-determination as the anti-colonialist forces in the United Nations become more numerous and more vocal.

In the first instance, the principle/right dispute arose over the meaning of the United Nations Charter's use of "self-determination," especially in article 1, paragraph 2. This provision, which falls under the "Purposes and Principles" chapter of the Charter, seemed to embody an answer to the question by referring to the "principle of equal rights and self-determination of peoples." The French text of the Charter, however, spoke of respect for the "principe de l'égalité de droits des peuples *et leur droit* à disposer d'eux-mêmes" (literally, the principle of equal rights of peoples and their right to self-determination).[321] With an ambiguity thus apparently enshrined in the Charter, the field was left open for the inevitable combat of juristic commentators. The most intractable opponents of the "right" of self-determination argued not only that it does not have the status of a legal right now but that it never will have it. The "right of self-determination," claims J. H. W. Verzijl, "has always been the sport of national or international politics and has never been recognized as a genuine political right of 'peoples' of universal and impartial application, and it never will, nor can be so recognized in the future." [322] Similarly, Rupert Emerson believes that self-determination is, as yet, incapable of constitutional formulation and "is essentially miscast in the role of a legal right which can be made an operative part of either domestic or international systems." [323] Elsewhere, Emerson concludes that "what emerges beyond dispute is that all peoples do *not* have the right of self-determination. They have never had it, and they will never have it." [324] The right of self-determination, L. C. Green has also maintained, is a political right. "It is not a right under international law. Customary law certainly does not recognize such a right, and, as yet, there are but few treaties that concede it." [325]

321. 15 U N C I O Docs. 367 (1945) (emphasis mine).

322. J. VERZIJL, 1 INTERNATIONAL LAW IN HISTORICAL PERSPECTIVE 324 (1968).

323. R. EMERSON, FROM EMPIRE TO NATION 307 (1970).

324. R. EMERSON, SELF-DETERMINATION REVISITED IN THE ERA OF DECOLONIZATION 64, Occasional Papers in International Affairs No. 9 (1964). *Cf.* Emerson, *Self-Determination*, 65 AM. J. INT'L L. 459, 464 (1971): "Despite the fact that the self-determination of the World War I peace settlement seems clearly to have involved secession, and that it is nonsense to concede the right to 'all peoples' if secession is excluded, the customary verdict has been that self-determination does not embrace secession, at least as any continuing right."

325. L. C. Green's comments are printed in INT'L L. ASS'N, REPORT OF THE 47TH CONFERENCE 58 (1956). For examples of other jurists who deny a general right of self-

In the opposing camp, a number of jurists (and probably a growing number) have accepted the status of self-determination as a right within the law of the United Nations either because (1) they believe that it had attained this status in pre-Charter customary international law; (2) they consider this to have been the intended import of paragraph 1(2) of the Charter; or (3) subsequent practice has indicated this to be the proper interpretation of that provision.[326] In addition to the large number of resolutions emanating from the United Nations which employ the "right" terminology, the International Covenants on Human Rights[327] and the 1960 *Declaration on the Granting of Independence to Colonial Countries and Peoples*[328] can be seen as supporting this viewpoint. Of course, by affirming a legal right to self-determination these writers do not necessarily assert that the parameters of the right are as yet clearly defined. Rosalyn Higgins, for example, concludes from her study of United Nations practice that it "seems inescapable that self-determination has developed into an international legal right." [329] Nevertheless, she is quick to point out that "the extent and scope of the right is still open to some debate." [330]

A more fundamental, if less plausible, attack on the Charter's endorsement of self-determination in article 1(2) has come from those who continue the dispute begun at the San Francisco Conference over the significance of the terms "nations," "States," and "peoples" in the

---

determination *see* G. Schwarzenberger, A Manual of International Law 74 (5th ed. 1967); Eagleton, *supra* note 109, at 593; Kaur, *supra* note 4, at 488; Sinha, *Self-Determination in International Law and Its Applicability to the Baltic Peoples*, Res Baltica 256, 264–65 (A. Sprudzs, A. Rusis eds. 1968).

326. Kurt Rabl writes that the development in United Nations law lead to the conclusion that "self-determination, conceived as a 'right' in 1917–19, reduced by the UN Charter in 1945 to a mere 'principle', has been—thus transforming the Charter provisions—declared to be a 'right' again." K. Rabl, Das Selbstbestimmungsrecht der Völker 786 (1972). For a full discussion of the opposing view (that neither the Charter, nor subsequent U.N. resolutions, nor State practice have confirmed a right of self-determination) *see* Gross, *The Right of Self-Determination in International Law* in New States in the Modern World 136 (M. Kilson ed. 1975).

327. *See* notes 163 and 164 *supra*.

328. *See* note 172 *supra*.

329. R. Higgins, The Development of International Law through the Political Organs of the United Nations 103 (1969). *See also* Johnson, *supra* note 4, at 41–55; Lachs, *The Law in and of the United Nations,* 1 Indian J. Int'l L. 419 (1961); Magarasević, *A View on the Right to Self-Determination in International Law,* Jugoslovenska Revija za Medunarodno Pravo 27, 32 (1956); Rivlin, *supra* note 115, at 207–18. *Cf.* J. Halderman, The United Nations and the Rule of Law 142 (1966).

330. Higgins, *supra* note 329.

Charter vocabulary. Hans Kelsen, for example, propounded during the early years of the Charter his well-known thesis that the phrase "self-determination of peoples" in article 1(2) should be interpreted to mean sovereignty of States. "Self-determination of peoples," Kelsen writes, "usually designates a principle of internal policy, the principle of democratic government. However, Article 1, paragraph 2, refers to the relations among states. Therefore the term 'peoples,' too—in connection with 'equal rights'—means probably states, since only states have 'equal rights' according to general international law." [331] The development of the self-determination concept in United Nations practice, however, and in particular the now common application of the principle by the General Assembly to national liberation groups *within* States or colonies,[332] appears conclusively to refute the thesis that self-determination of peoples is merely a euphemistic alternative to sovereignty of States.

The more important question for our purposes is not just whether the current trend of juristic opinion recognizes a right of self-determination, but rather whether those commentators who do accept this right see it as encompassing a right of secession. Some writers, of course, do not perceive any substantive divisions within the concept, even into its secessionist/nonsecessionist components. As a result, the *possibility* of a secessionist interpretation of the principle leads some jurists not only to exclude separatist movements from the scope of self-determination but to abjure entirely the suggestions of any legal content for the concept.[333] A less restrictive view, however, accepts self-determination as a legal right but does not interpret it as including any right to secession. Thus, Rosalyn Higgins, despite her belief in the legal nature of this right, nevertheless thinks, at the present stage of international law and relations, "Self-determination refers to the right of a majority within a generally accepted political unit to the exercise of power. In other words, it is necessary to start with stable boundaries and to permit political change within them." [334] This definition then leads her to the conclusion that "there can be no such thing as self-determination for the Nagas." [335]

Some writers advocate a kind of juridical abstention in dealing with

331. H. KELSEN, THE LAW OF THE UNITED NATIONS 51–52 (1951).
332. *See* text accompanying note 67, chapter 1 *supra*.
333. This seems to be true, for example, in the writings of EMERSON, *supra* notes 323 and 324, and VERZIJL, *supra* note 322.
334. HIGGINS, *supra* note 329, at 104.
335. *Id.* 105.

a concept as controversial as secessionist self-determination. Rather than inquire into whether international law recognizes any positive legitimacy in this concept, they prefer instead a negative formulation to the effect that international law does not condemn either secessionist attempts or suppression of such attempts by the central government. "There is no rule of international law," says Michael Akehurst, "which forbids secession from an existing State; nor is there any rule which forbids the motherstate to crush the secessionary movement, if it can. Whatever the outcome of the struggle, it will be accepted as legal in the eyes of international law." [336]

Even among those jurists willing to countenance some legitimacy for the concept of secessionist self-determination, several different attitudes are apparent. One approach has been to propose that nothing in the general principle of self-determination demands the exclusion of secession and that this aspect only awaits reasonable juridical limitation to be fully endorsed. Thus, secession will attain a recognized place within the broader principle if, and when, some acceptable limitations are articulated which would allow the international community to distinguish between legitimate and illegitimate separatist claims. One writer who adopts this approach, M. K. Nawaz, warns that a proponent of this view should not be interpreted as saying that the principle of self-determination can always be smoothly applied, or that every demand for secession in the name of the principle should be considered rational. He goes on to say, however, that "it is strongly urged that difficulties in the application of the principle of self-determination are by no means unique to that principle alone. What is required is the devising of useful criteria for determining the rationality of a demand for self-determination." [337] A similar optimism is expressed by Piet-Hein Houben who argues, "However difficult it may be to agree on a definition, efforts should at least be made to establish criteria for and characteristics of situations to which the principle is generally felt to be applicable or in which the legitimate question of the principle's implementation may arise." [338]

336. M. AKEHURST, A MODERN INTRODUCTION TO INTERNATIONAL LAW 72 (1970). *Cf.* Potter, *Legal Aspects of the Beirut Landing,* 52 *Am. J. Int'l L.* 727, 728 (1958): "It has to be admitted, to the distress of the shades of Jefferson, Paine, and many other patriots in many lands, that legally there is no right of revolution, at least in the absence of illegal action on the part of the established government."

337. Nawaz, *supra* note 114, at 91–92. "Within the United Nations it should become feasible to devise useful criteria and methods for ascertaining who the 'peoples' are that are entitled to self-determination." *Id.* 92.

338. Houben, *Principles of International Law concerning Friendly Relations and Co-operation among States,* 61 AM. J. INT'L L. 703, 725 (1967).

Similarly, Alfred Cobban concludes in his book on national self-determination:

> The truth seems to be that if we take the right of sovereignty on the one hand, and the right of secession on the other, as absolute rights, no solution is possible. Further, if we build only on sovereignty, we rule out any thought of self-determination, and erect a principle of tyranny without measure and without end, and if we confine ourselves to self-determination in the form of secessionism, we introduce a principle of hopeless anarchy into the social order. The only hope, it seems, must be in a combination of the two principles, allowing each to operate within its own proper field, and recognizing neither as an absolute right, superior to the rights of individuals, which are the true end of society.[339]

Other commentators take a step further and affirm the existence of a right of secession subject to certain conditions. Writing during the League of Nations period, Georges Scelle declared firmly that "The right of peoples, or collective self-determination, therefore implies not only the condemnation of the classic principle of forced annexation or cession, but *the freedom of secession*." [340] Scelle believed that one consequence of the development of the principle during the League era was the removal of the previously recognized power of State governments to oppose secession and to maintain the union of the State by force.[341] Nevertheless, despite this extraordinarily broad statement of the right of secession, he also acknowledges its practical limitations. The regulation of the right of self-determination, he argues, must seek a balance between the aspirations of secessionist minorities and the needs of the collective majority.[342] The existence of the State is itself one form of the right of peoples to self-determination and it would be a curious application of this right which would attempt to satisfy in all cases the aspirations of dissident groups, however tiny, at the risk of sacrificing the conditions of the existence of the State (which serves the needs of the more numerous majority). The demands of every irreducible minority, he thinks, could be met only by a regression to the homogeneous social milieu of primitive humanity.

Robert Redslob, writing at about the same time, developed a fairly

339. COBBAN, *supra* note 52, at 138.
340. G. SCELLE, PRECIS DE DROIT DES GENS: PRINCIPES ET SYSTEMATIQUE 259 (1932) (translation mine).
341. *Id.* 260.
342. *Id.* 269.

detailed theory of the right of secession. The first consideration to be kept in mind when determining the legitimacy of a proposed secession, he argues, is the geographical condition of the remaining State after the separation. The principle of nationality as a justification for secession would not be applicable where the projected division would seriously cut into the organic structure of the State, that is, where the natural frontiers of the State would suffer a grave impairment by the separation.[343] However, even this principle is not absolute. Secession, Redslob notes, can be justified even in circumstances where the vital interests of the remaining State are injured, if that State has committed serious abuses and offended against basic human laws. Where it is guilty of this sort of oppression, it cannot plead for the integrity of its geographical configuration as against a minority demand for secession. But suppose, he asks, that the separation would not mutilate the geographical body of the remaining State; does this mean that every instance of a national will must be satisfied by permitting a secession from the State even in the absence of governmental oppression? The answer he proposes would limit the right of secession to those groups having a distinct personality and strong desire for separation. Evidence of these distinguishing traits he believes may be found in a discernible history of the ethnic group, and perhaps a difference of religion or language. Finally, their desire for separation must be profound and sincere, and must be expressed in unequivocal actions.[344]

In his book entitled *Self-Determination in International Law,* U. Umozurike argues that secession can be legitimated in some circumstances, primarily as a method of redress for the violation of human rights.

> There is no rule of international law that condemns all secession under all circumstances. The principle of fundamental human rights is as important, or perhaps more so, as that of territorial integrity. Neither a majority nor a minority has the legal right to secede, without more, since secession may jeopardize the legitimate interests of the other part. . . . [A] majority or minority ac-

---

343. Redslob, *Le Principe des Nationalités,* 37 ACADEMIE DE DROIT INTERNATIONAL, RECUEIL DES COURS 1, 35 (1931) [hereinafter ACAD. RECUEIL]. His thesis is developed more extensively in R. REDSLOB, LE PRINCIPE DES NATIONALITES 119–28 (1931); R. REDSLOB TRAITE DE DROIT DES GENS 419–22 (1950).

344. 37 ACAD. RECUEIL 36–37. For a similar analysis *see* M. SIBERT, 1 TRAITE DE DROIT INTERNATIONAL PUBLIC: LE DROIT DE LA PAIX 304–05 (1951).

corded its normal democratic rights cannot legally request the international community to help it to secede.[345]

Charles Rousseau also accords a measure of legitimacy to secession but he includes the crucial qualification that the exercise of this right must be voluntarily acknowledged by the unified State. He begins by arguing that the right of self-determination in international law contains two aspects; one negative and the other positive. Viewed negatively, it encompasses the right of a population not to be exchanged or ceded against its will. In addition, he claims, the right of self-determination contains a positive aspect in the right of secession. He means by this the "right of a population to change governments, that is, to separate from the State to which they belong, either to incorporate themselves in another State, or to form an autonomous State." [346] Rousseau is then quick to point out that the exercise of this right must be limited and that only the interested State can acknowledge or refuse the right of a fraction of its population to determine its own political status by a plebiscite or otherwise. Consequently, he concludes, the problem is rarely susceptible of juridical solutions.[347]

Finally, jurists in the communist bloc have, predictably, supported a legal right of secession subject to certain conditions. D. B. Levin writes, "The question of the object of the right of nations to self-determination is reduced to the question what rights and interests of a nation, people, nationality, etc., are included in their right to self-determination. Undoubtedly, the most important element of this right is freedom of state secession and the formation of an independent state." [348] Aleksandar Bozovic argues that a number of elements may be considered in determining whether a claim to self-determination by

345. UMOZURIKE, *supra* chapter 1, note 8, at 199. *Cf.* I DELUPIS, INTERNATIONAL LAW AND THE INDEPENDENT STATE 17 (1974): "A right to secession must be enjoyed *before* independence is reached. . . . The right to secede must therefore be enjoyed only by certain fairly consolidated groups of people, which to themselves and to the world appear to be emerging 'nations.' "

346. C. ROUSSEAU, DROIT INTERNATIONAL PUBLIC 81 (1953) (translation mine).

347. *Id. See also* JOHNSON, *supra* note 4, at 61: "A secessionist movement may demand a plebiscite but it is not an immediate international issue if this demand is not honored. A plebiscite, in such a case, is unilateral. If this leads to the formation of a new state, the results are international whereas the means are not."

348. Levin, *supra* note 299, at 47. *See also* H. BOKOR-SZEGÖ, NEW STATES AND INTERNATIONAL LAW 32 (1970): "Modern international law . . . recognizes the right of peoples

a particular group should be recognized. Among these, he suggests, are whether the remaining State would be deprived of fluvial and sea communications, natural or artificially fortified frontiers, areas containing raw materials, and the like.[349] Despite the importance of these considerations, however, Bozovic warns that they should not be accorded absolute deference. In the final analysis, the issue of whether a claim to a right of self-determination should be recognized by the international community is a factual, rather than a purely legal, question, and should be decided with an eye on the lesson that a failure to respect the right constitutes a threat to international peace and security.[350]

In conclusion, juristic opinion shares with the other possible sources of the claim to regard secessionist self-determination as an international right the characteristic of neither being uniformly in favor nor uniformly in opposition to the "right." There is certainly no dearth of commentators who would deny its legitimacy entirely, but a significant percentage uphold its status as an international right subject to heavy limitations and, perhaps more importantly, others seem prepared to accord it such a status if an international consensus on limiting conditions were forthcoming.

There is a pardonable reluctance on the part of these commentators to let slip the dogs of secession without first forging the links of a juridical leash to ensure their proper conduct. Nevertheless, the fact remains that current world history is constantly punctuated by secessionist attempts, many of which seek their justification in the principle of self-determination. In the present order of things, these entail a constant threat of intervention and with it the possibility of global conflict escalation. At the very least, as the recent cases of Biafra and Bangla Desh disturbingly attest, a secession can result in a savage civil war involving an enormous loss of life and injury to fundamental human dignities — all of which tends to mock finely wrought juridical schemes of "world order." At the present time, international jurists lack even the rudimentary consensus required to determine whether a legal or

---

and nations to secede from the State in which they live and to form independent states of their own."; Magaraŝević, *supra* note 329, at 31; Šuković, *supra* chapter 1, note 21, at 371–72.

349. Bozovic, *Some Tendencies in the Development of the Right of Self-Determination*, 5 Ju-GOSLOVENSKA REVIJA ZA MEDUNARODNO PRAVO 30, 34 (1958).

350. *Id.* 34–35.

simply a moral claim has been presented in these cases. If the former, the further question of whether the right of self-determination has been *legitimately* invoked in a particular case is also at present largely unanswerable.

It is obviously too much to hope that an international framework for discerning such legitimacy would prevent any future instances of contested secession attempts, but it could significantly reduce the frequency of these phenomena by removing the possibility of external aid for an illegitimate secession (and this, presumably, could be known beforehand by both secessionist and unionist alike). Given the urgent international implications of these appeals to an international legal right, the world community ought not to remain incapable of adjudging the legitimacy of such claims.

3 Self-Determination in Dispute: Case Studies

Before undertaking an inquiry into possible factors bearing upon the legitimacy of claims to secessionist self-determination under international law, it would be helpful to review the factual circumstances of some contemporary separatist movements and thereby acquaint ourselves with the wide disparities in the nature and goals of these movements. It seems fair to say that examples of the collective desire of a minority to separate from a larger political entity can be found in every society from the beginning of mankind's political adventure. Dissatisfaction with the structure or operation of a political union is probably almost as old as the initial desire for unification itself. Add to this the countless instances of conquest and national subjugation which enliven the chronicle of human social existence and one finds a fertile soil of parochial discontent in which the secessionist impulse has taken root. The significant difference between these historical separatist attempts, however, and similar recent claims is that the latter have typically sought to justify themselves under a legal doctrine of self-determination. It may indeed be said that the very promulgation of this doctrine has acted, for better or worse, as a stimulus to group demands of this kind. It appears more profitable, therefore, to concentrate our attention on recent examples of secessionist behavior undertaken in an international atmosphere which, at least in theory, accords great importance to the right of self-determination.

Even after narrowing the time period to the post-1945 era, one can find a significant number of political phenomena which may properly be categorized as having a separatist character.[1] The first lesson to be

1. There is a large, and growing, literature on the problem of separatist challenges to independent States. For some recent studies of individual movements see: Beckett, *Northern Ireland*, 6 J. CONTEMP. HIST. 121 (1971); Caplan, *Barotseland: The Secessionist Challenge to Zambia*, 6 J. MOD. AFRICAN STUDIES 343 (1968); Davies, *Welsh Nationalism*, 39 POL. Q. 322 (1968); Latouche, *Quebec and the North American Subsystem: One Possible Scenario*, 28 INT'L ORGANIZ. 931 (1974); Mackintosh, *Scottish Nationalism*, 38 POL. Q. 389 (1967); Mallory, *The Canadian Dilemma: French and English*, 41 POL. Q. 281 (1970); Morgan, *Welsh Nationalism: The Historical Background*, 6 J. CONTEMP. HIST. 153 (1971); Payne, *Catalan and Basque Nationalism*, 6 J. CONTEMP. HIST. 15 (1971); Qureshi, *Pakhtunistan: The Frontier Dispute between Afghanistan and Pakistan*, 39 PAC. AFF. 99 (1966); Schwarz, *The Scottish National Party: Nonviolent Separatism and Theories of Violence*, 22 WORLD POL. 496 (1970); Wilson, *French-Canadian Separatism*, 20 W. POL. Q. 116 (1967).

drawn from a review of these movements is that no region of the world is free from demands of this nature. The strong tribal and regional sentiments that still thrive in many areas of Afro-Asia have made these the continents most commonly associated in popular imagination with endemic separatist problems. It should be noted, however, that Western Europe currently harbors the unsatisfied nationalisms of the Basques, Bretons, Welsh, Northern Irish, Scots, Catalans, Lapps, Sicilians, Corsicans, Frisians, Walloons, and the German-speaking inhabitants of Alsace-Lorraine (to name just a few). Canada remains troubled by the demands of the French-speaking citizens of Quebec; the United States is occasionally importuned in this regard by American Blacks or its native Indians; and even the communist bloc has not been entirely successful in quelling nationalistic sentiment in areas like the Ukraine, Georgia, Croatia, Estonia, Latvia, and Lithuania. Similarly, the Communist Chinese have been embroiled in a guerrilla war with the Khambas of Tibet ever since the Chinese conquest of that country in the 1950s.

The second lesson to be learned from this history is that some States have managed to preserve their territorial integrity by defusing the separatist demands of their minorities. In most instances, this has been accomplished by granting a larger measure of regional autonomy to the area concerned. For example, the once active separatism in the South Tyrol and Sardinia has in this way gradually been mollified. More recently, the Swiss have compromised with the Jurassians to form the country's first new canton in 160 years; and the decentralization of governmental power (a process called "devolution") is at the heart of the current British attempt to satisfy the separatist rumblings of Wales and Scotland.

Of course, not every nationalist movement anticipates the territorial dismemberment of its governing State. Many groups have been content with demanding some degree of political autonomy or protection for native culture without necessarily meaning by this a demand for complete independence. Some have sought to achieve their ends primarily within the internal constitutional framework of their governing State without recourse to violent rebellion or external military support (although the danger of extremists within a movement pursuing violent tactics to achieve recognition of their goals is an increasing risk in an age of widespread political terrorism).

There have, nevertheless, been some groups who have actually attempted a territorial separation from their governing State and backed this claim with armed force. Because of the obvious threat to

KATANGA

Provinces of the Congo, 1960

world peace and security posed by secessionist attempts of this kind, and because of the serious consequences of international legal abstention in such cases, the examples below have been chosen from this final category. They have been selected to illustrate the complexity of historic, ethnic, and political factors that may contribute to these claims. Among other things, these cases serve to point up the problems surrounding active United Nations involvement in a dispute of this nature (the Congo); ineffective United Nations action (Bangla Desh); and the total absence of such involvement (Biafra). They exemplify the peculiar difficulties presented when ethnic regions overlap national frontiers (the Kurds, Somalis, Nagas); when the desire for secession amounts to an irredentist demand for unification with an ethnically similar State (Somalia); when the basis for the secession is largely conditioned by the wealth of the seceding province (Katanga), or is a direct result of its impoverishment (Bangla Desh).

This discussion is not intended to pass judgment retrospectively on the legitimacy of any of these movements but rather to provide some basic data to guide our subsequent inquiry into the standards of secessionist legitimacy.

THE CONGO

On June 30, 1960, King Baudouin of Belgium proclaimed the independence of the Republic of the Congo, thus setting in motion a hurricane of events which would eventually force the international community into a face-to-face confrontation with the specter of secession. The reaction of the United Nations and the individual members of the world community to the secession of the province of Katanga from the newly independent Republic of the Congo warrants attention for several reasons. First, the events in the Congo during the period 1960–63 revealed the tangled interrelationship between the purely political act of secession and its strategic, economic, and emotional roots. This in turn led to an appreciation of the rather limited utility of international legal analysis in the actual healing of a secession once it has taken place (as opposed to its possible role in minimizing the danger of secession in the future). As the United Nations was to learn in the Congo, in dealing with the phenomenon of secession one may either attempt to negotiate a reconciliation, taking into account the emotional and economic factors that spawned the desire for separation, or one may dictate a settlement after the crucial question of the secession has been resolved by military force. As it happened, the United Nations tried both approaches during the Congo crisis. By the time it was over, however, it was clear that the services of a diplomat qua priest, or those of a general, are far more valuable in resolving a conflict than the skills of an academic lawyer. The legalistic characterization of such events is more often a hindsight attempt to fit the *fact* of a secession into the *theory* of a world regulated by an international legal order; it is rarely in the minds of the secessionists as they pursue their separation and probably never taken into account in forming the emotional commitment to secede. Nor is it, as the Congo crisis was to show, likely to be the primary consideration in the mind of the world community as it frames its collective reaction to the secession.

Second, the United Nations' role in the Congo affair was not simply that of a forum for the exchange of rhetoric or rationalizations, nor was it even to have the luxury of being an instrument for the detached pronouncement of collective judgment. It was, rather, a participant in these events and it quickly became apparent that the very existence of Katanga as an independent State would depend upon the action, or inaction, of the United Nations. In this capacity the organization was forced to assume an uncomfortable responsibility for the actual course of events in the Congo — events for which it was largely the efficient cause — rather than merely give its approval or disapproval to someone else's behavior. The organization thus came to appreciate in its own sphere the same kind of unbridgeable gap which often separates the child psychologist from the parent.

Finally, the Katangan secession serves as an excellent example of the need to balance economic realities against parochial or political sentiments. With a population of 1,709,659, the Katanga was in 1960 one of the most sparsely populated of the Congolese provinces and accounted for only 13 percent of the total population of the country. Despite this thin population, the Belgian Congo administration prior to independence is reported to have derived 60 percent of its revenue from the province, and foreign mining interests reportedly took out $47 million in net profits from Katanga in 1960.[2] The mineral output of the region was estimated to be 80 percent of the total value of minerals extracted from the Congo in 1957.[3] It was thus apparent at the time of independence that the new republic could not easily survive without Katanga and equally apparent, especially to the foreign in-

2. These figures are taken from T. FRANCK, J. CAREY, THE LEGAL ASPECTS OF THE UNITED NATIONS ACTION IN THE CONGO 5 (1963).

3. *See* Lemarchand, *The Limits of Self-Determination: The Case of the Katanga Secession,* 56 AM. POL. SCI. REV. 404, 405 (1962).

vestors in the province, that Katanga would be more prosperous (and more amenable to Belgian influence) if dissociated from the remainder of the country. Whatever the significance of tribal or regional sentiments in the ensuing secession, it may safely be assumed that the economic facts of life were never far from anyone's mind.

The events in the Congo during the early 1960s are well-known and are the subject of an extensive literature.[4] A brief recapitulation of the more important developments as they relate to the Katanga separation will suffice to illuminate the international response to the secessionist attempt. After it became clear that the Congolese movement for independence could not long be resisted without a great deal of effort, the Belgian authorities in January of 1960 called the native political leaders of the Congo to a Round Table Conference in Brussels to discuss the procedure for achieving independence and the nature of the political institutions in the subsequent independent State. The conference produced a number of resolutions ultimately embodied in a constitution or "Loi fondamentale," which was passed by the Belgian Parliament and signed by the King of Belgium in May of 1960. Although the question of secession was not mentioned per se in the Loi, article 6 did proclaim that "the Congo constitutes within its present boundaries, an indivisible and democratic State." [5] This provision was later to be of considerable importance in providing a justification for the suppression of the secession. The Loi was intended to serve until a formal constitution could be drafted by the National Parliament.

The elections held during May 1960 resulted in the rise of Patrice Lumumba to the position of prime minister. Lumumba had associated himself with a platform advocating a strong central government and a

4. *See, e.g.,* FRANCK & CAREY, *supra* note 2; K. GORDON, THE UNITED NATIONS IN THE CONGO: A QUEST FOR PEACE (1962). C. HOSKYNS, THE CONGO: A CHRONOLOGY OF EVENTS, JANUARY 1960–DECEMBER 1961 (1962); C. HOSKYNS, THE CONGO SINCE INDEPENDENCE (1965) [hereinafter HOSKYNS]; G. MARTELLI, EXPERIMENT IN WORLD GOVERNMENT: AN ACCOUNT OF THE UNITED NATIONS OPERATION IN THE CONGO 1960–1964 (1966); C. YOUNG, POLITICS IN THE CONGO: DECOLONIZATION AND INDEPENDENCE (1965). For discussions of the legal aspects of the Congo operation *see* Miller (Schachter), *Legal Aspects of the United Nations Action in the Congo,* 55 AM. J. INT'L L., 1 (1961); Wright, *Legal Aspects of the Congo Situation,* 4 INT'L STUDIES 1 (1962).

5. Extracts from an unofficial translation of the Loi fondamentale may be found in FRANCK & CAREY, *supra* note 2, at 108. On the significance of article 6 with regard to the question of secession *see id.* 13; HOSKYNS, *supra* note 4, at 44.

minimization of concessions to tribal or regional differences. His proclivities toward a centralized government were not, however, shared by Joseph Kasavubu, who was elected head of state on June 24, 1960. Shortly thereafter, on June 29, this coalition government signed a Treaty of Friendship with Belgium which contained a crucial provision that Belgian metropolitan troops could be used in the Congo only at the express request of the Congolese minister of defense.

The new government could have foreseen the impending crisis in the Katanga even before independence. Rumors that the region's leaders were going to proclaim the province independent on June 28, two days before the date set for the granting of independence to the entire Congo, caused the Belgian administration to take steps to thwart the attempted declaration of Katangan independence.[6] The events immediately following the June 30 proclamation of Congolese independence more than justified any fears of the central government with regard to the continued unity of the country. Civilian riots and mutiny in the armed forces followed within days of independence, causing many Europeans to flee the Congo in panic. The premier of the province of Katanga, Moise Tshombe, called for Belgian troops to intervene in the province and threatened to request assistance from neighboring Rhodesia if Belgium did not comply. On July 10, therefore, Belgian troops actively intervened in Katanga and elsewhere in the Congo. This was immediately followed by a formal proclamation of independence by Katanga and the next day the leaders of the central government, Lumumba and Kasavubu, appealed to the United Nations for military assistance to counter the intervention of Belgium which, they said, had "carefully prepared the secession of Katanga with a view toward maintaining a hold on our country."[7] The Security Council responded to this request by adopting a resolution (S/4387) on July 14, 1960, which called upon the government of Belgium to withdraw its troops and also authorized the U.N. Secretary General to "take the necessary steps" to provide the Congolese government with military and technical assistance until the national security forces, in the words of the resolution, "may be able . . . to meet fully their tasks."[8]

Secretary General Dag Hammarskjöld, in his first report on the im-

6. See HOSKYNS, supra note 4, at 81.
7. Telegrams dated July 12 and 13, 1960, 15 U.N. SCOR, Supp. July–Sept. 1960, at 11, U.N. Doc. S/4382 (1960).
8. Id. 16, U.N. Doc. S/4387 (1960).

plementation of Security Council resolution S/4387, stated that one of the principles essential to the operation was that "the United Nations units must not become parties in internal conflicts, that it cannot be used to enforce any specific political solution of pending problems or to influence the political balance decisive to such a solution." [9] The consensus at this point clearly was that the U.N. operation was intended to counter external aggression from Belgium, not to suppress an internal secession. [10]

The situation was further complicated by an appeal to the Soviet Union by Lumumba and Kasavubu to intervene should the "Western camp not stop its aggression." [11] This appeal was favorably received by Soviet Premier Khrushchev. Partially in response to this threat of escalating intervention, and after the initial arrival of U.N. troops in the Congo on July 18, the Security Council unanimously passed its second resolution on July 22. This resolution reaffirmed the earlier call upon the government of Belgium to withdraw its troops and further requested all States to refrain from any action that might tend to impede the restoration of law and order in the country or undermine the territorial integrity or political independence of the Congo. [12]

Meanwhile, events in Katanga were assuming a clear direction. Tshombe on July 27 stated that he would not allow U.N. troops in the Katanga and on August 3 he warned Hammarskjöld that their arrival would touch off a general uprising in the province. The secretary general responded to this, significantly, by reminding Tshombe that the Security Council has authority applicable directly to governments and a fortiori to "subordinate territorial non-governmental authorities of Member nations," and that resistance by "subordinate territorial organs of a nation" has serious legal consequences. [13] The same day that this message was received by Tshombe, August 4, a constitution for an independent State of Katanga was approved by the Katanga Assembly to replace the Loi fondamentale. Although the constitution

9. *Id.* 19, para. 13, U.N. Doc. S/4389 (1960). This was the so-called Lebanon precedent arising out of the United Nations' efforts to avoid taking sides in the Lebanese situation in 1958. *See* 13 U.N. SCOR, 818th, 823–25th, 827–38th meetings (1958). The precedent is described by Hammarskjöld in 15 U.N. SCOR, *supra* note 7, at 64–65, para. 3, U.N. Doc. S/4417/Add. 6 (1960).

10. *See* telegram dated July 13, 1960 from the president and prime minister of the Congo to the U.N. secretary general, *supra* note 7, at 12, U.N. Doc. S/4382 (1960).

11. Quoted in FRANCK & CAREY, *supra* note 2, at 16.

12. *Supra* note 7, at 34–35, U.N. Doc. S/4405 (1960).

13. *Id.* 48–49, para. 6, U.N. Doc. S/4417 (1960). *See generally* GORDON, *supra* note 4, at 37–39.

purported to establish Katanga as an independent and sovereign State, it announced rather mysteriously that the State "adhered to the principle of association with the other regions of the former Belgian Congo."[14] Tshombe was thereafter elected president of the new entity and unsuccessfully appealed for recognition of his State by members of the international community.

The secretary general delivered his second report to the Security Council on August 8. In it he attempted to walk the thin line between adherence to the principle of noninterference in the internal affairs of the host country, and a fulfillment of his mandate to help the central government in the face of a Katangan decision to refuse entry to U.N. troops. Prima facie it seemed clear, of course, that by sending troops into the self-proclaimed independent State of Katanga at the request of the central government, the U.N. would effectively beg the question of the legitimacy of the Katangan secession. Hammarskjöld was aware of this difficulty and attempted to avoid its apparent import with two arguments. First, he stressed that justification for a United Nations entry into Katanga was solely based upon the continued presence of Belgian troops in the province. When applied to the situation in the Katanga, Hammarskjöld said, the principle of noninterference in internal affairs

> means that the United Nations is directly concerned with the attitude taken by the provincial government of Katanga to the extent that it may be based on the presence of Belgian troops, or as being, for its effectiveness, influenced by that presence. . . . Therefore, in the application of operative paragraph 4 [of Security Council resolution S/4426, August 9, 1960[15]] . . . it can be concluded that if the Belgian troops were withdrawn . . . the question between the provincial government and the Central Government would be one in which the United Nations would in no sense be a party and on which it could in no sense exert an influence.[16]

Furthermore, he took the opportunity to respond to those who suggested that the United Nations should assist the central government in exercising its power in Katanga because this duty would seem to follow from the Loi fondamentale as the legal constitution. The United

14. Quoted in HOSKYNS, *supra* note 4, at 165.
15. *Infra* note 22.
16. *Supra* note 7, at 65, 70, para. 6, U.N. Doc. S/4417/Add. 6 (1960).

Nations has to observe, Hammarskjöld said, that, de facto, the provincial government is in active opposition to the central government and is using its own military means to achieve political aims. Once the Belgian presence has been removed, the United Nations must not interfere in this struggle by aiding the central government to suppress the secession or by inhibiting the central government from taking action by its own means against Katanga.[17] His position, as he was later to argue, was that it must be assumed that the Security Council did not authorize the secretary general to intervene with armed force in an internal conflict, when it had not specifically adopted enforcement measures under articles 41 and 42 of chapter 7 of the Charter.[18]

In addition, Hammarskjöld argued that a strict regulation of U.N. activities would not prejudice the ultimate question of the secession which, in his mind, had to be solved in a constitutional fashion. The question of secession, he said in a remarkably guarded way, "is a constitutional one with strong undercurrents of individual and collective political aims."[19] He did not confront the apparent significance of U.N. intervention in Katanga as equivalent to a denial of the legality of the secession but rather chose to comment upon the much less explosive issue of whether such a U.N. involvement would jeopardize the possibility for "other constitutional solutions than a strictly unitarian one, e.g. some kind of federal structure providing for a higher degree of provincial self-government than now foreseen.[20] Having once begged the question in favor of "constitutional" solutions, the secretary general could then claim that the United Nations would not prejudge these solutions as long as it acted with "clarity and tact."

Against the backdrop of allegations by the communist Powers that Belgium and its NATO allies acting on behalf of "foreign monopolies" had engineered and were supporting the secession,[21] the Security Council at its meeting on August 8, 1960, passed its third resolution. This resolution, almost with a sense of grateful relief, follows the direction indicated by the secretary general and declares that the entry of United Nations forces into the province of Katanga is necessary for the full implementation of the resolution. It then goes on to combine

17. *Id.* 70, paras. 6, 7.
18. *See* 15 U.N. SCOR, 887th meeting at 9–10, para. 44, U.N. Doc. S/PV. 887 (1960).
19. *Supra* note 7, at 53, para. 10, U.N. Doc. 4417 (1960).
20. *Id.*
21. *See* comments of the representatives of Poland, 15 U.N. SCOR, 868th meeting at 19, para. 96 (1960), and the Soviet Union, *id.* 42–43, paras. 218, 223.

the two strands of Hammarskjöld's argument by saying that the U.N. force will not in any way influence the outcome of any internal conflict, "constitutional or otherwise."[22]

At this same time, and almost as a confirmation of the often repeated warnings that secession is an infectious ailment, Albert Kalonji declared the independence of his "Mining State"—an area compromising South Kasai Province adjacent to Katanga.

In the event, Hammarskjöld was not forced to intervene in the Katanga *only* on the request of the central government, for he had meanwhile opened negotiations with Tshombe, and on August 12 they reached an agreement for the entry of U.N. troops into Katanga on certain conditions. The secretary general apparently assured Tshombe that the United Nations was not taking sides in the dispute and, that although the U.N. did not recognize the constitution of Katanga, it would not interfere in the administration of government in the province.[23] The very fact that the secretary general negotiated with the Tshombe regime, however, and the subsequent conduct of the U.N. troops taking over policing duties from the Belgians in the Katanga, drove Lumumba into a furious rage. He asserted that these acts gave some colorable legitimacy to the Katanga government and, moreover, allowed that government a crucial breathing space in which to consolidate its position.

At base, Lumumba interpreted the mandate given to the secretary general in a way very unlike Hammarskjöld's own perception of his task. The latter was concerned primarily with removing the threat to international peace caused by outside intervention in the province, whereas Lumumba clearly intended that the United Nations should help the central government regain control over the prodigal territory. The dispute erupted in the Security Council on August 8, when the secretary general explained his position and his interpretation of the Security Council's mandate.[24] The Soviet Union on the following day wholeheartedly backed Lumumba's call for United Nations help in suppressing the Katanga rebellion. Referring to Tshombe as a "puppet who is sustained by foreign bayonets and who executes the will of foreign monopolies,"[25] the Soviet representative claimed that

22. 15 U.N. SCOR, Supp. July–Sept. 1960, at 91, 92, U.N. Doc. S/4426 (1960).
23. *See* HOSKYNS, *supra* note 4, at 172.
24. 15 U.N. SCOR, 887th meeting at 2–13, U.N. Doc. S/PV. 887 (1960).
25. *Id.* 888th meeting at 13, para. 53, U.N. Doc. S/PV. 888 (1960).

the States supporting Belgium were trying to prove that "Tshombe's treason" was unconnected with the Belgian aggression and thus was an internal matter preventing the United Nations from suppressing the revolt. With this "cheap artifice" the Soviet Union took the strongest exception.[26] The Lumumba government was thereafter directly supplied by the Soviet Union with military aid to help suppress the secession of Katanga and the Mining State. [7]

The events between September 1960 and February 1961 constitute a confusing record of power struggles within the central government of the Congo. During the phase now known as the "constitutional crisis," the Lumumba/Kasavubu coalition disintegrated, with each discharging the other, and a rival (Soviet-backed) government was established at Stanleyville in the northern province of Orientale. All was not well in Katanga either, which itself suffered the secession of North Katanga during January of 1961.[28] With the assassination of Lumumba in February 1961, the Security Council again met to consider the situation with the tenor of debate running strongly against the Katanga regime. The Council passed, on February 21, a resolution that recognized the "imperative necessity of the restoration of parliamentary institutions in the Congo in accordance with the fundamental law of the country." [29] This was followed by attempts at reconciliation of the various rivalrous factions, and a number of proposals to structure the Congo along the lines of a federal model were discussed.[30] It took until August of that year for some semblance of stability to return. The National Parliament was reconvened (without the support of Katanga) and Cyrille Adoula formed a new government which promptly announced its intention to end the Katanga secession.

The Adoula government opened its campaign by proclaiming that all non-Congolese mercenaries serving in the Katanga Forces were un-

26. *Id.* 15, paras. 63–67. For general discussions of the Hammarskjöld/Lumumba dispute see FRANCK & CAREY, *supra* note 2, at 20–21; GORDON, *supra* note 4, at 44–48; HOSKYNS, *supra* note 4, at 178–80; R. MILLER, DAG HAMMARSKJÖLD AND CRISIS DIPLOMACY 283–89 (1962).

27. For a discussion of the general Soviet response to the Congo situation see R. LEGVOLD, SOVIET POLICY IN WEST AFRICA 76–80 (1970).

28. *See generally* YOUNG, *supra* note 4, at 540–44 for background.

29. 16 U.N. SCOR, Supp. Jan.–March 1961, at 147–48, U.N. Doc. S/4741 (1961). *See generally* MARTELLI, *supra* note 4, at 72–84.

30. For a detailed discussion of attempts to structure Congolese federalism see YOUNG, *supra* note 4, at 475–532; and in particular on Tshombe's proposals during this period see MARTELLI, *supra* note 4, at 85–98.

desirable aliens and ordering their expulsion from Congolese territories.[31] United Nations assistance was requested for this endeavor,
which thus involved U.N. forces in heavy fighting in Katanga. It was
during this new crisis in the Katanga situation that Secretary General
Hammarskjöld was killed on September 17, 1961. The Security Council was provoked by this latest turn of events to pass a resolution on
November 24 (by 9 votes to 0, with 2 abstentions) authorizing the use
of force if necessary to apprehend mercenaries. Of crucial importance
was the United States' decision at this point to align itself with the
Afro-Asian and communist blocs in the United Nations, thus creating
an almost unanimous front against the continued existence of
Tshombe as a political force.[32] The November 24 resolution, therefore, marks a radical shift in the Security Council's approach to the
Katanga problem. No longer was there any agonizing over draftsmanship to assure an impartiality between the central government and the
secessionists. Rather, the resolution begins by reaffirming that one
purpose of the United Nations operation is "To maintain the territorial integrity and political independence of the Congo." It then goes
on to deplore all armed action in opposition to the authority of the
government of the Republic of the Congo, "specifically secessionist activities and armed action now being carried on by the provincial administration of Katanga with the aid of external resources and foreign
mercenaries, and *completely rejecting* the claim that Katanga is a 'sovereign independent nation.' "[33] Paragraph 8 of the resolution, in unequivocal language, "*declares* that all secessionist activities against the
Republic of the Congo are contrary to the "Loi fondamentale" and
Security Council decisions and specifically *demands* that such activities
which are now taking place in Katanga shall cease forthwith."[34]

31. Text in Hoskyns, The Congo: A Chronology of Events, *supra* note 4, at 45–46.
32. On the reasons for the American abandonment of a "neutral" position toward
the Katanga regime see Martelli, *supra* note 4, at 104–05. The official version of the
United States position on the Congo may be found in 45 Dep't State Bull. 1061–69
(1961), and Gardner, note 290, chapter 2 *supra*.
33. 16 U.N. SCOR, Supp. Oct.–Dec. 1961, at 148, U.N. Doc. S/5002 (1961) (emphasis in
original).
34. *Id.* 149. Rosalyn Higgins writes with reference to paragraph 8: "It will be noted
that the secession is not declared illegal *because it is fomented by foreign elements* (which is
surely the crucial point), but rather because it is contrary to the Basic Law. . . .
[I]nevitably the paragraph gives support to those who insist that the United Nations
wants to end the Katanga secession and not merely to expel the foreign elements from
influence in Katanga so that the Congolese may negotiate among themselves." Higgins,
supra note 329, chapter 2, at 109.

With this radically altered mandate, the new secretary general, U Thant, began a program to end the secessionist efforts in the Katanga. It is significant that, although altered, the U.N. policy was still opposed to ending the secession by armed force. During the first half of 1962, some progress toward national unity seemed to be made when negotiations were resumed between Prime Minister Adoula and Katanga's President Tshombe. When these talks broke up without agreement on the relationship of Katanga to the rest of the Congo, Tshombe went ahead with plans for a celebration of the second anniversary of Katangan "independence." The secretary general responded by introducing his own Plan for National Reconciliation,[35] while backing it up with threats of economic sanctions with the explicit goal of ending the secession in Katanga which was, in his words, the "crux of the Congo trouble."[36]

The Adoula government expressed its willingness to accept the Plan for National Reconciliation and a draft constitution was prepared by experts from the United Nations.[37] The reception given to the plan by the Katangan authorities was somewhat colder, but before U Thant's scheme for economic sanctions could be brought into play renewed fighting between the Katangan gendarmerie and U.N. troops erupted in late December 1962. By the middle of January 1963 the political and military position of the Tshombe regime was very uncertain. Tshombe and his ministers were forced, therefore, on January 14 to indicate their willingness to end the secession and cooperate with the United Nations to implement its plan. By the end of the month U.N. troops had occupied the most important positions held by Katangan forces and the secession was for all practical purposes over.

In retrospect, the United Nations action in the Congo stands as a major precedent against an international recognition of secessionist legitimacy in circumstances similar to those surrounding the Congo at independence. It now seems clear that the United Nations did not at the outset wish to prejudice by its action the ultimate question of the status of Katanga. Hammarskjöld's valiant attempts to restore order and remove the threat to international peace while maintaining a pol-

---

35. See 17 U.N. SCOR, Supp. July–Sept. 1962, at 16–18, paras. 77–91, U.N. Doc. S/5053/Add. 11 (1962). The secretary general's plan is spelled out in more detail (complete with proposals for economic sanctions) in 17 U.N. SCOR, Supp. Oct.–Dec. 1962, at 37–42, U.N. Doc. S/5053/Add. 13 (1962).

36. 17 U.N. SCOR, Supp. July–Sept. 1962, at 15, para. 76, U.N. Doc. S/5053/Add. 11 (1962).

37. See id. 53–85.

icy of noninterference can only be explained by his desire to avoid having the final decision regarding Katanga's future rest on the shoulders of the United Nations. It was a difficult, and perhaps an impossible, path to tread. Hammarskjöld seemed unwilling to confront, or at least unable to resolve, the logical inconsistency between taking steps to restore order in the face of a recalcitrant secessionist province and attempting to maintain a posture of noninterference in the affairs of that province and the central government. Even while he was alive, although no one seriously questioned in principle his policy of noninerference, a number of States among the Afro-Asian and communist blocs strongly expressed their view that it was inapplicable to the Katanga secession. After the assassination of Lumumba, the weight of opinion in the United Nations began to swing strongly in favor of opposing the secession regardless of any consequent injury to the principle of noninterference. This was clearly the mandate thrust upon U Thant, and he interpreted it as such. Thus, by February 1963, U Thant could report to the Security Council that "the United Nations has avoided any intervention in the internal politics of the country" and follow it immediately with a crucial qualification, "beyond the *opposition to secession in general* required by the Security Council resolutions and the constitutional suggestions embodied in the Plan for National Reconciliation."[38]

The reasons for the world community's disapproval of the Katanga secession may in one sense be seen as limitations upon the precedential effect of the United Nations' Congo action. There was first of all a good deal of concern for the economic future of the Congolese Republic if stripped of its most valuable province. Second, the majority of the members of the U.N. undoubtedly viewed the Tshombe regime as not representing the true wishes of the majority of the Katangan population and therefore regarded the secession as intrinsically illegitimate regardless of its effect on the remaining republic. Inseparable from this, and adding to the unpopularity of the Tshombe government in the U.N., was the belief that the secession was being supported (if not instigated) by certain Western nations to protect business concerns in the region. This seemed a perfect case with which to justify the "neocolonialist" paranoia of many newly independent African States. Finally, the Congo showed every indication of being further beset by separatist demands if the legitimacy of the Katanga se-

38. 18 U.N. SCOR, Supp. Jan.–Mar. 1963, at 103, para. 37, U.N. Doc. S/5240 (1963) (emphasis mine).

cession had been recognized. For these reasons, once the United Nations had resigned itself to the belief that its policy of noninterference ought not or could not be strictly maintained, the deck was noticeably stacked in favor of supporting the central government and suppressing the secession.

THE KURDS

Kurdistan is a geographical term denoting a territory of approximately 74,000 square miles covering parts of Iraq, Iran, Syria, Turkey, and the Soviet Union. It is the home of the Kurdish people, a distinct ethnologic group that has inhabited the area since virtually the beginning of recorded history.[39] Of Indo-European origin and speaking a language with Aryan Indo-European roots, the Kurds trace their ancestry back to the tribes known as the Medes, who had probably settled in the mountains of Iran by the seventh century B.C. It is the inhospitable, mountainous nature of much of Kurdistan that has indirectly produced the strongest evidence both for and against the persistent claims for Kurdish autonomy. In one respect, the very wildness of the territory was conducive to the fierce, tribal independence which has become embedded in the Kurdish character and which has kept to a minimum the level of governmental interference by the various foreign peoples who have historically had nominal rule over Kurdistan. This same feature, however, has militated against the cohesiveness of the Kurds as a people. Thus, their disposition toward tribal factiousness has been equally efficient in preventing any sustained government of all the Kurds by the Kurds.

The salient feature of the last three thousand years of Kurdish history is that, despite their numbers, continuous occupation of a homeland, and distinct culture and language, the Kurds have never enjoyed any lasting measure of self-government.[40] They have found themselves alternately subsumed within the empires of the Assyrians, Persians, Greeks, Romans, Arabs, Mongols, and Turks. It is therefore perhaps even more surprising that throughout this long history the Kurds have tenaciously clung to their cultural individuality—often acting the part of a rebellious minority defending its national identity against an imperial governor.

At the present time, the Kurds represent a substantial minority in

---

39. *See generally* H. ARFA, THE KURDS: AN HISTORICAL AND POLITICAL STUDY 1–32 (1966).

40. *Cf.* Elphinston, *The Kurdish Question,* 22 INT'L AFF. 91, 93 (1946).

KURDISTAN

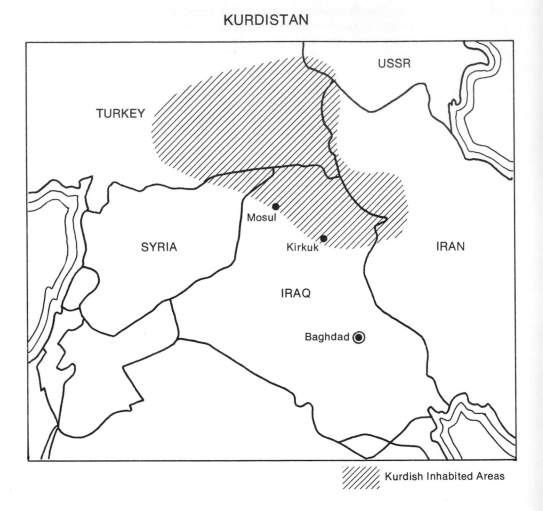

TURKEY

USSR

SYRIA

IRAN

Mosul

Kirkuk

IRAQ

Baghdad ◉

/////// Kurdish Inhabited Areas

Iraq, Iran, and Turkey, with smaller groups in Syria and the Soviet Union. The actual number of Kurds living in each of these countries is a matter of some dispute. Estimates of the size of the Kurdish population taken as a whole range from about 7 million to 16 million people, with the majority of these in Turkey but approximately 2 million living in Iraq and probably somewhat more than that in Iran.[41] Although in terms of real numbers there are many more Kurds in Turkey than in Iraq (where the recent fighting has taken place), nevertheless the Kurdish community in this latter country represents a significant minority of one-fifth of the total Iraqi population.

The history of the present Kurdish situation may conveniently be traced back to Woodrow Wilson's famous Fourteen Points at the end of the First World War. Point 12 of the president's scheme called for an assurance of "an absolute unmolested opportunity of autonomous development" for the non-Turkish minorities contained within the Ottoman Empire.[42] To the ears of the leaders of the Greeks, Slavs, Armenians, Arabs, and Kurds, Wilson's program was tantamount to an assurance of political independence. Kurdish hopes were further sustained by the text of the Treaty of Sèvres signed in August 1920.[43] Paragraphs 62 through 64 of the treaty dealt with "Kurdistan":

> 62. A commission . . . composed of three members appointed by the British, French and Italian Governments respectively shall draft within six months from the coming into force of the present Treaty a scheme of local autonomy for the predominantly Kurdish areas. . . .
>
> 64. If within one year from the coming into force of the present Treaty the Kurdish peoples within the areas defined in Article 62 shall address themselves to the Council of the League of Nations in such a manner as to show that a majority of the population of these areas desires independence from Turkey, and if the Council then considers that these peoples are capable of such independence and recommends that it should be granted to them, Turkey agrees to execute such a recommendation, and to renounce all rights and title over these areas.[44]

41. Minimum/maximum figures for the Kurdish population can be found in M. SHORT, A. McDERMOTT, THE KURDS (Minority Rights Group Report No. 23) 6 (rev. ed. 1975).

42. *See* note 57, chapter 2, *supra*.

43. Note 73, chapter 2, *supra*.

44. *Id.* 666–67.

Paragraph 64 further specified that, after the establishment of an autonomous Kurdistan, the Kurds of the Mosul Vilayet (province)—then under British control—were to be free to adhere to the new autonomous entity.

With the rise of Mustafa Kemal Ataturk, the Treaty of Sèvres was never ratified by the Turkish National Assembly. It was subsequently replaced by the Treaty of Lausanne (1923) which omitted any reference to an autonomous Kurdistan and contained customary provisions in articles 37–45 for the guarantee of the protection of minority rights within Turkey.[45] In addition, the treaty left the future of the Mosul Vilayet (which had been awarded by the Treaty of Sèvres to Iraq but which Turkey now insisted on keeping) as a matter for direct negotiation between Turkey and Great Britain, then acting as mandatory power for Iraq. When these negotiations broke down the matter was referred to the League of Nations, whose Council, in 1925, awarded the territory to Iraq.[46] The award was made on the condition, as recommended by the League Commission of Enquiry, that "regard must be paid to the desires expressed by the Kurds that officials of the Kurdish race should be appointed for the administration of their country, the dispensation of justice and teaching in the schools, and that Kurdish should be the official language of all these services."[47] The British Mandate came to an end in 1932 and Iraq was admitted to the League but, again, Iraq was required in its declaration upon termination of the mandatory regime to give assurances for the protection of minority rights and in particular rights of the Kurdish minority.[48]

Since the end of the First World War Kurdish nationalism has exhibited itself in spasmodic armed rebellion in Turkey, Iran, and Iraq. It is only in Iraq, however, that the Kurdish resistance has been widespread and persistent, lasting through a number of changes of Iraqi central government until the present time.[49] The Kurdish nationalist

45. 28 L.N.T.S. 12, 31–37 (1924).

46. 7 LEAGUE OF NATIONS OFF. J. 187, 191–92 (1926). *See generally* C. HOOPER, L'IRAQ ET LA SOCIETE DES NATIONS (1928); F. WALTERS, 1 A HISTORY OF THE LEAGUE OF NATIONS 305–10 (1952).

47. 7 LEAGUE OF NATIONS OFF. J. 190 (1926).

48. 13 LEAGUE OF NATIONS OFF. J. 1342–50 (1932).

49. There has been a certain amount of speculation as to why the Kurds in Iraq have sustained such a successful rebellion and not the more numerous Kurdish communities in Turkey or Iran. C. J. Edmonds explains this curious fact by saying that "it is only in Iraq that the Kurds were officially and legally recognized as an ethnic minority having certain rights *qua* Kurds." Edmonds, *The Kurdish War in Iraq: The Constitutional Background,* 24 WORLD TODAY 512, 513 (1968). Lettie Wenner attributes it to the more ac-

sentiment was fueled by a sense of dissatisfaction with the Iraqi government's imperfect attempts to implement the guarantees of minority rights given to the League of Nations in 1925 and 1932, and later by the post–World War II renewal of international concern with subject peoples, expressed in documents such as the Atlantic Charter.[50] The overthrow of the monarchy in Iraq[51] in 1958 was significant for two reasons: first, the new Iraqi government made representations about the Kurds as co-partners with the Arabs in the framework of Iraqi unity and mentioned guarantees of their communal rights;[52] second, the Kurdish tribal leader Mulla Mustafa Barzani was brought back from an eleven-year exile in the Soviet Union. Of these two events, the promises made by the government proved illusory and were quickly forgotten, but Barzani stayed to become an important part of the Kurdish rebellion which flared into open fighting in 1961.

The period between 1961 and 1975 presents a confusing record of Iraqi promises, ceasefires, Kurdish disillusionment, renewed fighting, Iraqi victories, Kurdish victories, more attempts at compromise, and so on. In between their periodic essays at destroying the Kurdish resistance by military force, the successive Iraqi governments have proffered various schemes for "communal rights," "decentralization," "just and peaceable settlements," and so on.[53] For their part, the Kurds have listened to these proposals—sometimes seriously—but on the whole have shown an understandable inclination to keep their powder dry during negotiations. The presence of a large oil field in Kirkuk (a region within the claimed Kurdish territory) has also contributed to the continuation of the conflict by significantly raising the stakes for both sides.

---

tive political leadership exhibited by Iraqi Kurds and the fact that they form a larger (proportionate to the general population) minority group in Iraq than in Turkey or Iran. Wenner, *Arab-Kurdish Rivalries in Iraq,* 17 MIDDLE EAST J. 68, 69 (1963). The most complete list is provided in Naamani, *The Kurdish Drive for Self-Determination,* 20 MIDDLE EAST J. 279, 287 (1966); in addition to those just mentioned, it includes these factors: (1) the Kurds of Iraq are more geographically concentrated, mostly in mountainous areas; (2) they resent rule by the Arabs who, like themselves, were a subject people under the Turks; and (3) they fear Arab nationalism more than that of the Turks or Iranians, whom they consider ethnic brothers.

50. *See* Elphinston, *supra* note 40, at 91.

51. For a discussion of the Kurdish situation during the period of the Iraqi monarchy *see* Note, *Iraqi Kurdistan: A Little-Known Region,* 12 WORLD TODAY 417 (1956).

52. *See* Edmonds, *supra* note 49, at 514.

53. For discussions of events during this period *see generally* Cruikshank, *International Aspects of the Kurdish Question,* 3 INT'L REL. 411 (1968); Edmonds, *supra* note 49; Edmonds, *Kurdish Nationalism,* 6 J. CONTEMP. HIST. 87 (1971).

The Kurdish conflict has not been entirely free from outside involvement. Until 1975, Iran supported the Kurdish rebellion by sending aid (much of it of American origin) to Barzani and his compatriots. Recent reports indicate that this covert military support supplied to the Kurds by the United States was undertaken, not out of any commitment to the ideal of self-government for distinct national groups, but rather as a convenient way of weakening Iraq—a country for whom the American ally Iran bore no great affection. A document purportedly drafted by the U.S. House of Representatives Intelligence Committee and unofficially leaked to the American press was recently quoted as having summarized the Kurdish policy of the United States and Iran. These two countries, the report said, rather than hoping for a complete Kurdish victory, "preferred instead that the insurgents simply continue a level of hostilities sufficient to sap the resources of our ally's [Iran] neighboring country [Iraq]. This policy was not imparted to our clients [the Kurds], who were encouraged to continue fighting."[54]

In 1970 the Iraqi central government and the Kurds signed a fifteen-article Peace Agreement which promised extensive guarantees of Kurdish national rights and protections for Kurdish national identity.[55] The agreement also claimed to recognize that Iraq was composed jointly of the Arab nationality and the Kurdish nationality. In addition, it provided that those regions in which the Kurds constituted a majority were to be made self-governing within four years from the date of the agreement. At the end of the four-year period, in March of 1974, the central government unilaterally promulgated its Law for Autonomy in the Area of Kurdistan. The area of Kurdistan, the law promised, "shall be considered an integral Administrative unit, enjoying a juridical personality and autonomy within the framework of the legal, political and economic integrity of the Republic of Iraq."[56]

The Kurds viewed the Autonomy Law as an insufficient implementation of the 1970 agreement. "No real power was granted to the autonomous administration" of Kurdistan, they asserted in justifying their rejection of the settlement. The Kurds also claimed that the Autonomy Law deprived Kurdistan of executive power in areas such as irrigation affairs, regional planning, administration of justice, indus-

54. Shawcross, note 293, chapter 2 *supra*, at col. 6. *See also Mr. Nixon 'told CIA to send arms to Kurds,'* Times (London), Nov. 3, 1975, at 6, col. 8.
55. Peace Agreement of Mar. 11, 1970, reprinted in THE KURDS, *supra* note 41, at 25–26.
56. *Id.* 27.

try, and "local security," while failing to provide for the economic development of Kurdistan. In the wake of this rejection of the Autonomy Law, fighting resumed between the Kurdish forces and the army of the Iraqi central government.[57]

The most significant recent event in the Kurdish drama occurred on March 6, 1975, when an Iraq-Iran reconciliation was reached at a summit meeting of the Organization of Petroleum Exporting Countries in Algiers. The Shah of Iran, whose perception of his political interests had apparently shifted away from backing the Kurdish rebellion, promised to withdraw his military and political support for the Kurds, thus shutting off their major supply of military equipment. With this crucial support removed, the Iraqis accelerated the pace of events. Shortly after the Algiers agreement, the Kurds were reported to have abandoned warfare from behind fixed positions in favor of guerrilla tactics,[58] while directing appeals to the United States to use its influence to pressure the Iranians into renewing support.[59] The Iraqis, determined to crush the Kurdish resistance, stepped up military operations, using tanks, jet warplanes, and artillery. Apparently surprised at the speed and ferocity of the Iraqi response, the Shah of Iran asked for a two-week truce to allow Kurds to leave the country.[60] At the end of this period, the Iraqi military quickly completed the seizure of the Kurdish territory and the long conflict seemed at last to be over.[61]

Reaction to the Kurdish defeat was confined primarily to outraged newspaper editorials and appeals by pro-Kurdish organizations for public support.[62] In the aftermath of the defeat, a certain amount of stability apparently returned to Iraq. Reports of the treatment of the

57. INFO. DEPT. OF KURDISTAN DEMOCRATIC PARTY, ON THE KURDISH QUESTION AT THE UNITED NATIONS 3-4 (1974).

58. See N.Y. Times, Mar. 12, 1975, at 3, col. 1.

59. See N.Y. Times, Mar. 18, 1975, at 5, col. 1.

60. N.Y. Times, Mar. 14, 1975, at 3. Nevertheless, the borders of the States surrounding Iraqi Kurdistan were quickly sealed off. See, e.g., Turkey Acts to Prevent Entry of Fleeing Kurds, N.Y. Times, Mar. 28, 1975, at 6, col. 4.

61. Iraqi Forces, Truce Over, Told to Seize Kurdistan, N.Y. Times, Apr. 1, 1975, at 3, cols. 1-2; Iraqis Complete Seizure of Kurdish Rebel Area, N.Y. Times, Apr. 3, 1975, at 3, cols. 1-2.

62. See, e.g., the New York Times editorial entitled ". . . Kurds Betrayed?" N.Y. Times, Mar. 12, 1975, at 38; Sulzberger, To Be Obscurely Hanged, N.Y. Times, Mar. 12, 1975, at 39. See also an advertisement in the N.Y. Times, Apr. 9, 1975, at 52, headed "For a Barrel of Oil . . . the World Remains Silent," which reduced the positions of the parties to the following: "The Iraqi government wants the oil soaked lands of the Kurds. The Kurds want self-determination and the right to live on their own lands as did their fathers before them."

vanquished Kurds have been mixed (although they do indicate some measures for the preservation of the Kurdish language and culture.[63]) Nevertheless, there have been disturbing reports that large numbers of Kurds have been forced to leave their mountainous homes and settle in the arid southern plains of Iraq.[64] Kurdish appeals to the United Nations have accused the Iraqis of attempting a "mass arabisation" of Kurdistan in violation of the United Nations Charter, international treaties and conventions on human rights, and the "Right of Nations to self-determination."[65]

From the perspective of the international jurist, the Kurdish conflict demonstrates the sometimes obscure distinction between a demand for regional autonomy and a claim for outright secession. There has never been any agreement regarding the exact nature of the Kurdish demands for "autonomy." One commentator, writing in 1966, concluded that "Throughout the years the Kurds insisted that they wanted autonomy within the boundaries of Iraq, without in any way affecting the political or territorial integrity of the country. Officially they never pressed for a separate State carved out of Iraq; nor did they formally speak of a pan-Kurdish entity."[66] Another viewpoint sees the Kurds as seeking an autonomy akin to that enjoyed by the states within the United States.[67] In contrast, the refusal of the Kurds to accept the 1974 Autonomy Law provoked one commentator's interpretation that "Barzani has held out for independence." [68]

Probably the most accurate assessment that can be made about the Kurdish definition of autonomy is that it has changed over the years in response to the Kurds' sizing up of their own chances for complete independence and the capability of the Iraqi military to preserve the union. Thus, when the journalist David Adamson asked a Kurdish leader for his definition of autonomy he was met with the response,

63. *See* Mortimer, *Uneasy Stability Comes Back to Iraq,* Times (London), Dec. 3, 1975, at 16, col. 1; editorial entitled "The Kurds Pay the Price," Times (London), Mar. 8, 1976, at 13; and a reply by the Iraqi ambassador to Great Britain in a letter to the editor, printed in Times (London), Mar. 11, 1976, at 15, col. 4.

64. *See* Times (London), Nov. 28, 1975, at 8, col. 4.

65. Patriotic Union of Kurdistan, Memorandum to the United Nations on the Situation of the Kurdish People in Iraq 1 (1977).

66. Naamani, *supra* note 49, at 290. *See* Elphinston, *supra* note 40, at 91: "The Kurdish Nationalists are not unreasonable. They simply desire to be allowed to live as Kurds, speak the Kurdish language, read and publish books and newspapers in that language and not to be assimilated as Arabs, Persians or Turks."

67. *Supra* note 41, at 23.

68. *Time* (Europe), Mar. 24, 1975, at 18.

"We have never given a definition. It depends on our strength and that of our enemy."[69]

In its rather limited response to Kurdish appeals, the international community has confined itself to considering the application of international pressure on the Iraqi central government to ameliorate the Kurdish grievances. Discussion of the Kurdish situation in various organs of the United Nations has therefore been conducted in the context of international concern with human rights, genocide, and the prevention of racial discrimination, rather than self-determination. For example, Mongolia requested the inclusion of an item on the provisional agenda of the eighteenth session of the General Assembly dealing with "the policy of genocide carried out by the Government of the Republic of Iraq against the Kurdish people."[70] This was not a plea for the recognition of separatism, however, but rather was explained by the delegate from Mongolia as an expression of his country's firm conviction "that when the fate of a whole ethnic group in any country is in question, no one has the right to stand aside unconcernedly if he respects the principles of justice and humanity." [71] The representative of Iraq responded by claiming that the limited military operation being carried on against "a traitorous group of rebels" was a matter of an exclusively internal character.[72] Neither the Mongolian proposed item, nor a similarly worded request from the Soviet Union to include the matter on the agenda of the thirty-sixth session of the Economic and Social Council,[73] was successfully pursued.

Significantly, the Kurds themselves seem to have abandoned any hope of securing international support for a demand involving the creation of an independent Kurdistan, in favor of arousing concern for the protection of the Kurds and Kurdish culture within Iraq. It must be conceded that the international community has historically shown a greater willingness to discuss measures to protect human rights and prevent racial discrimination than to entertain claims based upon a right of secessionist self-determination. In terms of minimizing the danger to international peace, however, this preference is useful only when external influence is successful in ameliorating the grievances of the petitioning group. If international pressure on the gov-

69. D. ADAMSON, THE KURDISH WAR 92 (1966).

70. Cable dated June 29, 1963, U.N. Doc. A/5429 (1963).

71. 18 U.N. GAOR, 1222d meeting at 9, para. 102, U.N. Doc A/PV. 1222 (1963).

72. *Id.* 15, paras. 156, 157.

73. 36 U.N. ECOSOC, Annexes, Agenda Item No. 1, U.N. Doc. E/3809 (1963).

erning State proves insufficient to accomplish its goals and the group resorts to a self-help remedy such as armed rebellion, the distinction between violence in defense of minority rights and violence in furtherance of a right of self-determination is unlikely to be visible in the actual course of events.

BIAFRA

In 1967, when the Katanga crisis was still a disturbingly fresh memory, Africa was again shaken by a forceful claim to separatist self-determination. The next "victim" of a secessionist attempt was the Federation of Nigeria, a large, populous, and wealthy former British colony which had enjoyed independence since 1960. The claimant group, the Ibo tribe of Eastern Nigeria, sought to establish a sovereign, independent State called the Republic of Biafra and did in fact succeed in opposing the unionist desires of the Nigerian federal government during the course of a painful thirty-month civil war.

The roots of the Biafran secession stretch deep into the tribal, cultural, and religious history of the region. When it achieved independence, Nigeria contained within its borders three major ethnic groups: the Hausa-Fulani in the Northern part of the country, the Yoruba in the West, and the Ibo in the East. In addition to their geographical isolation, each group was separated from the others by differences of culture, language, and religion, differences that made them rather uneasy political bedfellows, even during the years of British colonial rule. The Hausa and Fulani in the North are primarily Moslems, reflecting the inroads of Islam into Northern Nigeria during the past millennium. The majority of the Ibos, on the other hand, profess Christian beliefs, and the Yorubas contain about an even mixture of Christian and Moslem allegiances.[74] Adding to the problems arising from the cultural diversity of these groups has been, in recent years, an uneven educational and economic development of the regions marked by a more rapid progress of the Ibos in comparison with the Northern population. Finally, within each of these three main ethnic areas are numerous smaller tribal groups, distinguishable both in language and in culture from the dominant population, and commanding strong local loyalties.

Given such a highly pluralistic society, it is not surprising that the political union of these regions was, from the beginning, a very fragile creation. Each major group within the territory had at one time or an-

---

74. *See* Kirk-Greene, *The Peoples of Nigeria*, 66 AFRICAN AFF. 1, 5–6 (1967).

BIAFRA

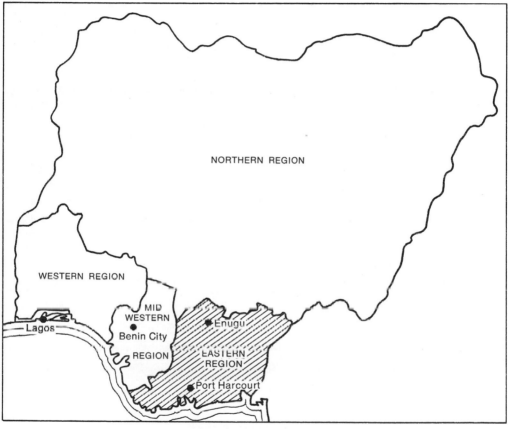

Regions of Nigeria, 1966

other brandished the threat of secession—occasionally to achieve a specific political goal, but often out of a simple dread of "domination" by one of its partners. When the British introduced a scheme for the political amalgamation of the North and the South in 1914, for example, the North seriously considered seceding to protect its own interests. The former premier of the Northern Region of Nigeria, Sir Ahmadu Bello, (who was destined to die in the civil disturbances preceding the Ibo secession) depicted the sentiments current in his region at this time in a way that prefigures some of the same considerations influencing Northern policy fifty years later. First, with regard to the crucial question of the economic situation of the North if divorced from the other regions, Bello concluded: "We were certainly 'viable', to use the current phrase. . . . We had the men and production and minerals and the will to act."[75] The major concern, however, both when the North itself considered seceding and when the East actually attempted it, was the possibility that the North would become a landlocked territory without port facilities for exporting its products. The "rub," as Bello calls it, arose from the uncertainty regarding the South's willingness to allow transport for Northern goods over its territory and use of seaports for external trade.[76]

The smoldering ethnic hostilities erupted again during the early 1950s, when the Western region threatened secession if the capital of Lagos were not retained within its political ambit.[77] Continuing into the postindependence period, separatist sentiments were occasionally given voice during the series of attempts to establish a framework for Nigerian federalism acceptable to the mutually distrustful provinces.[78] It is significant, however, that they were heard most frequently from the leaders of the Northern and Western regions during this period, not from the East.

It is against this history of volatile intergroup rivalry and conflict, in which at least the threat of disassociation was a commonplace instrument of political coercion, that the Biafran secession must be considered. The events constituting the proximate cause of the Ibo sepa-

75. A. BELLO, MY LIFE 135 (1962).

76. Id. 136.

77. See Tamuno, Separatist Agitations in Nigeria since 1914, 8 J. MOD. AFRICAN STUDIES 563, 567–70 (1970).

78. See id. 573–77; J. HATCH, NIGERIA: A HISTORY 197–234 (1970); NIGERIAN POLITICS AND MILITARY RULE: PRELUDE TO THE CIVIL WAR 8–13 (S. Panter-Brick ed. 1970); A. NWANKO, S. IFEJKA, THE MAKING OF A NATION: BIAFRA 34–105 (1969) [hereinafter BIAFRA].

ration were very much a product of the ethnic hostilities that had blighted Nigerian political development all along. Five years after achieving independence, on January 15, 1966, civilian rule in Nigeria was ended by a military coup of young officers ostensibly intended to remove governmental corruption and hasten national unity. The main difficulty with the coup, as perceived by the Northerners, was that most of the young officers involved were Ibos and most of the politicians and senior officers killed during the coup were Northerners. One of the intended Ibo victims of the coup, Major General Aguiyi Ironsi, survived to assume power at the request of a disoriented federal government. Ironsi's personal diagnosis of Nigeria's ailment centered upon its deleterious attachment to "regionalism" and he quickly set about trying to remedy this illness.[79] By a "Unification Decree" of May 24, 1966, the Ironsi government abolished the federation and renamed it the Republic of Nigeria. The decree also declared the formal abolition of the "regions" and sought to centralize regional and federal administrative functions into a unified system.[80]

Dissatisfaction with the Ironsi regime grew rapidly in both the North and the South. The Northerners interpreted the Unification Decree as tantamount to Ibo domination of the country, and Southerners accused Ironsi of delaying needed reforms so as not to offend Northern opinion. Anti-Southern sentiment in the North soon erupted in a wave of mob violence, resulting in the death of hundreds of Ibo residents in the North. Ironsi was assassinated when a second military coup occurred on July 29, 1966, this time led by Northern officers. He was replaced by Lieutenant-Colonel Yakubu Gowon, a Northerner, whose intention it was that the coup result either in a reestablishment of Northern predominance over the country or, alternatively, in a secession of the North from the other regions.[81] In the event, he may have been dissuaded from declaring the separation of the North only at the last minute by American and British diplomatic pressure.[82] Nevertheless, in a speech broadcast on August 1, Gowon left little doubt regarding his belief that the historically thin bonds of

79. *See* Press Statement of General Ironsi, Feb. 21, 1966, in which he declared: "It has become apparent to all Nigerians that rigid adherence to 'regionalism', was the bane of the last regime and one of the main factors which contributed to its downfall." NIGERIAN POLITICS, *supra* note 78, at 189.

80. For a summary of the decree's major features *see id.* 179–80.

81. *See* BIAFRA, *supra* note 78, at 156–57.

82. *See id.* 161; A. WAUGH, S. CRONJE, BIAFRA: BRITAIN'S SHAME 65 (1969). *But see* J. ST. JORRE, THE BROTHERS' WAR: BIAFRA AND NIGERIA 74–75 (1972).

Nigerian unity had worn even thinner. "Suffice it to say," he concluded, "that putting all considerations to test, political, economic as well as social, the basis for unity is not there, or is so badly rocked not only once but several times. I therefore feel that we should review the issue of our national standing."[83]

While Gowon was debating withdrawing his region from its association with the rest of the country, widespread rioting recurred in the North, bringing in its wake the massacre of at least 10,000 Easterners residing in that province, and the expulsion of many times that number more, during the period September–October 1966.[84] In an attempt at keeping the country from drifting further into anarchy, an Ad Hoc Conference on the Nigerian Constitution was called in September. The Eastern region, under the command of Lieutenant-Colonel Odumegwu Ojukwu, sent a delegation to the conference to meet with representatives of the North, West, Midwest, and the capital city of Lagos. When the delegations tabled their initial memoranda containing proposals for the structuring of the constitution, the East, West, and North had all suggested the inclusion of a right of secession. The Northern proposal, significantly in light of the North's later staunch defense of a "one Nigeria" policy, suggested that Nigeria should be a union or association of the existing regions and such other states as might be formed subsequently, with a "right to secede completely and unilaterally." The Northern memorandum then stated:

> Right of self-determination of all people in the country must be accepted and a referendum or plebiscite shall be the method through which the wishes of the people concerned shall be ascertained. These rights include the right of any State within the country to secede. But the implementation of these principles shall not delay the determination of the future of Nigeria. All necessary guarantees shall, however, be written in the future con-

83. The quotation is taken from an excerpt of Gowon's August 1 speech printed in S. CRONJE, THE WORLD AND NIGERIA: THE DIPLOMATIC HISTORY OF THE BIAFRAN WAR 1967–1970, at 17 (1972).

84. S. K. Panter-Brick cites Colonel Ojukwu as setting the figure of Ibos killed in the North at 10,000. Panter-Brick, *The Right to Self-Determination: Its Application to Nigeria*, 44 INT'L AFF. 254, 262 n. 5 (1968). K. W. J. Post mentions a figure as high as 40,000 Easterners killed and 1 million expelled from the North. Post, *Is There a Case for Biafra?* 44 INT'L AFF. 26, 32 (1968). The Biafran authorities set it at 30,000; 6 INT'L LEG. MAT. 668 (1967).

stitution to establish the right of self-determination by any section.[85]

During an adjournment of the conference between September 29 and October 24, the worst outbreak of anti-Eastern violence enveloped the North, and when the Ad Hoc Constitutional Committee reconvened in October the Eastern delegates were not in attendance. After a brief and inconclusive series of meetings, Gowon therefore decided that, in the absence of the representatives from the East, the committee would remain adjourned indefinitely. Gowon had by this time adopted a personal commitment to the idea of a unified Nigeria with a strong central government. In a November 30 broadcast calling for support for the federal military government's efforts at unification, he struck an ominous note by saying, "I shall do everything in my power and use the resources of the Federal Government to guarantee the continued existence of Nigeria as one political and economic unit."[86]

In an effort to reconcile the Eastern region (which was by now deeply aggrieved by the treatment of its citizens in the North), Gowon and Ojukwu met for direct negotiations at Aburi on January 4–5, 1967. The agenda of their discussion included, among other things, problems relating to the recognition of Gowon as "supreme commander and head of the federal military government," and the powers that would be accorded to the federal and regional governments. The negotiations ended on a hopeful note with agreement apparently having been reached on a number of key issues. It took only until the end of the month, however, for Gowon and Ojukwu to dissent sharply in public statements over the interpretation of the Aburi agreements; Gowon felt that the question of governmental structure had been resolved in favor of effective central authority, while Ojukwu interpreted the agreement to envision a kind of confederation.[87] Each was subsequently to accuse the other of a deliberate breach of the agreements.

Events from this point on snowballed rapidly into the eventual proclamation of the secession of the Eastern region in May of 1967.

85. Reprinted in NIGERIAN POLITICS, *supra* note 78, at 156. *See also* Nixon, *Self-Determination: The Nigeria/Biafra Case*, 24 WORLD POL. 473, 478–79 (1972).

86. The text of the Nov. 30, 1966, speech is reprinted in NIGERIAN POLITICS, *supra* note 78, at 190, 195.

87. *See* BIAFRA, *supra* note 78, at 216–20.

Within days of the impending secession, Gowon unilaterally announced a restructuring of the federal scheme into twelve states (three of which were in the Eastern region) based on the ethnic divisions of the country. This did not, however, halt the Biafran separation nor did it have its arguably intended effect of measurably increasing minority (non-Ibo) unrest within the Eastern region. On May 30, therefore, Ojukwu, after borrowing from Rousseau and Jefferson to tell his fellow citizens of Eastern Nigeria that "you are born free and have certain inalienable rights which can best be preserved by yourselves," declared the Republic of Biafra an independent, sovereign State.[88]

The military history of the Biafran struggle is beyond the scope of this discussion.[89] It is sufficient to say that after an incredibly costly civil conflict, in terms of both military and civilian casualties, the war ended on January 12, 1970, when the Biafran army's chief of staff surrendered to representatives of the Nigerian federal government with the words, "The Republic of Biafra ceases to exist."[90] Of more relevance to the present consideration is the international response evoked by this sanguine spectacle of a long and ferocious civil war carried on in the name of self-determination.

With its fingers still smarting from burns suffered in the Congo crisis, the United Nations did not at any time consider the events in Nigeria during this period. Secretary General U Thant sought to defer the matter to the Organization of African Unity (OAU) and reacted in an exceptionally defensive way to questions regarding United Nations inaction. At a January 9, 1970, press conference, for example, when asked if the United Nations anticipated taking any action with regard to the Biafran conflict, U Thant emphatically stated:

> The question is that the issue must be brought to the attention of the United Nations. So far, not one single Member State out of 126 has brought the question of the civil conflict in Nigeria to the United Nations, not one Government. . . . [S]ince the eruption of this crisis, not one single Member State has brought up the ques-

88. The Proclamation of the Republic of Biafra may be found in 6 INT'L LEG. MAT. 665, 679–80 (1967).

89. For an excellent documentary history of the Biafran secession *see* A. KIRK-GREENE, CRISIS AND CONFLICT IN NIGERIA: A DOCUMENTARY SOURCE-BOOK 1966–1970 (2 vols. 1971).

90. N.Y. Times, Jan. 16, 1970, at 13, cols. 1–2.

tion. . . . So far, not one single Member State out of 126 has brought this to the attention of the Security Council or the General Assembly.[91]

The reason for this hesitancy of member States to bring the Nigerian crisis before the U.N., according to the secretary general, was their knowledge that the United Nations would simply refuse to discuss it. In the absence of overt military intervention by outside States (beyond the supply of arms and military equipment), U Thant's prediction that the United Nations would not discuss the crisis was probably a realistic, if disturbing, judgment. U Thant himself, of course, had the power under article 99 of the Charter to bring the matter to the attention of the Security Council but it is doubtful whether many members would have welcomed such an initiative. The reaction of the OAU to the Biafran situation seems to confirm the belief that they would not.

Given the general prejudice of the Organization of African Unity against any further "Balkanization" of the continent, the Biafrans were likely to find little sympathy in that quarter. In the event, they found none. The heads of the OAU assembled at Kinshasa on September 11–14, 1967, and passed a short resolution which began by solemnly reaffirming their adherence to the principle of respect for the sovereignty and territorial integrity of member States; "*Reiterating their condemnation of secession in any Member States*"; and recognizing that the situation was an "internal affair," the solution of which was primarily the responsibility of the Nigerians themselves.[92]

The resolution also set up a Consultative Committee which met at Lagos on November 22–23, 1967. Emperor Haile Selassie set the tone of the meeting by declaring: "The national unity and territorial integrity of member states is not negotiable."[93] Not surprisingly, the Consultative Committee failed to achieve a resolution of the conflict at its Lagos meeting or at subsequent meetings at Niamey, Niger, on July 15, 1968, Addis Ababa on August 6, 1968, or Monrovia, in April 1969. The OAU passed a number of inconsequential resolutions on

---

91. 7 U.N. MONTHLY CHRONICLE, Feb. at 40 (1970).

92. Reprinted in 6 INT'L LEG. MAT. 1243 (1967).

93. Nayar, *Self-Determination beyond the Colonial Context: Biafra in Retrospect*, 10 TEX. INT'L L.J. 321, 328 (1975). Ethiopia, of course, was not without its own interest in seeing an acceptance of this proposition. *See* text accompanying notes 116–29 *infra*.

the Nigerian situation,[94] but its effectiveness as an instrument for inducing the parties to negotiate was clearly prejudiced by its unquestioned assumption that Biafra must first renounce the secession.[95]

The reactions of individual members of the world community to the Biafran situation were mixed. Five States chose to recognize the Republic of Biafra as a sovereign member of the community of nations. The first to do so was Tanzania on April 13, 1968, followed by Gabon, the Ivory Coast, Zambia, and Haiti. Most of the declarations announcing the granting of recognition stressed the ferocity of the Nigerian/Biafran conflict and saw little basis for any future political unity of the country.[96] France called for a resolution of the conflict "on the basis of the right of peoples to self-determination" and noted that the suffering of the Biafrans had shown their will to affirm themselves as a people.[97] Similarly, China, once Soviet support for the Nigerian federal government became apparent, offered verbal encouragement to the Biafran regime.[98]

In the absence of any collective international judgment on the legitimacy of the secession, there was little to inhibit outside powers from intervening on behalf of whichever side seemed to offer the best chances for furthering the intervenor's own interests. Thus, France was reported to have indirectly supplied the secessionists with arms via the Ivory Coast and Gabon.[99] Portugal permitted the Biafrans to use Lisbon as a base for propaganda activities and for arranging the purchase of arms and supplies.[100]

The United Kingdom, as the former colonial Power, felt a particular responsibility for the events in Nigeria and sought to maintain what it at one point called a "neutral" position in the conflict. By this the British government meant that it would do all in its power to end the fighting in Nigeria, but its neutrality did not demand a suspension

94. See 2 KIRK-GREENE, supra note 89, at 244–45, 328–29, 445.

95. See Nayar, supra note 93, at 329. Nayar gives this restrained opinion with reference to the OAU's unquestioning condemnation of the secession: "Such a partisan stand imposed certain limitations upon the effectiveness of the mediatory role of the O.A.U. Consultative Committee." See generally WAUGH & CRONJE, supra note 82, at 81–95.

96. Ijalaye, Was "Biafra" at Any Time a State in International Law? 65 AM. J. INT'L L. 551, 553–54 (1971). See also 2 KIRK-GREENE, supra note 89, at 206–13, 220–21.

97. See July 31, 1968, statement of the French secretary of information, Ijalaye, supra note 96, at 554.

98. CRONJE, supra note 83, at 275–76. Ojukwu's response thanking Chairman Mao for his support is reprinted id. 383–84.

99. Id. 205.

100. See Nixon, supra note 85, at 495.

of its sales of military weapons to the federal government. As the British secretary for commonwealth affairs, George Thomson, was to tell the House of Commons in 1968, there was nothing dishonorable in Britain as "the creator of the original Nigerian union" hoping passionately that the people would find a way of living with each other.[101] Nevertheless, the government was determined that, should passionate British hopes fail to reunite the parties, at least the continued supply of British weapons to the federal authorities would help prevent their separation from being permanent. The sale of British arms to the Nigerian federal government was justified to a somewhat hostile House of Commons with a number of arguments. First, the continued supply of weapons was necessary to preserve British influence with the federal government (particularly when the Soviet Union seemed eager to fill any vacuum in this regard). Second, Britain had been the traditional supplier of arms for the Nigerian army and could not now leave them in the lurch. Third, even if shipments were curtailed, this would not measurably affect the ultimate outcome of the Nigerian conflict. Fourth, a suspension of arms shipments would have shaken the faith of other Commonwealth countries in Britain's willingness to support them in times of crisis. In a later debate in the House of Commons, Thomson summarized the British government's position in this way:

> The Nigerian forces, like the forces of many Commonwealth countries, were trained and equipped on British lines before independence. Under successive British Governments, they have naturally looked largely to us for resupply. When the time came that they most needed supplies, they counted on our willingness to allow them to purchase from the United Kingdom.
>
> Neutrality was not a possible option for Her Majesty's Government at that time. We might have been able to declare ourselves neutral if one independent country was fighting another, but this was not a possible attitude when a Commonwealth country, with which we had long and close ties, was faced with an internal revolt. What would other Commonwealth countries have thought?[102]

Britain's major, but not exclusive, competitor in supplying arms to the federal government was the Soviet Union. Following an initial pe-

101. 769 PARL. DEB., H. C. (5th Ser.) 109–10 (1968).
102. 769 PARL. DEB., H. C. (5th Ser.) 1146 (1968).

riod of indecision, the Soviets found it in their interest to sell artillery, jet warplanes, infantry weapons, and armored vehicles to the federal authorities. To some extent, the British and Soviet arms shipments tended to have an escalating effect on each other—each country seeking through its generosity to minimize the growth of the other's influence with the Gowon government.[103]

Shortly after hostilities began, the United States imposed an embargo on the sale of American weapons to the combatants and this policy of refusing to sell arms to either side was maintained throughout the conflict. This did not of course imply any American recognition of Biafra—as the State Department was quick to point out—nor did it signify a withdrawal of American recognition of the federal government. An early statement from that agency reiterated that "The United States Government has in no way encouraged, supported, or otherwise been involved in this rebellion." [104] Although generally deploring the intervention of outside Powers in the dispute by the supply of arms to the combatants, the United States did not encompass within this criticism the British sale of arms to the federal government. In a 1968 speech, a State Department official echoed the British justification for their behavior: "I do not really see how they could have made any other choice. . . . If they had stopped sales they could, in fact, be helping to support the dismemberment of a fellow Commonwealth country with which they have had a special relationship since independence." [105]

The military success of the Nigerian government in suppressing the Biafran resistance removed the immediate need for any further inquiry into the legal legitimacy of the secession. Two issues have nonetheless continued to arouse some interest among international jurists: (1) Did the "Republic of Biafra" in fact enter the community of States for a brief period before leaving it again under duress?[106] (2) Despite its unsuccessful conclusion, was the secession a legitimate act of self-

103. See CRONJE, supra note 83, at 252–80.
104. 58 DEP'T STATE BULL. 278 (1968).
105. Katzenbach, The Tragedy of Nigeria, 59 DEP'T STATE BULL. 653, 656 (1968).
106. On this issue, a 1971 study concluded that "it is difficult to establish that Biafra attained statehood in international law." Ijalaye, supra note 96, at 559. Another commentator has interpreted the same set of circumstances as justifying the belief that "The factual conditions constituting the basis of independence and sovereignty . . . are factual conditions which were present in the case of Biafra." C. OKEKE, THE EXPANSION OF NEW SUBJECTS OF CONTEMPORARY INTERNATIONAL LAW THROUGH THEIR TREATY-MAKING CAPACITY 165 (1973).

determination by the Biafran people?[107] With regard to this second question, the inevitable comparison of the Biafran secession with that of the Katanga suggests a strong argument for Biafran legitimacy. The main features of this argument can be revealed by a survey of the objections to the Katanga separation which were raised in international forums. Unlike the Tshombe regime, the Eastern Nigerians did not attempt to divide the country virtually at the moment it became independent; the Biafran secession occurred sixteen years after independence and presumably after the benefits and burdens of union had been experienced by all concerned. Additionally, the economic viability of the Federation of Nigeria was never seriously in doubt even if denied the industry and oil fields existing in the Eastern region (except insofar as the secession might have induced a further general break-up of the federation into its ethnic components). The Republic of Biafra itself showed every sign of being able to survive as a separate entity—it had a population of 12 to 14 million, port facilities, natural resources, a relatively high educational level, and so on.[108]

Second, the international community had grave doubts about the true extent of popular support for the Tshombe regime among the people of Katanga and, indeed, questioned whether the population possessed enough ethnic or historical identity to substantiate a claim to being a "people." To the extent that the majority of Biafrans (approximately 64 percent) were Ibos, its cultural and historical differentiation from the other regions of Nigeria was apparent. (It is noteworthy, however, that the non-Ibo tribes within the area of the "Republic of Biafra" probably had as little in common with the Ibos as with other Nigerian groups.)

There do not appear to be persuasive reasons for doubting the popularity of the secession among the Biafran people in general. At each stage of the events leading up to the separation, the actions of the Ojukwu regime were authorized by the only functioning political bodies in Eastern Nigeria at the time: the Consultative Assembly and the Advisory Committee of Chiefs and Elders. Indeed, it was a joint session of these bodies which on May 27, 1967, passed the resolution mandating Ojukwu "to declare at the earliest practicable date Eastern Nigeria a free, sovereign and independent state by the name and title

107. *See* Wodie, *La Sécession du Biafra et le Droit International Public*, 73 REVUE GENERALE DE DROIT INTERNATIONAL PUBLIC 1018, 1025–29 (1969).

108. *See generally* Anber, *Modernisation and Political Disintegration: Nigeria and the Ibos*, 5 J. MOD. AFRICAN STUDIES 163 (1967).

of the REPUBLIC OF BIAFRA."[109] The Easterners also had a colorable claim to excessive oppression at the hands of the Northerners in
light of the widespread killings and expulsions of Easterners residing
in the North prior to the secession. Furthermore, it is significant that
these attacks victimized both Ibo and non-Ibo Easterners alike. This
was, in fact, one of the elements cited by the resolution of May 27 justifying the East's declaration that the federation had forfeited any
claim to their allegiance.[110] In the final analysis, the strongest piece of
evidence supporting the Biafrans' claim to being a distinct group with
an overwhelming desire for independence was their willingness to suffer almost three years of civil war, disease, and famine to achieve that
independence.

Finally, the common currency of secessionist talk in all of the Nigerian regions right up to the actual separation of the East in 1967 gave
the Biafrans a reasonable ground for believing that secession was recognized in Nigeria as a legitimate method of altering one region's
relationship to the others, or at least that it would not be strenuously
opposed. They were certainly justified in thinking that some rearrangement of the political structure toward a looser union of the regions was in order when the head of the federal government, Gowon,
publicly expressed his belief that "the basis for unity is not there."[111]

Despite these differences, a comparison of the Katanga with Biafra
reveals two lingering uncertainties, present in both secessionist attempts, which may continue to haunt the world community in dealing
with similar situations in the future. First, would a recognition of the
secessions by the international community or the respective central
governments of the Congo or Nigeria really have opened the flood-
gates for an inevitable separatist disintegration of these countries?
Both States at the time of their crises showed signs of further internal
disunity beyond the disaffection of the provinces immediately involved
in the secession. The proliferation of rival governments in the various
Congolese provinces during the post independence crisis seemed to
remove any doubts regarding the possibility of a unified Congo had
secession been condoned. Similarly, almost all of the Nigerian regions
had embraced secession in theory at one time or another. The danger
of setting off further separatist reactions was made clear at the first

109. *Supra* note 88, at 13–14.
110. *Id.* 14.
111. *See* text accompanying note 83.

meeting of the Ad Hoc Constitutional Committee in 1967, when Chief Awolowo of the Western Region, speaking for the Western political body which bore the rather Orwellian title of the "Leaders of Thought," indicated that if the East seceded from the federation the West would not be far behind. Had this occurred, which it did not, the North would again have been left to confront the problems arising from a landlocked geographical position with potentially hostile neighbors blocking its access to the sea.[112]

The second uncertainty responsible for some of the international uneasiness in these cases was the problem of minority groups finding themselves within territory claimed by the seceding provinces. Within the region calling itself the Republic of Biafra, for example, were large numbers of non-Ibo tribal groups whose fate after the separation was unclear. Additionally, with regard to the Ibos living outside of the East (such as the Ibo population of the Midwest), would these people have had a valid irredentist claim to join the Republic of Biafra once independent?[113]

In conclusion, perhaps the most important lesson to be learned from the Biafran secession is that such phenomena are rarely as much of an "internal affair" as one might hope. Moreover, an abstention from collective international involvement in disputes of this magnitude on the basis of the "internal affairs" doctrine is in practice likely to guarantee that the matter does not remain internal. Without some indication of the international community's collective judgment about the legitimacy of a particular claim to self-determination, or at least about the need to avoid third-party involvement, external intervention on behalf of either side is virtually unassailable on legal grounds. Although it is true that the external involvement in Biafra did not take the form of overt military intervention, as it did in the Congo, nevertheless the supply of arms to the antagonists in the conflict clearly affected the conduct of the war and initiated a process which, under different circumstances, might have involved a confrontation of major power blocs. A precedent of an international consideration of cases like the Biafra secession, in which a massive civil war waged largely with foreign weapons results in the death of hundreds of thousands

112. See NIGERIAN POLITICS, supra note 78, at 101–02; Nixon supra note 85, at 490. For an excellent criticism of the "domino theory" of one secession spawning others, see Kamanu, Secession and the Right of Self-Determination: An O.A.U. Dilemma, 12 J. MOD. AFRICAN STUDIES 355, 366–70 (1974).

113. See Panter-Brick, supra note 84, at 262–65.

of people, would not seem to justify the apprehensions of those who fear a perpetual United Nations involvement in every internal squabble. The significant practical and diplomatic problems that surround any collective international action taken to minimize a threat to world peace (problems graphically illustrated by the Congo operation), must finally be balanced against the cost in terms of human suffering and international disruption of maintaining an overly timid policy of strict noninterference. At the very least, the human cost of this policy of abstention ought to suggest a careful review of the meaning of the phrase "internal affair" as applied to these situations.

THE SOMALI-KENYA/ETHIOPIA DISPUTE

My face is burning and will not be happy
Until I see all the five parts sharing the flag over us
Until I see brothers taking the oath to die together.
I shall not be happy until our spears are wet and we do our duty
I shall not feel well until we go to war to unite Somalis
Until the leader gives us news of his determination.
I shall be depressed until young and old men alike,
Women and children, all put on signs of mourning and revenge.[114]

Thus begins a poem celebrating the theme of the liberation of the Somali peoples. The "five parts" of the Somali nation for which the poet demands unification are British Somaliland and Italian Somalia (now united in the Somali Democratic Republic); the contiguous region of the Republic of Djibouti (formerly the French Territory of the Afars and Issas);[115] the Ethiopian territories of Ogaden, the Haud, and the "Reserved Area"; and the Northern Frontier District (NFD) of Kenya. The poem reflects a nationalistic desire for an amalgamation of the territories occupied by Somali peoples—the desire, in short, for a nation-State of "Greater Somalia" in the Horn of Africa. When such irredentist wishes are voiced by Somali tribesmen living in Ethiopia and Kenya, they are in effect demands for a secession of these areas from their present governing States and their incorporation within the Somali Republic. It is the Somali insistence on secession as the ultimate fulfillment of self-determination for these peoples that brings its disputes with Kenya and Ethiopia within the purview of the present discussion.

114. Legum, *Somali Liberation Songs*, 1 J. MOD. AFRICAN STUDIES 501, 505 (1963).
115. The Republic of Djibouti achieved its independence from France on June 27, 1977.

SOMALIA

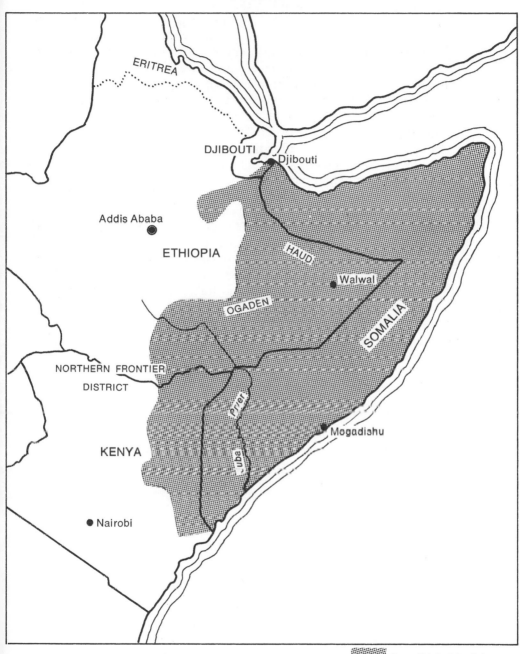

ERITREA

DJIBOUTI
Djibouti

Addis Ababa

ETHIOPIA

HAUD

OGADEN

Walwal

SOMALIA

NORTHERN FRONTIER
DISTRICT

KENYA

Pref.

Juba

Mogadishu

Nairobi

Somali Inhabited Areas

Somalia-Ethiopia

During the nineteenth century, the Horn of Africa endured a troubled history at the hands of the European colonialists and it has had an even more tortured contemporary history as the former colonial Powers have sought to extricate themselves from their unpopular position while leaving behind some semblance of order. The present Ethiopia-Somalia dispute over the territories comprising the southeastern portion of Ethiopia (Ogaden, the Haud, and the Reserved Area) is a legacy of the previous colonial administration.

By treaties concluded between 1884 and 1886, a number of Somali tribes placed themselves under the protection of the British Crown,[116] although the exact territorial delimitation of the British protectorate was never really clear. The French reached similar agreements with the Somali clans around Djibouti (1885), and the Italians with the sultans on the Indian Ocean (1889). During the 1890s, Emperor Menelik II acceded to the throne of Ethiopia and began a policy of Ethiopian expansion into lands occupied by the Somali nomads, some of whom had recently placed themselves under the protection of the colonial Powers. An Italian military defeat at the hands of the Ethiopians at Adowa in 1896 eventually induced the British and Italians to draw back the lines of their protectorates in the Haud and Ogaden. A negotiated settlement between Menelik and Rennell Rodd, the British special envoy to the emperor, resulted in a British cession to Ethiopia of the areas now known as the Haud and the Reserved Area — totaling some 25,000 square miles.[117] In these regions the 1897 British/Ethiopian Treaty recognized the traditional rights of the Somali nomads to graze and water their herds, with each party obligating itself to respect these rights.[118] The British neither consulted the Somalis on the terms of the 1897 agreement nor undertook to brief them on it afterward. As Ethiopia did not immediately attempt any rigorous control over the area, however, life for the Somali herdsmen went on much as before.

Despite the nationalistic disturbances of a Somali leader, Sheikh Mohammed Abdillee, between 1900 and 1920, this relatively peaceful

116. *See* 76 BRIT. ST. PAPERS 101–07 (1884–85); 77 BRIT. ST. PAPERS 1263–69 (1885–86).

117. *See generally* J. DRYSDALE, THE SOMALI DISPUTE 25–32 (1964).

118. *See* 89 BRIT. ST. PAPERS 37, 38 (1897). In a previous letter Emperor Menelik assured the British envoy that "The Somalis who may by boundary arrangements become subjects of Ethiopia shall be well treated and have orderly government." *Id.* 33.

situation lasted into the 1930s, when the Ethiopians began to take a more active interest in the ceded territories. This prompted the formation of an Anglo-Ethiopian Commission designed to clarify the 1897 boundary, which had never been demarcated with any precision. The Somali nomads, however, reacted violently to the formation of the commission and what they perceived as an attempt to restrict their transfrontier grazing rights.

For their part, the Italians had signed a convention with the Ethiopians in 1908 which purported to give a definitive delimitation of the Italo-Ethiopian border.[119] This proved a vain hope, however, when an Italo-Ethiopian Commission tried unsuccessfully several years later to establish the boundary line on the ground. Italian and Ethiopian interests in the region eventually brought the two countries into conflict over the camel-watering center of Wal Wal in November of 1934. The Italians had occupied the wells as part of Italian Somaliland since 1930 and maintained a garrison of Somalis in the area. This garrison resisted an attempt by Ethiopian troops to take over the wells and sharp fighting broke out, resulting in loss of life on both sides. After the Wal Wal incident, the deterioration of relations between the two countries finally resulted in open conflict and the Italian conquest of Ethiopia in 1935–36.

With the commencement of World War II and Italy's declaration of war on England in 1940, the Italians successfully invaded British Somaliland. A British offensive recovered the territory in 1941, however, and took the rest of Italian Somaliland shortly thereafter. At the war's end, the British proposed that the various Somali territories (except, significantly, the Somali-inhabited NFD of Kenya) be amalgamated into a single trusteeship. British Foreign Secretary Ernest Bevin explained the plan to the House of Commons in 1946:

> In the latter part of the last century the Horn of Africa was divided between Great Britain, France and Italy. At about the time we occupied our part, the Ethiopians occupied an inland area which is the grazing ground for nearly half the nomads of British Somaliland for six months of the year. Similarly, the nomads of Italian Somaliland must cross the existing frontiers in search of grass. In all innocence, therefore, we proposed that British Somaliland, Italian Somaliland, and the adjacent part of Ethiopia, if Ethiopia agreed, should be lumped together as a trust territory,

119. 101 BRIT. ST. PAPERS 1000–01 (1908).

so that the nomads should lead their frugal existence with the least possible hindrance and there might be a real chance of a decent economic life, as understood in that region.[120]

The Bevin Plan failed to meet with the approval of Ethiopia or the other major Powers, and in 1948 Britain agreed to return Ogaden to Ethiopia. The Treaty of Peace with Italy had already stipulated that the final disposition of the Italian territorial possessions in Africa and the appropriate adjustment of their boundaries would be made by the Four Powers "in the light of the wishes and welfare of the inhabitants."[121] When the Four Powers failed to reach agreement concerning the disposition of the territories, the matter was referred to the General Assembly of the United Nations. By its resolution 289 of November 21, 1949, the Assembly determined that Italian Somaliland would become independent ten years from the date of an approval of a trusteeship agreement by the General Assembly, and that Italy would be the administering authority during the term of the trusteeship.[122]

The British thereafter succumbed to Ethiopian pressure to return the Haud and Reserved Areas to Ethiopian sovereignty, doing so by an agreement dated November 29, 1954.[123] When news of the agreement reached the Somali people, political protests broke out in most centers in the territory. Communications addressed to the United Nations by local political groups called for the repeal of the agreement on the grounds that (1) the regions involved were Somali territory; (2) the Haud region was included in the contested frontier area; (3) no decision thereon should be taken prior to the settlement of the question of the border between Ethiopia and Somaliland; and (4) the inhabitants of these regions had never been consulted.[124] Nevertheless, the U.N. Advisory Council for the Trust Territory of Somaliland concluded that the effect of the 1954 agreement was "in no way prejudicial to whatever decisions or disposition might be taken on this vi-

120. 423 PARL. DEB., H.C. (5th Ser.) 1840–41 (1946).

121. Treaty of Peace with Italy, signed Feb. 10, 1947, Annex 11, 49 U.N.T.S. 214 (1950).

122. G.A. Res. 289, U.N. Doc. A/1251 (1949). For a discussion of the history of the Italian trusteeship *see* Castagno, *Somalia,* 1959 INT'L CONC. No. 522, at 348–85.

123. 207 U.N.T.S. 284 (1955). The rights of tribes to cross the Ethiopia-Somaliland frontier for the purpose of grazing was reaffirmed in article 2. For a more detailed discussion of the 1954 agreement *see* Brown, *The Ethiopia-Somaliland Frontier Dispute,* 5 INT'L & COMP. L. Q. 245, 258–64 (1956).

124. Report of the U.N. Advisory Council for Somaliland, 16 U.N. TRUSTEESHIP, Annex, Agenda Item No. 17, at 8, para. 54, U.N. Doc. T/1172 (1955).

tal question,"[125] although the council conceded that "it would undoubtedly be most interesting to know the opinion of the people affected, as this question calls for the exercise of the right of self-determination."[126]

During the period following the war, Somali nationalism became a potent political force. The Somali Youth Club (after 1947 called the Somali Youth League, or SLY), which was eventually to hold the majority of Legislative Assembly seats at the time of independence, staunchly advocated the unification of all territories inhabited by the Somali peoples. A 1948 memorandum of the SLY expressed its convictions: "We wish our country to be amalgamated with the other Somalilands and to form one political, administrative and economic unit with them. We Somalis are one in every way. We are the same racially and geographically, we have the same culture, we have the same language and the same religion. There is no future for us except as part of a Greater Somalia."[127]

Ultimately, despite the efforts of the General Assembly to induce Ethiopia and Italian Somaliland into a settlement concerning the proper demarcation of the boundary,[128] no understanding was reached and the dispute was inherited by the Republic of Somalia when it attained independence in 1960. The constitution of the new republic, in article 6, promised that "the Somali Republic shall promote, by legal and peaceful means, the union of Somali territories."[129]

Somalia-Kenya

Somalia's quarrel with its southern neighbor, Kenya, is also of colonial origin. An 1891 agreement between Italy and Great Britain set the northern border of British East Africa at the Juba River. This geographical feature had the virtue of being a convenient, clear demarcation of the boundary but it shared with the Ethiopia-Somaliland border the drawback of arbitrarily cutting across ethnic regions. Somali tribesmen inhabited the areas both to the North and to the South of the Juba and migrations of Somali tribes southward from Italian Somaliland and Ethiopia greatly increased the Somali population of

125. *Id.* para. 55.
126. *Id.*
127. *Quoted in* S. TOUVAL, SOMALI NATIONALISM 95 (1963).
128. *See* Castagno, *supra* note 122, at 386–91 for a discussion of the General Assembly's efforts during the term of the Italian trusteeship.
129. 11 CONSTITUTIONS OF THE COUNTRIES OF THE MODERN WORLD, Somalia (A. Blaustein & G. Flanz ed. 1971).

the British territory after the establishment of a protectorate in 1895. Part of this region, known as "Jubaland," was ceded to Italian Somaliland in 1924,[130] pursuant to a prior secret agreement between Italy and Great Britain which promised the territory in return for Italy's entering the First World War on the Allied side.

The remainder of the Somali-inhabited territory in the British protectorate of Kenya, designated the Northern Frontier District, did not feel any noticeable governmental intrusion until the 1940s. It is significant, however, that from 1924 onward Great Britain treated this area as an administrative unit separate from the rest of Kenya. In the mid-1940s, the SLY established branches in the Northern Frontier District. Their activities in that region managed to incur the government's disapproval and the SLY was officially proscribed in July of 1948. Somali nationalist sentiment in the province remained quiescent until stimulated by the imminent union of British and Italian Somaliland into the Republic of Somalia in 1960, and the granting of independence to Kenya shortly thereafter.

As the British authorities began to receive petitions demanding the incorporation of the Northern Frontier District into Somalia, a new political party openly espousing the cause of pan-Somalian unification was formed in 1960 with the alliterative title of the Northern Province People's Progressive Party. Prosecessionist sentiments were much in evidence at a 1962 constitutional conference held in London to prepare the way for Kenyan independence. A Commission of Inquiry was despatched to ascertain local public opinion regarding the future of the NFD. The commission concluded that the NFD could be divided into areas that favored secession and amalgamation with Somalia, those that favored remaining part of Kenya and participating in its constitutional development, and areas of mixed opinion. The areas found to be supporting the "Somalia Opinion" were the largest in total population and size. "We found," the commission reported, "that the people there almost unanimously favour the secession of Kenya from the NFD, when Kenya attains independence, with the object of ultimately joining the Somali Republic, but they want the NFD to have a period under British authority in which to build up its machinery of government so that it can join the Somali Republic as a self-governing unit."[131]

130. Treaty between Italy and the United Kingdom, signed July 15, 1924, 36 L.N.T.S. 380 (1925).
131. NORTHERN FRONTIER DISTRICT COMMISSION, REPORT, CMND. NO. 1900, at 18 (1962). This document should be compared with a contemporaneous report of the Re-

Thus, the British found themselves in the rather embarrassing position of having ascertained a majority desire for secession within the NFD and yet not wanting to offend Kenyan and Ethiopian sentiments which strongly objected to any dismemberment of Kenyan territory. In the end, the latter consideration carried more weight. On March 8, 1963, therefore, the British colonial secretary, Duncan Sandys, announced that the Somali-inhabited areas of Kenya would be formed into a separate region of the country to be granted a larger amount of local autonomy. This action provoked the Somali Republic to break off diplomatic relations with Great Britain. At a conference in August called by the British, the Somalis proposed that, pending a final settlement of the problem, the NFD should be placed under a special joint Somali/Kenya administration or under a United Nations administration.[132] The Kenyans were reported to be unimpressed with this proposal. Consequently, on December 12, Kenya attained independence with the NFD intact.

By 1964, therefore, the fledgling Republic of Somalia had antagonized both its neighbors by demanding the right of self-determination for their minority groups which, as things stood, amounted to a demand for the cession of large parts of their territory.[133] The areas claimed by Somalia on the basis of ethnic affinity are of a not inconsiderable size. But it must be conceded that, large as the areas are, they are inhabited principally by Somalis. The Somali-inhabited regions of Ethiopia comprise about 80,000 square miles—nearly one-

---

gional Boundaries Commission which noted, "The Somali delegations seen by us in these areas were unanimous in their desire not to be included in any region of Kenya. Apart from one of these delegations, which wished the area to remain under British control for the time being, all these delegations wished the Northern Frontier District to be joined with the Somali Republic." REGIONAL BOUNDARIES COMMISSION, REPORT, CMND. No. 1899, at 16 (1962).

A publication of the Somali Republic interprets the NFD commission's report, albeit with questionable calculations, as disclosing that 87 percent of the population wished to secede from Kenya and form an association with the Somali Republic. MINISTRY OF FOREIGN AFFAIRS (Somali Republic), THE SOMALI PEOPLE'S QUEST FOR UNITY 11 (1965). Cf. I. LEWIS, THE MODERN HISTORY OF SOMALILAND: FROM NATION TO STATE 191 (1965).

132. See DRYSDALE, supra note 117, at 157.

133. See speech of Somali president Aden Osman at the OAU Inaugural Summit Conference, Addis Ababa, 1963: "Let there be no misunderstanding about our intentions. . . . The Somali Government . . . must press for self-determination for the inhabitants of the Somali areas adjacent to the Somali Republic. . . . If the Somalis in those areas are given the opportunity to express their will freely, the Government of the Republic pledges itself to accept the verdict." Reprinted in CASE STUDIES IN AFRICAN DIPLOMACY: THE ETHIOPIA-SOMALI-KENYA DISPUTE 1960–67, at 32, 33 (C. Hoskyns ed. 1969) [hereinafter AFRICAN DIPLOMACY].

fifth of the whole of Ethiopia. The Kenyan territory that would be likely to accrue to Somalia in the event of an act of "self-determination" by the inhabitants would be approximately 45,000 square miles and, again, almost one-fifth of the total area of Kenya. Aside from the economic and strategic importance of the areas involved,[134] the polyethnic character of both of these States has effectively chilled any temptation to acknowledge a right of secession to their disaffected minorities.[135] The Republic of Somalia, on the other hand, is probably the most ethnically homogeneous country in Africa. It has enjoyed the rare luxury of being able to advocate a right of secessionist self-determination for cohesive minority groups without having to fear that it might itself become the victim of such claims.

The recent developments in these two disputes are interrelated and may be discussed together. In 1963, as Kenyan independence approached, an "Ethio-Kenya Agreement of Co-operation and Mutual Defense Assistance" was signed by the two governments, vaguely promising mutual assistance against the demands of the "offending nation," Somalia.[136] Relations between the Republic of Somalia and Ethiopia gradually became more strained during the early years of independence. Clashes between Ethiopian forces and armed groups of Somali nomads began to increase in frequency and severity as both sides conducted hostile radio campaigns. Tension mounted into a full-scale clash all along the Ethiopia/Somalia border in February–March 1964, with Ethiopian jets bombing targets well inside Somalia. Meanwhile, the Somali tribesmen in the NFD began guerrilla activities against the Kenyan army and police during the years 1963–67. These guerrillas, or *shifta* as the Kenyans called them, were supported both militarily and psychologically by the Republic of Somalia.

A ceasefire along the Somali/Ethiopia border followed a February 14, 1964, resolution adopted at the Second Extraordinary Session of

---

134. *See* Mariam, *The Background of the Ethio-Somalian Boundary Dispute*, 2 J. Mod. African Studies 189, 216–17, for a statement of the Ethiopian position on this matter.

135. "There are practical reasons why Ethiopia cannot easily accommodate Somali claims for an independent Ogadenia—the main one being that this might encourage separatist movements among other ethnic groups in Ethiopia. However, as in Kenya, the other ethnic groups are not as politically sophisticated as the Somalis, and do not have neighbouring States comprised of the same ethnic groups." Castagno, *The Somali-Kenyan Controversy: Implications for the Future*, 2 J. Mod. African Studies 165, 188 (1964). The Ethiopians, of course, have also been troubled by another secessionist movement in the northern province of Eritrea.

136. *See* African Diplomacy, *supra* note 133, at 44.

the Council of Ministers of the OAU held in Dar es Salaam. The resolution called upon the governments of Ethiopia and Somalia to enter into negotiations for the peaceful settlement of their dispute and to refrain from all campaigns of a provocative or insulting nature.[137] A second resolution adopted on the following day was addressed to the governments of Kenya and Somalia and called upon them to "take the necessary steps to settle the present dispute." [138] At the Second Ordinary Session of the Council of Ministers of the OAU (Lagos, February 24–29, 1964) a further resolution congratulated Somalia and Ethiopia on ordering a ceasefire and again advocated a peaceful settlement of both disputes.[139] At the Cairo OAU Heads of State meeting later in 1964, the negotiations between the Somalis and Ethiopians totally failed. The Ethiopians maintained that there was no dispute beyond a simple problem of demarcating the frontier on the basis of the 1897 treaty. The Somalis rejected the treaty as incompatible with the right of self-determination, a right which they felt to be part of the *jus cogens* of international law.

On the theoretical level, Somalia has consistently advanced the claim that the Somali tribesmen in the disputed regions should be given an opportunity to exercise their right of self-determination by plebiscite or referendum. The Kenyans and Ethiopians have countered by insisting that the regions involved were unquestionably part of their territory and that the principle of self-determination was completely inapplicable to the disputes because self-determination has no function in an independent State. The clear implication of this position was that its role was confined to securing the independence of a subject people from colonial rule. Furthermore, it has been their contention that the only way for Somali nomads living in these regions to exercise a legal right of self-determination would be, as Jomo Kenyatta eloquently phrased it, to "pack up your camels and go to Somalia." [140] The principle of self-determination, they maintained, has relevance

137. Reprinted, *id.* 60.

138. Reprinted, *id.* 61.

139. Reprinted, *id.* 62–63.

140. A memorandum submitted by the Kenyan delegation to the 1963 OAU Inaugural Summit Conference expressed the following view: "The Somalis are Africans. Those who live in Kenya are Kenya Africans. Either they integrate with the rest of the Africans in the country or, as Mr. Jomo Kenyatta told them in 1962, 'pack up your camels and go to Somalia'. This is the only way they can legally exercise their right of self-determination." Reprinted, *id.* 36, 37.

only to foreign domination and not to territorial disintegration by dissident citizens.[141]

By 1967, Somalia had been involved in an exhausting conflict all along its borders ever since independence. Its insistence on unification had been costly in both money and international goodwill. In terms of outside support, the United States chose to continue supplying military aid to the Ethiopians, and the Soviet Union, despite some military assistance, refused to endorse the generally unpopular idea of a Greater Somalia. Furthermore, the early opinion of the African community supporting the Somalis' desire to overcome the separation of its peoples resulting from artificial colonial boundaries, gradually hardened into a firm opposition to any alterations in the boundaries of African States.[142]

In 1967, therefore, a new Somali government, headed by President A. Shermarke and Prime Minister M. Egal, undertook to ease the tensions aroused by the policy of pan-Somalia unification. They did not renounce the goal of Somali unification; they merely acknowledged that it was not to be attained immediately by force of arms. In 1968, Prime Minister Egal explained his government's position by saying:

> Naturally, the aims and the political objectives of the Somali people are unalterable and are enshrined in our constitution, viz., that we are obligated to seek the unification of the Somali territories through peaceful and legal means. It was however open to us to alter the policy of confrontation and to seek accommodation for a detente with our neighbors as a preliminary to creating a suitable atmosphere without abandoning the context of our political aspirations and objectives.[143]

Prime Minister Egal attended a meeting of OAU Heads of State at Kinshasa in September of 1967 and there discussed the lowering of tensions between his country and Ethiopia and Kenya. A partial rec-

141. One curious feature of the Somali case has been their seeming unwillingness to contest directly this limited definition of self-determination. In THE SOMALI PEOPLE'S QUEST FOR UNITY, *supra* note 131, at 14–15, for example, the Somali Ministry of Foreign Affairs answered their antagonists' claim by saying: "It has been said that the right [of self-determination] has no application to a free, multi-racial society. Perhaps, but the Somali peoples of Kenya and Ethiopia are not a free, willing part of those societies: their participation is enforced by troops, even British troops, in the N.F.D."

142. *See, e.g.,* O.A.U. *Resolution on Border Disputes,* note 243, chapter 2 *supra.* The resolution was passed over the objection of both Somalia and Morocco.

143. Egal, *Somalia: Nomadic Individualism and the Rule of Law,* 67 AFRICAN AFF. 219, 225 (1968).

onciliation of the parties in the Kenya-Somalia dispute was evidenced by a declaration issued at Kinshasa and a later (October 1967) agreement signed at Arusha, Tanzania, promising to reduce tensions and normalize relations between the two countries.[144]

President Shermarke was assassinated in October of 1969 and five days later Somali military leaders established a "Revolutionary Council" as the new government of the country. The council began its administration by suspending the constitution, dissolving the National Assembly, arresting all the members of the cabinet (as well as Prime Minister Egal), and renaming the country the "Somali Democratic Republic." The new regime promised to continue the policies of President Shermarke and to support all liberation movements in countries under colonial rule and those in "illegally-occupied territory." [145] This promise did not, however, portend any radical change in the former government's policy of easing tensions with Somalia's neighbors. Nevertheless, there were indications that even the Egal government, before being deposed, had become disillusioned with its policy of detente. There was a sense that it had been used by Kenya and Ethiopia to strengthen their military position along the frontiers.

The dispute with Ethiopia, however, has continued to simmer despite OAU efforts at mediation. At the Eleventh Assembly of OAU Heads of State and Government meeting in Addis Ababa in May 1973, an eight-member "good offices committee" was established to mediate between the parties. In its statements to the OAU, Ethiopia has continued to deny that the conflict is a border dispute; it prefers to see the issue as a simple matter of border demarcation. A report of the "Committee of Eight" to the Twelfth Assembly of the OAU Heads of State held in Mogadishu (June 1974) conceded that the committee had failed to bring about negotiations between the parties.[146]

The Somali government's case for demanding the reunification of the Somali-inhabited regions rests upon several arguments. First, the validity of the treaties by which former colonial Powers ceded large segments of Somaliland to the Ethiopians is disputed because the Somalis were never consulted about the purported transfers. Second, the colonial Powers, it is argued, were not entitled to cede the areas they had recently undertaken to protect merely because Ethiopia had them at a temporary military disadvantage. Finally, it is claimed that the se-

144. AFRICAN DIPLOMACY, *supra* note 133, at 82–83.
145. 17 KEESING'S CONTEMP. ARCHIVES 26372 (Nov. 15–22, 1969).
146. 20 KEESING'S CONTEMP. ARCHIVES 26612 (July 8–14, 1974).

ries of agreements that left Somali regions within the borders of Kenya and Ethiopia violated the right of these peoples to self-determination. The legal right of peoples to self-determination, the Somali government asserts, "imposes a corresponding legal duty on all States, including Kenya and Ethiopia, to recognise and give effect to this right." [147] They are nevertheless quick to point out that a reunification of the Somali peoples would not work any serious economic harm to Kenya or Ethiopia, nor would it result in an economically or politically unrealistic entity.[148]

When viewed from this perspective, the Somali case is very enlightening. It provides an opportunity to measure the strength of the antisecessionist argument after excision of considerations relating to the viability of the regions following the secession, or the fear of large minorities becoming trapped within the seceding province. There seems little doubt that the regions in question would annex themselves to Somalia soon after their secession from Kenya and Ethiopia, and they both have large Somali majorities. With an excellent case for the ethnic cohesiveness of these areas and their desire to become part of "Greater Somalia," it is, in the final analysis, really only the respect for territorial integrity and the arguable effect of a secession on other dissident groups within Kenya and Ethiopia which undermines the theoretical soundness of the Somali claim. It is significant, however, that these two elements alone have been sufficient to prevent Somalia from enlisting any widespread international support for its goal of pan-Somali unification.

Of considerable interest for the theorist of self-determination has been the Somalis' willingness to base their case for secession on grounds other than a simple parochial sentiment in the regions concerned. First, the Somali argument takes great pains to assure the world community that it need not be troubled by the prospect of Ethiopia or Kenya losing a crucial economic region in the event of an act of self-determination in disputed areas (thus skillfully attempting to avoid one objection to the Katangan secession). Second, unlike Biafra or Katanga, the Somalis stress that very few non-Somalis will be affected by the territorial transfer they propose. Finally, the impor-tance attached by the Somalis to the almost certain unification of the disputed regions with the existing Somali Republic is intended to assuage any international fears that the secession would produce an economically untenable State. Although the Somalis are a long way from

147. THE SOMALI PEOPLE'S QUEST FOR UNITY, *supra* note 131, at 14.
148. *Id.* 15.

achieving any international acceptance of their argument, much less its acceptance by Kenya and Ethiopia, it is significant that they have attempted to respond to issues they assume the international community finds relevant in considering the acceptability of a secessionist claim.

THE NAGAS

The Indian state of Nagaland is situated on the northeast frontier of India between Assam and Burma. The tribal peoples giving the area its name, the Nagas, now number somewhat more than 500,000. Since 1947, they have raised one of the most insistent demands for political independence on the Indian subcontinent, a region so widely heterogeneous in population that it stands in constant fear of separatist agitations from the racial, linguistic, cultural, and religious groups which the tides of history have left domiciled there.

Like the Kurds, the Nagas inhabit an inhospitable mountainous region. This circumstance, combined with the historical antipathies that have characterized the relationship between the Nagas and their neighbors, has left the Nagas little in common with the other groups comprising the Indian Union. Of Tibetan or Mongolian origin, they preserve a distinct cultural heritage and, due to the efforts of American Baptist missionaries since the turn of the century, Christianity has a strong hold in the area. The Nagas also share with the Kurds and Somalis the discomfort of occupying an ethnic region that overlaps national boundaries, in this case the frontier between India and Burma. There are now at least fourteen major tribal groups that identify themselves as Nagas, although their long history of tribal isolation in the mountainous terrain has produced linguistic differences and such sharp dialectal variations as to render most of the groups mutually unintelligible.

By all accounts, the Nagas have had a history of fiercely resisting any attempts by their neighbors in Assam and Burma to exert control over the Naga territory. Thus, it was in accordance with a long-established precedent that when the British first came into contact with the tribesmen in the 1830s they too became the victims of Naga raids and hostile forays. Such actions provoked sporadic British reprisals over the next several decades in the form of punitive expeditions into the Naga Hills.[149] By 1873, the British had adopted a policy embodied in the "Inner Line Regulation" of that year which sought to isolate the

149. For excerpts from contemporary accounts see THE NAGAS IN THE NINETEENTH CENTURY 114–95 (V. Elwin ed. 1969).

NAGALAND

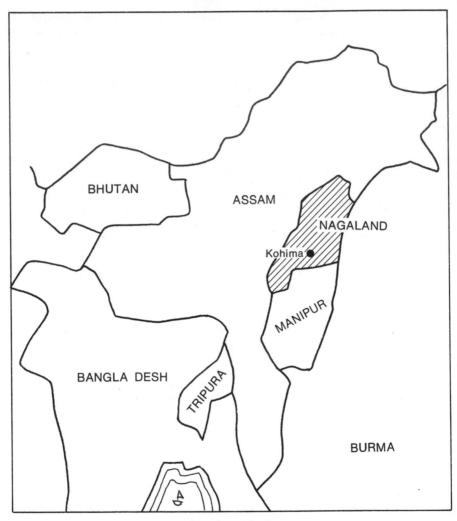

Northeast India

Naga hillsmen from their neighbors in Assam by preventing the tres-
passing of outsiders on Naga territory and restraining Naga raids on
the surrounding Assamese tea plantations. It was clear to the British
that any intensive domination of the Naga Hills would be difficult to
achieve and would involve a costly maintenance of large military contingents in the area. They chose therefore to accept a nominal incorporation of the region within the empire while preventing any irri-
tating intercourse between the Nagas and other British subjects. The
territory eventually came to be administered by the British as an "Excluded Area" under the terms of an 1880 regulation which permitted
the inhabitants of hill tracts to be excluded from the operation of all
laws unsuitable to their less civilized mode of life.[150]

The development of a communal sentiment among the Nagas, replacing the endemic hostility and internecine conflicts among the various tribes, is of a fairly recent origin. The first local political organization evidencing a feeling of Naga nationalism was the "Naga Club,"
founded in 1918 by government officials and some headmen of Naga
villages. It was this club that presented a memorandum to a British
commission on constitutional reforms headed by John Simon which
visited the regional capital of Kohima in January of 1929. The memorandum pleaded for a continued separation of the Naga territory
from the other provinces of the British colony in any reformed constitutional scheme. More significant, however, was an acknowledgment
of the two sets of circumstances that continue to influence the Nagas'
claim to political independence. In one respect, the memorandum
concedes, "our country within the administered area consists of more
than eight tribes, quite different from one another with quite different languages which cannot be under-stood by each other, and there
are more tribes outside the administered area which are not known at
present. We have no unity among us and it is only the British Government that is holding us together now." [151] Nevertheless, despite the
lack of unity among the Nagas themselves, the memorandum argues
that there is even less in the way of communal bonds between the
Naga hillsmen and the inhabitants of "the plains." "Our language is
quite different from those of the plains," it asserts, "and we have no
social affinities with either Hindus or Muslim." [152]

150. *See* B. CHAKRAVORTY, BRITISH RELATIONS WITH THE HILL TRIBES OF ASSAM
SINCE 1858, at 194 (1964).
151. The memorandum is reprinted in NAGA INSTITUTE OF CULTURE, A BRIEF HIS-
TORICAL ACCOUNT OF NAGALAND 163–64 (1970) [hereinafter NAGALAND].
152. *Id.* 164.

The Second World War did much to erode the traditional isolation of the tribesmen. The Naga territory became the site of intense fighting as the British sought to prevent the Japanese invasion which had swept across Burma from cutting into the Indian heartland. Shortly after the war's end in 1945, the deputy commissioner of the Naga Hills, C. R. Pawsey, is reported to have aided the establishment of the Naga Hills District Tribal Council. This organization of tribal leaders, which later changed its name to the Naga National Council (NNC), was formed with the goals of unifying the Nagas and repairing war damage. From these modest beginnings, it was to develop into a rallying point for Naga nationalistic sentiments during the next few years as the British raj gave way to Indian independence. The political character of the organization was such that by June 1947 the NNC made a public demand for the separation of Nagaland from India when that country achieved independence.

The Nagas were not the only group to see the withdrawal of the British from India as the most auspicious moment to declare independence from the new Indian Union. When a delegation of Nagas, headed by Z. A. Phizo, traveled to Delhi in July 1947 to place a request for separation before the Indian National Congress, they found that body already struggling with other separatist claims, most notably the demand of the Muslim League for partition of the country along religious lines. The delegation met with Mahatma Gandhi on July 19, and he is reported to have assured them that force would not be used to retain the Naga territory within the Indian Union if the Nagas chose to pursue their own independence.

While the Naga delegation was in Delhi, the governor of Assam, Sir Akbar Hydari, conducted negotiations in Kohima with the NNC. The result of these discussions was the so-called Hydari Agreement signed in late June 1947. After a preambular announcement that "the right of the Nagas to develop themselves according to their freely expressed wishes is recognized," the agreement sets out conditions that would provide a fair amount of local autonomy for the Naga region.[153] It also contains, however, one of those ambiguous clauses so useful in making a document acceptable during negotiations, and so vexing when the time arrives to put the agreement into effect. Paragraph 8 of the Hydari Agreement provides that "the Governor of Assam as the Agent of the Government of India will have a special responsibility for a period of 10 years to ensure the due observance of

153. Reprinted in M. HORAM, NAGA POLITY 141–42 (1975).

this agreement; at the end of this period, the Naga National Council will be asked whether they require the above agreement to be extended for a further period, or a new agreement regarding the future of the Naga people arrived at." [154] The "whether" clause of this paragraph was interpreted by the Nagas as an option to secede from the union after ten years, and by the Indian government as a promise that the Nagas might renegotiate their status *within* the union at the end of that period.

Long before the expiration of the ten-year period, however, the NNC came under the control of those leaders advocating complete separation from India. A. Z. Phizo was unanimously elected president of the council in December 1950, and a month later he announced that a plebiscite would be held in the Naga territory to determine the question of its relationship to the union. The Indian government refused to recognize the plebiscite which was held on May 16, 1951, nor did it respond to the NNC's report that the "verdict of the people has been for the constitution of the Nagaland into a separate sovereign state in which they can live their own lives, and guide their own destiny." [155]

During the early 1950s, the NNC attempted to bring pressure upon the Indian government by conducting a campaign of civil disobedience — a move that only prompted punitive measures by the government and the stationing of units of the Indian police in Nagaland to deal with what was felt to be an impending crisis. It had become apparent to some of the more moderate members of the NNC that Jawaharlal Nehru would not be shaken in his conviction that the component areas of India, as bequeathed to it by the British administration, might achieve some measure of local autonomy within the union but not outright independence. In order to avoid the violence which they saw as the probable result of a Naga insistence on complete separation, a number of these moderates resigned from the NNC in 1955 leaving it a largely prosecessionist organization. Events took a further turn for the worse when the open fighting between the Naga separatists and Indian forces during 1955 provoked the Nehru government to increase the number of Indian army contingents stationed in the Naga Hills.

In March 1956, the Naga leaders demanding total separation announced the formation of the Naga Federal Government (NFG) com-

154. *Id.* 142.
155. *Quoted in* Means, Means, *Nagaland: The Agony of Ending a Guerrilla War*, 39 PAC. AFF. 290, 293 (1966–67).

plete with its own flag, constitution, and army of the Naga Home Guards. The following year saw the formation of the less radical Naga People's Convention (NPC) intended to act as an intermediary between the Indian government and the rebellious NFG. At its first meeting in August 1957, the 1,760 delegates to the NPC passed a resolution requesting the establishment of a separate administrative unit called the "Naga Hills-Tuensang Area" to be administered by the governor of Assam. The convention's hopes for mediating a compromise between the Indian government and the separatists centered upon achieving a recognition of the Naga-inhabited territories as a separate political unit within the Indian Union. If this could be accomplished, they felt, it would foster local self-government for the Nagas and thus quiet their fears concerning domination by "the plainsmen" and the gradual absorption of their cultural identity. Moreover, the convention believed that if a solution along these lines succeeded in stopping the violence in the Naga Hills it would be acceptable to the majority of the Naga people, who had never given unanimous support to the secessionist cause.

At its second and third meetings in 1958 and 1959, therefore, the Naga People's Convention passed a sixteen-point memorandum intended to form the basis for negotiation with the government of India. The memorandum advocated the establishment of a separate state within the Indian Union to be known as "Nagaland." The proposals of the NPC would give the state of Nagaland a good deal of local autonomy; they included a provision that no act of the Indian Union Parliament would apply to the Nagas without their consent in areas such as the religious or social practices of the Nagas, Naga customary laws and procedure, civil and criminal justice insofar as these concern decisions according to the Naga customary laws, and the ownership and transfer of land and its resources.[156]

Despite significant opposition within Indian public opinion to the creation of a state with an area of about 6,000 square miles and a population of less than one-half million (which would be, by far, the smallest Indian state), the Nehru government acquiesced in the NPC proposals with a few modifications. The Indian constitution was consequently amended in 1962 to provide for the formation of the state of Nagaland,[157] and in December 1963 the state was officially inaugurated by the president of India, S. Radhakrishnan. The president

156. The memorandum of the NPC is reprinted in NAGALAND, *supra* note 151, at 190–95.

157. *See* B. RAO, THE FRAMING OF INDIA'S CONSTITUTION: A STUDY 590–91 (1968).

took the opportunity to express his hope that, "now that the wishes of the Nagas have been fully met, normal conditions will return to the state, and that those who are still unreconciled will come forward to participate in the development of Nagaland." [158]

Any hope that the concessions of the Indian government in establishing the state of Nagaland would end the rebellion of the Naga Federal Government was quickly stifled. The NFG denounced both the statehood compromise and the compromisers, while persisting in its claim for full independence. The guerrillas did not respond well to Nehru's promise of amnesty and their campaign of hostilities and terrorism against the government forces continued as before. Early in 1964, therefore, a conference of the Naga Baptist churches passed a resolution establishing a three-man Peace Commission to expedite an end to the violence in the Naga territory. The commission eventually achieved an agreement on a ceasefire signed by representatives of the Indian government and the NFG on May 24, 1964.[159] As part of this agreement, the commission was also to mediate in negotiations between the parties on a political settlement once the ceasefire came into effect.

During the next several years, a series of negotiation efforts, including a number of talks between the new prime minister, Indira Gandhi, and Naga leaders, failed to establish a basis for settlement of the dispute. The NFG clung to its demand for complete sovereignty, or at least a virtually sovereign status such as that enjoyed by Bhutan. The Nagas stressed that their territory had never been conquered by the Indian army or ruled by the Indian government but was attached to the Indian Union only as a result of a forcible annexation by the British colonizers. Thus, they claimed that their right of self-determination belonged to them separately as a people distinct from the independent State of India.[160] The Indian government opposed these suggestions because of the probable effect of acquiescence in the secession of such a small minority upon the numerous other Indian minorities and also because of a purported skepticism concerning the ability of an independent Nagaland to exist as a sovereign State. At one point the Indian government is reported to have offered the Nagas com-

---

158. Speech inaugurating the State of Nagaland, Dec. 1, 1963, MINISTRY OF INFO. & BROADCASTING (Gov't of India), PRESIDENT RADHAKRISHNAN'S SPEECHES AND WRITINGS, MAY 1962–MAY 1964, at 439 (1968).

159. *See* NAGALAND, *supra* note 151, at 202–03 for the provisions of the ceasefire agreement.

160. *See id.* 209.

plete autonomy apart from defense, external relations, communications, and currency, but this too was rejected by the Naga delegation as incompatible with their claim to independence.

The uneasy ceasefire in Nagaland remained in force from 1964 until 1972, having been extended whenever it expired by periods of one to three months. Neither side, however, respected the ceasefire completely and incidents involving armed skirmishes between the antagonists were common. During this period, the rebel leader Phizo tried unsuccessfully to bring the Naga claim into an international forum. A 1967 visit to the United States by Phizo resulted in only a chilly reaction by the American State Department and no noticeable progress in persuading the United Nations to interest itself in the dispute.

By 1967, the Nagas had begun to receive assistance from Pakistan and the Communist Chinese, provoking a sharp Indian protest to the Chinese government. A number of Naga rebels were reported to have crossed through Burma into China to secure arms, ammunition, and training in sabotage and guerrilla tactics. The Chinese were also reported to have aided the secessionist insurgents of the nearby Mizo district of Assam, who began their own campaign for an independent and sovereign State of "Mizoram" in 1966.

The military position of the Nagas deteriorated greatly during the last years of the ceasefire. The Naga and Mizo rebellions suffered two setbacks when Bangla Desh successfully seceded from Pakistan in 1971. First, the former area of East Pakistan could no longer be used as a staging area for the guerrillas, and, second, some of the Indian troops who had participated in the Bangla Desh conflict were reportedly diverted to Nagaland after their intervention in the former country, thus greatly increasing the strength of the Indian military in the Naga Hills. B. K. Nehru, the governor of Nagaland, announced in an August 31, 1972, broadcast that the suspension of operations against the Naga underground would not be extended. The Naga secessionist organizations, he went on to say, would be banned under the Unlawful Activities (Prevention) Act, which empowered the government of India to ban organizations advocating the secession of any part of India.[161]

What little strength was left in the secessionists gradually expired during the next three years. In November of 1975, the Indian government reopened negotiations with the Naga separatist leaders in an attempt to put a final end to the uprising. By November 19 it was announced that an agreement had been reached under which the Naga

161. *See* 18 KEESING'S CONTEMP. ARCHIVES 25516 (Oct. 7–14, 1972).

movement would surrender its arms in return for a grant of general amnesty, suspension of the Unlawful Activities (Prevention) Act, withdrawal of cases against the Nagas under trial, release of all political prisoners, and the rehabilitation of rebels leaving the underground. "They have now accepted," the *New York Times* reported, "that Nagaland is an integral part of India, and that Nagaland cannot be granted any special status." [162] It seemed likely, particularly after eighteen years of opposition, that the rebels' conversion to the cause of a unified India was closely tied to their military inability to continue the secession.

Judged from the point of view of efficacy in quelling the secession, the Indian government's Naga policy contained one clearly beneficial element largely offset by another damaging one. On the positive side, the granting of statehood to Nagaland apparently satisfied the political aspirations of many moderate Nagas. It was an obvious concession to Naga claims for local autonomy and preservation of cultural identity, and it did much to weaken the secessionists' use of ethnic fears in furthering the cause of complete separation. It was, moreover, perceived both by outsiders and by many Nagas as a reasonable compromise between complete Indian domination and an independent, sovereign Nagaland—particularly when the prospects for such an entity in terms of economic, military, and political viability were never very favorable.

However, the benefits following from this concession were to some extent offset by allegations that in subduing the secession the Indians employed undisciplined troops—some of whom were apparently drawn from ethnic groups historically antagonistic to the Nagas. Aside from the human suffering it may have caused, there were two tangible results of this policy. First, the Indian forces reportedly took on the character of brutal oppressors to some of the uncommitted Naga villagers, thus pushing them into sympathy with the separatists' cause. Second, the Nagas were skillful in bringing their allegations of Indian army rape, torture, and needless brutality to the attention of world journalists,[163] who often painted a fairly romantic picture of a small people valiantly defending itself against a barbarous aggressor.[164] The

162. N.Y. Times, Nov. 20, 1975, at 6, cols. 1–2.

163. *See, e.g.,* N. MAXWELL, INDIA AND THE NAGAS (Minority Rights Group Report No. 17), at 28–32 (1973), for a typical list of charges made by the NFG against the Indians.

164. *See, e.g.,* the series of articles in the *Observer* entitled "An Unknown War," by the British journalist Gavin Young. Observer, Apr. 30, 1961, at 8; May 7, 1961, at 7; May 14, 1961, at 7.

Naga leaders were shrewd enough to know that, in the balance of secessionist legitimacy, demonstrable oppression by the governing State
counterbalances a multitude of deficiencies within the historic, economic, and political elements of the separatists' case. Instead of seeming to be an obdurate, incurably provincial people making unrealistic
demands on a thoroughly reasonable, conciliatory central government—an image the Indians might have been able to put forward—
the Nagas succeeded in focusing some journalistic light upon their
own characterization of a tiny ethnic group heroically resisting the ad-
vances of a large, alien State into whose clutches a colonial Power had
thrust them.

The implications of the Naga case for the doctrine of self-determination may be seen only indirectly. The Nagas never managed to
arouse substantial international interest in their situation. They were
unable to advance many of the comforting assurances raised by the
Somalis relating to the cohesiveness of their population, clear majority
support of the cause of separation from India, and their economic
and political prospects as a viable independent State. For its part, the
Indian policy of granting a measure of local autonomy to the Nagas
within the framework of the Indian Union was a classic case of "steal-
ing the other fellow's thunder." It managed to defuse much of the
Naga separatist sentiment and seemed a reasonable concession, short
of outright separation, to a demand for self-determination.

Lacking a compelling case based on a single communal sentiment or
clear ability to withstand the rigors of independent Statehood, the
Nagas attempted to establish that the immoderate conduct of the Indian military in countering the secession constituted oppression sufficient to legitimate their claim for independence. As will be discussed
below, a similar argument was to some extent successful in influencing
world opinion in the context of the Bangla Desh secession. Without at
least certain other indicia of "selfhood," however, secession would
seem to be a generally inappropriate remedy where the ultimate goal
of the majority of the population is really to moderate certain offensive conduct of their governors.

BANGLA DESH

The case of Bangla Desh is unique among the separatist movements
discussed here for the obvious reason that it is an example of a successful secession and as such warrants attention at least for its likely
precedential effect on future claims. It has been noted earlier that the
mere *fact* of a successful conclusion to a secessionist attempt ought not

to be considered sufficient evidence of the jural legitimacy of the claimant's demand; nor does the failure of such an attempt resolve all questions in favor of a conclusion of illegitimacy. Nevertheless, where the circumstances indicate that the world community has accepted the grounds, as well as the fact, of a successful separatist undertaking, an inquiry into the background of the attempt may cast some light on the community's unwritten standards in judging these phenomena. A comparison of a significant number of such cases would undoubtedly do much to reveal the world community's sense of a threshold of legitimacy; but with only one current example (Bangla Desh) of a strongly contested secession receiving wide international support, any conclusions in this regard must obviously remain speculative.

The partition of the newly independent India in 1947, roughly along the lines of the Hindu-Muslim dominated regions, left the Muslim State of Pakistan in the curious position of being itself a divided country. The contiguous Muslim states located in the northwestern portion of India (minus Kashmir) along with part of the Punjab were formed into West Pakistan. More than a thousand miles away, on the other side of India, the province of East Bengal became East Pakistan. Communication and travel between the relatively sparsely inhabited West and the much more densely populated East were from the first very difficult and did little to contribute to the growth of a communal feeling among the Pakistani peoples. By itself, the geographical oddity of the new nation might not have proved lethal to the political unity of the country; but at the time of partition the two wings of Pakistan were divided by much more than the thousand miles of Indian territory lying between them.

In terms of geography, climate, population, and culture, the 55,000-square-mile entity of East Pakistan was an unlikely partner for the 310,000-square-mile area of West Pakistan. Whereas West Pakistan is a mountainous, arid region chronically afflicted by a scarcity of water, the alluvial plain forming East Pakistan suffers from an abundance of moisture which, during the monsoon season, can result in devastating floods. Although both regions share the common bond of Islam, their ethnographic similarities end there. The Easterners, speaking the Bengali language, could not for the most part understand the major languages of the West (Urdu, Punjabi, Sindhi, and Pushtu). Fiercely proud of their Bengali cultural heritage, the easygoing Easterners were the temperamental opposites of the more aggressive, martial peoples of the West (from whom, significantly, the Pakistani army was primarily drawn). Moreover, the Bengalis of East

BANGLA DESH

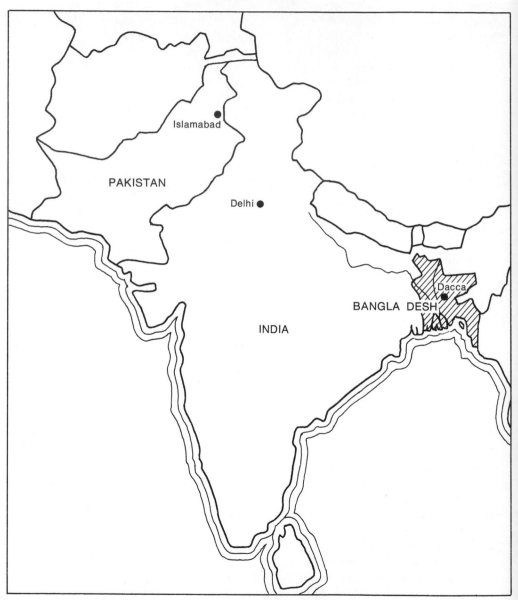

Pakistan constituted a compact, relatively homogeneous group, untroubled by the worries of its Western partner in trying to unify the four major ethnic groups within its land area—the Punjabis, Pathans, Sindhis, and Baluchis—each with its own distinct geographical area and separate language. Finally, the taller, lighter-skinned Westerners felt themselves to be racially distinct from (and superior to) the shorter, darker Bengalis, a fact that undoubtedly influenced their conduct toward East Pakistan during the 1971 conflict.

It is safe to say, therefore, that the stock of cohesive elements with which the leaders of the new country could mold a unified Pakistan was deplorably small, even at the time of partition. Unfortunately, these "natural" disparities between the two regions were further intensified during the early years of independence by an inequitable economic and political treatment of the East by the dominant Western wing. In the areas of education, employment, public expenditure, and promotion within civil and military ranks, the Westerners were almost uniformly more fortunate than their Eastern compatriots. To the Easterners, these disparities amounted to a campaign of economic exploitation which, rather than giving preference to the East's more pressing needs because of its larger population and greater economic disability, set about sedulously ignoring them. The details of the uneven development of the two wings of Pakistan have been documented elsewhere;[165] it is sufficient here to note that this pattern of conduct intensely aggrieved the population of East Pakistan and was a significant factor in the erosion of any last vestiges of interregional communal sentiment.

Civilian rule in Pakistan—tarnished by extensive corruption, nepotism and a general inability to remedy the economic ailments of the country—came to an abrupt end in 1958 when the commander in chief of the military, General Ayub Khan, effected a bloodless coup d'etat. The Ayub regime began auspiciously enough; the army took steps to deal with corruption and inefficiency in government, development programs were revitalized, and a leveling of the economic disparity between West and East Pakistan was made one of the chief goals of the administration. Unfortunately, the hydra of corruption

165. *See, e.g.,* S. CHOUDHURY, THE GENESIS OF BANGLADESH: A STUDY IN INTERNATIONAL LEGAL NORMS AND PERMISSIVE CONSCIENCE 9–19 (1972), where the author characterizes the relationship between the two wings of Pakistan as disclosing "an unmistakable pattern of colonial exploitation," *id.* 11; J. JAHAN, PAKISTAN: FAILURE IN NATIONAL INTEGRATION 9–49 (1972); Barnds, *Pakistan's Disintegration,* 27 WORLD TODAY 319–21 (1971).

soon reappeared and the inequalities between the two wings only worsened during Ayub's tenure as the leader of Pakistan. In 1959–60 for example, shortly after Ayub took control, the per capita income in West Pakistan was 32 percent higher than in the East. By 1969–70, this gap had nearly doubled, to a 61 percent higher per capita income in the West. The Ayub regime eventually crumbled in the late 1960s, due to the failure of its economic programs and Ayub's unpopularity after the Indo-Pakistan War of 1965 over Kashmir.[166] Forced to contribute toward the conflict even though they regarded the Kashmir issue as remote from their interests, the East Pakistanis were left isolated and virtually undefended during the seventeen days of the war. This greatly increased the sense of abandonment and neglect in the East and fueled the already hot fires of Eastern grievances.[167]

During the last years of Ayub's rule, two figures who would play key roles in the coming crisis in East Pakistan were imprisoned and then released in a final bid to bolster the flagging popularity of the government. Z. A. Bhutto, who had been Ayub's foreign minister but had defected from the regime after the Tashkent Agreement (1966) with India,[168] was arrested on November 13, 1966, two days after an unsuccessful assassination attempt on Ayub's life by a disaffected student. Sheikh Mujibur Rahman, leader of the East Pakistan nationalist organization called the Awami League, had been arrested shortly after placing his famous Six-Point Program for East Pakistan autonomy (of which more below) before a 1966 political convention in Lahore. He was, in 1969, facing charges of conspiracy to bring about the secession of East Pakistan. Each man had a large following among different segments of the population and both were released in February of 1969 in the face of growing public discontent. Nevertheless, this gambit proved insufficient to save the regime. Consequently, Ayub resigned on March 24, 1969, and the army chief, General Yahya Khan, replaced him as head of state.

President Yahya Khan's rule was also ushered in with promising developments. The imposition of martial law did much to restore order to the chaotic condition of the country; a return to civilian rule was pledged; and a general election on the principle of one man one vote was promised for October 5, 1970, to elect a constituent assembly.

166. For a detailed discussion of the "Fall of Ayub" see G. CHOUDHURY, THE LAST DAYS OF UNITED PAKISTAN 13–44 (1974).

167. *See generally* D. LOSHAK, PAKISTAN CRISIS 16 (1971).

168. For text *see* 21 U.N. SCOR, Supp. Jan.–Mar. 1966, at 273–75, U.N. Doc. S/7221 (1966).

The assembly was intended to have 300 seats, of which East Pakistan (because of its larger population) would elect 162 and the West 138. An unusually heavy monsoon coupled with a severe cyclone which struck East Pakistan in mid-November, however, worked to postpone the election until December 1970. When the results were finally counted, Sheikh Mujib's Awami League had won 160 out of 162 seats allotted to the East, and Bhutto's Pakistan's People's Party secured a somewhat lower majority of 81 of the 138 seats for the West.

It was President Yahya's intention, announced before the election, to hold a series of postelection talks between the leaders of the various parties to discuss the form of the new constitution before the document was actually drafted by the forthcoming National Assembly. However, the election campaigns of the two major figures, Mujib and Bhutto, had already revealed the dissimilarity of their ideas concerning the political future of Pakistan. Mujib won his overwhelming victory on the basis of the "Six Points," a program he characterized as guaranteeing regional autonomy to the component parts of Pakistan.[169] In summary, the Six Points demanded: (1) The constitution shall establish a federal government with a parliament directly elected on the basis of universal adult franchise. (2) The federal government shall be responsible only for defense and foreign affairs, and for currency subject to point 3. (3) There shall be two separate, freely convertible currencies or, alternatively, a single currency subject to a system preventing the transfer of resources and the flight of capital from one region to another. (4) Fiscal policy shall be the responsibility of the federating units, who shall provide the federal government with requisite revenue for meeting the requirements of defense and foreign affairs. (5) Each of the federating states shall have the power to negotiate foreign trade and aid, and each shall be able to maintain separate accounts of their foreign exchange earnings. (6) The federating states shall be empowered to maintain a militia or paramilitary force.

Obviously designed to remove any possibility of further exploitation of the East, the Six Points, had they been accepted, would have established in Pakistan a form of federalism much looser than that, for instance, practised in the United States of America. The federal government in the United States enjoys a taxing power along with sole responsibility for currency and foreign affairs. The central government of Pakistan under the Six Points would have been an extraordi-

169. Reprinted in S. RAHMAN, BANGLADESH, MY BANGLADESH 127–28 (1972).

narily weak creature, so weak in fact that the opponents of the Six Points interpreted them as tantamount to an acknowledgment of the secession of the East wing. Among the severest critics of the Awami League program was Bhutto, the man with whom Mujib would have to negotiate after the elections. Bhutto's predilection for a strong central government dictated his negative response to the Six Points, a plan he was later to describe as "meant to strike at the roots of our nationhood." [170] Bhutto also raised the telling argument that the presence of a strong central government was indispensable to hold the unruly component groups of West Pakistan (the Punjabis, Sindhis, Baluchis, and Pathans) together in some form of union.[171]

The result of the elections, therefore, was the confrontation of these two diametrically opposed programs for structuring the new constitution. The curious aspect of this situation was that the eventual deadlock in negotiations over the basic form of government was quite predictable before the elections took place. C. W. Choudhury, a participant in some of these events, maintains that President Yahya permitted the elections only after receiving Mujib's assurances that the Six Points were negotiable in postelection talks.[172] This version of the story seems plausible. Mujib's statement of December 19, 1970, after the election, that "there can be no Constitution except the one which is based on the Six-point Programme," [173] may be explained in terms of his altered political position at the time. He had not merely won the election in the East; he had won it by an overwhelming majority. In a sense, the very unanimity of opinion in the East removed any political flexibility he might have had: he believed that he had received an unqualified mandate to implement the Six Points and that to compromise them afterward in the formation of the constitution would be

170. *Quoted in* CHOUDHURY, *supra* note 166, at 123.

171. It is interesting to note that a ban on the West Pakistan successor to Mujib's Awami League after the secession (the National Awami Party) was upheld by the Pakistani Supreme Court in 1975. The court unanimously found that the NAP was guilty of attempting to establish an independent Pakhtunistan State in place of the North-West Frontier and Baluchistan provinces through large-scale insurgency, terrorism, and sabotage. *See* N.Y. Times, Oct. 31, 1975, at 8, cols. 2–4.

172. "The whole political dialogue between Yahya and Mujib from 1969 up to their crucial meeting in January 1971 *after* the elections were over was based on Mujib's unqualified and repeated pledge *to modify* his six-point plan." CHOUDHURY, *supra* note 166, at 137. Yahya himself made this accusation in a June 28, 1971, address during the East Pakistan war. *See Documents: Civil War in Pakistan,* 4 N.Y.U. J. INT'L L. & POL. 524, 559 (1971) [hereinafter *Documents*].

173. RAHMAN, *supra* note 169, at 26–27.

a direct betrayal of public trust. Rather than play the backsliding elected official, Mujib worked himself into an unshakable determination to impose his program upon the new constitution. At best, he might have hoped that the other figures in the political arena would view the election results with a similar sensitivity to the "general will" and capitulate on the basic issue of Six-Points federalism. Not surprisingly, this failed to happen.

As the preliminary negotiations became hopelessly deadlocked, Bhutto threatened to boycott the coming National Assembly. This gave Yahya an opening to announce on March 1, 1971, the indefinite postponement of the inaugural session of the National Assembly, scheduled for March 3. The president's speech produced an immediate hostile reaction in Dacca, the capital of East Pakistan. Sheikh Mujib issued a statement warning that "we cannot allow this to go unchallenged." [174] On March 2, as East Pakistan erupted into chaotic violence, he called for a provincewide *hartal* (a campaign of civil disobedience and noncooperation). An ineffective curfew was imposed upon Dacca the same day but did little to restrain the violence of the mobs roaming the city's streets. Amid mounting tension, Mujib reaffirmed on March 7,[175] and again on March 15[176] his support for what he termed a "non-violent and non-cooperation" movement. The effects of the general strike were somewhat eased after March 7, however, when the administration of governmental affairs was assumed by the Awami League.

The Yahya government spent the month of March increasing the strength of Pakistani armed forces in the East, a move obviously intended to provide Yahya with a contingency plan should a peaceful settlement prove elusive. The build-up continued even while a series of unfruitful negotiations between President Yahya, Bhutto, and Mujib was taking place from March 12 to March 25.[177] At first, these talks resulted in unexpected progress and there even seemed to be agreement on establishing an interim constitution until the National Assembly could be summoned to draft a new constitution. For reasons that are unclear, these negotiations were abruptly terminated on March 25, when Yahya and Bhutto suddenly left East Pakistan.

The significance of the army build-up was clearly revealed on the

174. *Id.* 77.
175. *See Documents, supra* note 172, at 551.
176. RAHMAN, *supra* note 169, at 105–11.
177. *See* Sobhan, *Negotiating for Bangla Desh: A Participant's View,* 4 S. ASIAN REV. 315 (1971).

night of March 25. The armed forces of West Pakistan on that night commenced a campaign of incredible brutality to suppress the secessionist tendencies of the East.[178] Sheikh Mujib was captured within hours of the first fighting, but not before he reportedly made a formal proclamation that "Bangladesh is a Sovereign and Independent Peoples' Republic." [179] By all reports, the agony of Bangla Desh during its early weeks was of an unexpected magnitude.[180]

President Yahya Khan addressed the country on the following day to explain his reasons for unleashing the army on the East. He began by describing as treasonable Sheikh Mujib's action of starting the non-cooperation movement. In addition to this crime, the President continued, "he and his party have defied the lawful authority for over three weeks. They have insulted Pakistan's flag and defiled the photograph of the Father of the Nation. They have tried to run a parallel government. They have created turmoil, terror and insecurity." [181] Mujib had attacked the solidarity and integrity of the country, Yahya claimed; he then added ominously, "This crime will not go unpunished."[182] As part of a series of martial law measures, the president announced that all political activities would be banned throughout the country; the Awami League was completely banned, and total press censorship imposed. The blame for this unfortunate situation, he concluded confidently, "rests entirely on the anti-Pakistan and secessionist elements." [183]

---

178. The Government of Pakistan later justified this action by alleging that information had reached them that the Awami League planned to launch an armed rebellion in the early hours of March 26. *See* INT'L COMM. OF JURISTS, EVENTS IN EAST PAKISTAN, note 214, chapter 2, *supra*, at 22–23.

179. RAHMAN, *supra* note 169, at 124.

180. There are many accounts of the nature of the Pakistani campaign in the East during this period; all paint a grim picture of incredible savagery. The International Commission of Jurists investigating these events concluded:

> The principle [sic] features of this ruthless oppression were the indiscriminate killing of civilians, including women and children and the poorest and weakest members of the community; the attempt to exterminate or drive out of the country a large part of the Hindu population; the arrest, torture and killing of Awami League activists, students, professional and business men and other potential leaders among the Bengalis; the raping of women; the destruction of villages and towns; and the looting of property. All this was done on a scale which is difficult to comprehend.

INT'L COMM. OF JURISTS, EVENTS IN EAST PAKISTAN, note 214, chapter 2 *supra*, at 26–27.

181. *Documents, supra* note 172, at 554–55.

182. *Id.* 555.

183. *Id.* 556.

The Bangla Desh military capability was never adequate to repel the West Pakistan army; but then neither was the latter strong enough to achieve the quick, total victory it had anticipated. Local guerrilla units (the Mukti Bahini) put up stubborn resistance. By mid-April, all of the important centers were in the hands of West Pakistan forces and the flow of refugees from Bangla Desh into India had become a torrent. A Provisional Government of Bangla Desh in exile (in India) issued on April 10 a proclamation reaffirming Mujib's declaration of independence "in due fulfillment of the legitimate right of self-determination of the people of Bangla Desh." [184]

Indian involvement in the dispute developed gradually over the next six months. Early in the war India had allowed Bangla Desh guerrillas to use Indian territory as a sanctuary, but as the months passed support for the guerrillas began to take the more positive form of supplying arms and ammunition to the secessionists. India clearly had a stake in the conflict, if for no other reason (and there were others) than the vast number of refugees pouring across its borders. On August 20, 7,900,000 refugees were reported in India; the figure increased to 9,700,000 by mid-November.[185] Amid this tense and confused setting, border clashes between Indian and Pakistani forces became more frequent with both governments exchanging allegations of frontier violations. The fighting in East Pakistan intensified after the Mukti Bahini launched an offensive (reportedly with Indian support) on November 21. President Yahya proclaimed a state of emergency on November 23, and open warfare between the two countries broke out on December 3, 1971, when Pakistani warplanes carried out a "pre-emptive" attack on airfields in India. Several days later, Indian Prime Minister Indira Gandhi announced her country's recognition of Bangla Desh [186]

This Indo-Pakistan War lasted less than two weeks. The Pakistani forces in the East capitulated by mid-December, with a ceasefire on the Western front following quickly thereafter.[187] The most important consequence of the war was the securing of Bangla Desh's independence from Pakistan—a result that would have been extremely unlikely without Indian intervention.

The Bangla Desh crisis lasted long enough, however, for the major

---

184. *Id.* 557.

185. 18 KEESING'S CONTEMP. ARCHIVES 24990 (Dec. 18–25, 1971).

186. I. GANDHI, INDIA AND BANGLA DESH: SELECTED SPEECHES AND STATEMENTS, MARCH TO DECEMBER 1971, at 132–34 (1972).

187. The parties eventually signed an agreement at Simla, India, on July 3, 1972, to improve relations between the countries. 11 INT'L LEG. MAT. 954–59 (1972).

world Powers to indicate their reactions to the secession of East Pakistan and the ensuing Indo-Pakistan War. The Soviet Union strongly supported India (with whom the USSR had signed a Treaty of Friendship in August 1971) against Pakistan. The motives behind the Soviet attitude are complex but a decision had apparently been made to abandon Soviet initiatives in Pakistan as that country moved closer to Communist China and the United States.[188] In addition to increasing the flow of arms to India during the months preceding the outbreak of hostilities, the Soviet Union used its veto in the Security Council to frustrate any attempt by the Council to impose a ceasefire until the Indian victory over Pakistani forces in Bangla Desh was secured.

For its part, Communist China condemned India as the "naked aggressor" [189] and vented a good deal of spleen on the Soviet Union which, they said, was trying to turn India into "its assistant and partner in committing aggression against Asia." [190] Not to be outdone, an article in the Soviet publication *Pravda* accused the Chinese of being "profoundly indifferent to the Pakistani people's real national interests," and of regarding Pakistan as just a puppet in their "filthy game on the international scene." [191]

The reaction of the United States to the conflict was also a product of several factors. Relations between India and the United States had been cooling for several years prior to these events, due in part to India's increased acceptance of Soviet aid. As India lost favor in American diplomatic eyes, Pakistan began to enjoy a status as America's principal ally in that area of the globe. Nevertheless, shortly after fighting erupted in East Pakistan in March of 1971, the United States ceased issuing or renewing licenses for military shipments to Pakistan and a hold was placed on arms previously committed until such time as Pakistan had resolved its internal conflict. This did not, however, affect the arms shipments "already in the pipeline" to Pakistan, and these "pipeline" shipments evoked a considerable hostile reaction among American legislators and journalists.[192] President Nixon himself conceded that the pipeline did not dry up completely until the

188. For an extended discussion of the factors influencing the major Powers' attitudes toward the crisis, see Choudhury, *The Emergence of Bangla Desh and the South Asian Triangle*, 27 Y.B. WORLD AFF. 62 (1973).

189. 18 KEESING'S CONTEMP. ARCHIVES 25069 (Jan. 29–Feb. 5, 1972).

190. *Id.* 25073.

191. *Id.* 25070.

192. *See* President Nixon's foreign policy report to Congress, Feb. 9, 1972. 66 DEP'T STATE BULL. 384 (1972).

early part of November — six months after the commencement of West Pakistan's campaign in the East.[193]

All outstanding licenses for the shipment of American military equipment to India were also suspended (along with all economic aid) when the Indo-Pakistan War broke out in December. It was only after India refused to comply with a December 7 ceasefire call of the General Assembly unless Pakistan withdrew its troops from the East that the United States openly accused India of primary responsibility for the continuance of the war. In the end, the United States' much criticized role in the Bangla Desh affair was dictated less by its theoretical disapproval of the secession (although this played a part[194]), than by its perception of Soviet and Chinese alignments in South Asia.

The involvement of the United Nations in the Bangla Desh crisis was limited and ineffective. On July 21, 1971, the secretary general sent a memorandum to the president of the Security Council saying that he was deeply concerned at the deterioration of the situation both from the humanitarian standpoint and as a potential threat to peace and security.[195] The Council did not, however, consider the matter at that point. The Third Committee of the General Assembly discussed the humanitarian aspects of the crisis (with particular reference to the refugee problem) in November of 1971, but the committee found it difficult to separate the humanitarian from the political questions involved in the dispute (and it was not authorized to discuss the latter).[196]

The Security Council first took up the Indo-Pakistan situation on December 4, 1971, after open warfare between the parties had begun.[197] When the first proposals for Council action were put forward, it became apparent that the Soviet Union would not accept a resolution that did not refer to the political situation in East Pakistan; and the United States and China adamantly refused to support one that did. Therefore, after two days of heated debate, the frustrated Council finally adopted (11 votes to 0, with 4 abstentions) a resolution pro-

193. *Id.*

194. *See* statement of Secretary of State Rogers, *id.* 54. "We did favor, we do favor, unity as a principle, and we do not favor secession as a principle, because once you start down that road it could be very destabilizing."

195. *Documents, supra* note 172, at 571, 573.

196. 26 U.N. GAOR, 3d Comm., 1876–78th meetings (1971).

197. 26 U.N. SCOR, 1606th meeting (1971). For an extended discussion of the United Nations involvement in the crisis (from a pro–Bangla Desh viewpoint) see K. MISRA, THE ROLE OF THE UNITED NATIONS IN THE INDO-PAKISTANI CONFLICT, 1971 (1973).

posed by Somalia,[198] which referred the matter to the General Assembly under the "Uniting for Peace" resolution because of a lack of unanimity among the permanent members of the Council. In response to this request and after a twelve-hour debate, the General Assembly passed a resolution on December 7 calling for an immediate ceasefire and withdrawal of troops by India and Pakistan from each other's territory.[199]

When the General Assembly resolution was accepted by Pakistan but not by India, the representative of the United States in the Security Council, George Bush, requested the Council to resume debate on the situation. A statement issued by the United States government explained this move by saying, "In view of India's defiance of world opinion, expressed by such an overwhelming majority, the United States is now returning the issue to the Security Council. With East Pakistan virtually occupied by Indian troops, a continuation of the war would take on increasingly the character of armed attack on the very existence of a Member State of the United Nations." [200] The Indian delegate responded by reiterating that the recognition of Bangla Desh, apart from being an acknowledgement of an "inevitable political reality," [201] was also an imperative requirement for the restoration of peace and stability in the area. Furthermore, he argued that, as a matter of international law, conditions are suitable for the emergence of a separate State when a "mother State has irrevocably lost the allegiance of such a large section of its people as represented by Bangla Desh and cannot bring them under its sway." [202] Bhutto, who now represented Pakistan in the Council debates, expressed puzzlement over what he called "this theory of the mother State." Although he conceded that it might be found somewhere in the archives, he did not know of any authentic or reliable evidence for the mother State concept. In addition, Bhutto pointed out,

> if there is such a concept, who is the mother and who is the child? The mother is East Pakistan and the child is West Pakistan, because it is in East Pakistan that the majority of our people live. Fifty-six per cent of our people live in East Pakistan and the rest

198. 26 U.N. SCOR, 1608th meeting at 15–16, para. 137 (1971).
199. G.A. Res. 2793, adopted by a vote of 104 votes to 11, with 10 abstentions. 26 U.N. GAOR, 2003d meeting at 44–45, para. 490 (1971).
200. 26 U.N. SCOR, 1611th meeting at 2, para. 16 (1971).
201. *Id.* 10, para. 100.
202. *Id.* 13, para. 124.

live in West Pakistan. The mother must naturally be the 56 per cent and not the 44 per cent.[203]

At its December 13 meeting, the Soviet Union's delegate proposed that the Security Council should hear from a representative of Bangla Desh. The president of the Council ruled against the Soviet suggestion on the grounds that he did not believe the necessary criteria for recognition of Statehood existed in the case of Bangla Desh.[204] The Council could reach no agreement on the draft resolutions before it during its next several meetings. On December 16, the Indian representative conveyed to the Council the information that Pakistani forces had surrendered in Bangla Desh and a ceasefire had come into force along the Western front.[205] It was only after this de facto termination of the war that the Council passed a compromise resolution on December 21,[206] calling for a strict observance of the ceasefire and the withdrawal of troops to their respective territories. India was not, however, required to withdraw its troops immediately from Bangla Desh because of the danger of reprisals in that country.

The Republic of Bangla Desh is now widely recognized by members of the world community and occupies a seat in the United Nations. Of course, under international law the mere fact of the recognition of a State need not entail approval of the new State's parentage or current administration. It is nevertheless true that the world community's support for Bangla Desh was on the whole noticeably warmer than that given, for instance, to Biafra or the Katanga, a fact which raises the inevitable question of whether the circumstances surrounding the birth of Bangla Desh legitimated (in the world community's eyes) its secession from West Pakistan. If so, then the issue of whether secession is *ever* legitimate would now seem to be answered. The remaining problem, of course, is to isolate which of the elements involved in the Bangla Desh case (or, more accurately, what combination of elements) succeeded in achieving this status of a legitimate secession.[207]

The most salient feature of East Pakistan in this regard was its geo-

203. *Id.* 19, para. 185.
204. *Id.* 1613th meeting at 9, para. 92–93.
205. *Id.* 1616th meeting at 1, para. 5.
206. S.C. Res. 307 (1971). The resolution was adopted by 13 votes to 0, with 2 abstentions. *Id.* 1621st meeting 2, para. 14.
207. Ved P. Nanda has concluded that the principle of self-determination was applicable to the Bangla Desh case in light of the following circumstances: (1) unlike all other claims for self-determination in a noncolonial context, in Pakistan the "parts" were physically separated; (2) deprivation of human rights was inflicted on a majority of

graphical separation from the West wing. As we have seen, this circumstance inhibited the growth of a communal sentiment among the Pakistani peoples and thus increased the likelihood of an eventual separatist attempt, but standing alone it would not seem to be a dispositive factor in legitimating the secession. Such a split in the territory of a State is certainly rare enough among land-based countries (although, as demonstrated by the position of Alaska, not unique) but it is the primary characteristic of archipelagic States like Indonesia. Nor can the racial or cultural distinctness of the Bengali population in East Pakistan be advanced as a sufficient answer to this problem. The Ibos, Nagas, Somalis, and Kurds, to name just a few, have all argued with little success for their secession from "alien" governors. Similarly, the economic disparity between the East and West wings of Pakistan can find analogies in the circumstances of many independent States. It seems safe to say that most countries have underdeveloped regions with lower per capita incomes and lower standards of living than their more prosperous areas. Although they may not be the victims of a systematic discrimination comparable to that endured by the East Pakistanis, the inhabitants of such underdeveloped regions often consider themselves the objects of exploitation or indifference by the more affluent majority.

There was little doubt that the people of East Pakistan desired an autonomous status within a Pakistani federation, as demonstrated by their response in the 1971 election. The Awami League officials therefore had a clear mandate to negotiate for that autonomous status; but it cannot be assumed that this necessarily authorized them to declare independence or even to insist on conditions of autonomy that amounted to independence. It should be remembered that acceptance of the regional autonomy envisioned by Mujib's Six Points would have made the complete disintegration of the heterogeneous West wing a very likely eventuality. Thus, the refusal of Western leaders to acquiesce in the Six Points in the face of the Awami League's intransigent demand for their acceptance cannot, by itself, be the sort of "oppression" which sways the judgment of the international community.

One is left, in the end, with the enormous savagery of the West Pakistani army's conduct between March and December 1971 as the

Pakistanis; (3) ethnic, linguistic, and cultural differences existed between the two wings; (4) the East suffered economic exploitation by the West; and (5) there had been a majority determination by vote regarding the political direction of Pakistan, which determination had been forcibly denied. Nanda, *Self-Determination in International Law: The Tragic Tale of Two Cities—Islamabad (West Pakistan) and Dacca (East Pakistan)*, 66 Am. J. Int'l L. 321, 336 (1971).

factor that was probably most influential in shifting a significant portion of world public opinion to the side of Bangla Desh. It is, of course, difficult to know whether the international community simply found it more dignified to accept the secession once Indian intervention had made it inevitable; or whether its reaction really was a comment upon the secession's intrinsic merits. As we have seen, this latter explanation, if accurate, would be consistent with the international response to previous secessionist attempts. To the extent that the Kurds, Nagas, and Biafrans suffered a similar harshness (but to a lesser degree) they each received more or less support in their claims for a legitimate secession. In the case of Biafra, this even took the form of recognition (both formal and informal) by several States. The Pakistani excesses in Bangla Desh not only were sufficient to prompt outside intervention on purportedly humanitarian grounds;[208] they also added the final element to an otherwise good case for secessionist legitimacy. The international community was even willing to let this factor outweigh other considerations such as the prospects for the economic viability of the new entity (Bangla Desh was at the time of independence, and remains now, largely dependent upon international aid to maintain its precarious existence), or the presence of "trapped minorities" within the seceding province (the Biharis of Bangla Desh, an Urdu-speaking minority group widely accused of aiding the Pakistani forces, have in fact been the victims of some reprisals since independence).

Even if this is an accurate analysis of the international reaction to Bangla Desh, it represents an undeniably disturbing conclusion. One could paint a rather demonic picture of international opinion demanding sanguinary evidence of a people's suffering—greater than that endured by the Biafrans, but perhaps less than that inflicted upon the East Pakistanis—before a claim to separation from their tormentors will be considered legitimate.[209] It may be a sufficient response for international jurists to say that a claim invoking the right

208. The risk of humanitarian intervention, which a central government had always run when supressing an insurrection with unnecessary force, is now arguably greater after the precedent of Bangla Desh. Cf. Franck, Rodley, *After Bangla Desh: The Law of Humanitarian Intervention by Military Force*, 67 AM. J. INT'L L. 275 (1973).

209. Cf. the following, probably widely held, sentiment expressed in the Separate Opinion of Judge Ammoun in the *Western Sahara* case [1975] I.C.J. 12, 100: "Nothing could show more clearly the will for emancipation than the struggle [for liberation from foreign domination] undertaken in common with the risks and immense sacrifices it entails. That struggle is more decisive than a referendum, being absolutely sincere and authentic. Many are the peoples who have had recourse to it to make their right prevail."

of self-determination obviously needs more than a sheer quantum of human suffering for its legitimacy. One can nevertheless understand how a group harboring separatist desires might perceive in this history the necessity of ultimately basing its case upon outraged humanitarian sentiment.

Several general conclusions regarding the current status of the principle of self-determination can be extracted from these cases. First, it is disturbingly apparent that the doctrine of self-determination as such has been of negligible value in contributing to the international community's collective response to these secessionist attempts. The secessionists and their patrons, of course, have often invoked the principle as at least a partial justification of their action. Without even a basic agreement on the boundaries of its own doctrine, however, the international community seems unable to incorporate the significance of such an appeal to self-determination into its assessment of the contestants' claims in a secessionist context. Consequently, the community is hampered in its efforts to regulate the conduct of the parties or outside States in accordance with the principle. In contrast, the community occasionally purports to recognize a "threat to the peace" requiring interventionary action (the Congo), and it seems capable of perceiving an "internal affair" justifying its refusal to intervene (Biafra). Unfortunately, it has rarely been able to utilize self-determination as a dispositive or even helpful concept in formulating its response or recommendations concerning a secessionist conflict.

Significantly, self-determination has not suffered from this infirmity in other contexts. In the colonial situation, an assertion of a right to colonial self-determination by a people was apparently often sufficient in itself to permit the community to authorize or condemn certain conduct by the colonial Power and outside parties. In these cases, of course, there was typically little question that the colonial peoples were entitled to invoke the principle. It therefore seems that self-determination, as a theoretical tool facilitating the international community's endorsement of certain behavior, is noticeably impaired only when the community cannot determine whether it is confronted with a legitimate claim to the principle. Once the crucial issue of legitimacy is decided, however, conclusions can be reached regarding the acceptable bounds of conduct by the parties, outside States, and international organizations.

Second, the world community generally seems to prefer that the grievance of a particular group be remedied by means which stop short of outright secession. As we have seen, schemes for greater regional autonomy rather than independence were strongly favored in the Congo and Biafran situations, and a concession along these lines was instrumental in resolving the Naga dispute. From the point of view of the separatist, the difficulty with this preference is that a simple rearrangment of the political subdivisions within a State, which does not involve a claim for independent existence, will almost certainly be viewed as an "internal affair" beyond the realm of legitimate international concern. Therefore, a group wishing to enlist the pressure of international public opinion to further its cause might perceive it necessary at least to allege a legitimate case for secession even where this is not the desired goal. Serious violations of minority rights may generate some international pressure on the delinquent State to moderate its policies but it cannot be expected that this will often involve a collective demand that a specific remedy, such as the restructuring of a State's internal political framework, be implemented. Moreover, such violations may not be present in every case of a demand for greater regional autonomy. Thus, the cruel choice which seems to face a group seeking an internal political rearrangement is whether to content itself with a request for regional autonomy (and thereby apparently forego its hope of international pressure to induce its governors to grant this request), or raise a claim for secessionist self-determination (and rely on international support for a compromise solution of regional autonomy).

Finally, even though the obscurity surrounding the application of self-determination to secessionist claims has often impaired the principle's utility in promoting a practical resolution of these conflicts, at least these cases do provide some evidence of the doctrine's evolving character. The justifications advanced in international forums by secessionists, unified States, and their respective patrons provide the basic data for isolating those elements which the international community may consider relevant in evaluating these claims. A clarification of these elements and their interrelationship is attempted in the concluding chapter.

4 The Standards of Legitimacy

A Conclusion

From the preceding discussion we can draw several conclusions. First, secessionist activity is an irrepressible feature of the contemporary world scene, and the future, from all indications, will not see an abatement in the frequency of these claims. Second, many of these movements seek legal justification in the international doctrine of self-determination. Third, at the present time there is neither an international consensus regarding the status of secession within this doctrine nor (should it be conceded such a status) is there an accepted teaching regarding the nature of a legitimate secessionist movement. Fourth, by its present inability to distinguish legitimate from illegitimate claims to secessionist self-determination, the international community is seriously handicapped in its attempt to minimize instances of unwarranted third-party intervention in secessionist conflicts under the aegis of the "peremptory norm" of self-determination. Finally, aside from the immense cost of secessionist wars to the immediate parties, the danger of unrestrained intervention inevitably brings in its wake a possibility of escalation and the confrontation of major power blocs. One is left, therefore, with the disturbing result that situations involving a potentially serious threat to international world order, situations which are by their nature arguably unregulated by the general legal restrictions upon the international use of force, remain equally unfettered by any specific doctrines of international law.

There are several apparent solutions to this problem. It is possible for the world community to make an ex cathedra pronouncement that secession has no place within the doctrine of self-determination, thus embracing a limitation of this principle to cases of overseas colonization, interracial domination, or some other arbitrary category. This approach is, I believe, both dangerous and highly unrealistic. Such a transparently artificial restriction of the principle to the relatively "safe" context of European-style colonialism, when articulated by the very entities (independent States) liable to be inconvenienced by its further extension, is not likely to convince minority groups within established States that their claims have been adjudged illegitimate by an impartial collective verdict. They will therefore tend to disregard all opinions coming from that body, whether concerning the outbreak, conduct, or settlement of separatist conflicts, as hopelessly self-protective. The international community would thus effectively cast itself in a role similar to that occupied by the Holy Alliance during the last century in its goal of guarding monarchic supremacy against "anarchic" nationalism; that is, the role of an entrenched power bloc flailing against threats to its dominance arising from the dissatisfactions of its own constituents. At the very least, the community will have to abandon its fondness for decrying the evils perpetrated by colonial Powers unless it can discover a convincing method of distinguishing, in principle, these evil policies from the equivalent deportment of "alien" governors occupying a contiguous land mass.

A second alternative is to leave the issue of the basic validity of secessionist self-determination to some future generation having greater wisdom, and concentrate upon the more immediate task of preserving the integrity of norms such as nonintervention and the proscription of the use of force. This might be attempted by an unequivocal declaration saying that the "higher" principle of self-determination may not be invoked to subvert these norms by States seeking to intervene in separatist conflicts on the basis of someone's right to self-determination. Overall, this approach has much to commend it and may by default be the least offensive course of action. It is marred by three difficulties: (1) the United Nations General Assembly has clearly *not* taken this position in the area of colonial self-determination; (2) any attempt to limit this declaration to cases of intra-State domination while affirming its direct opposite in the context of colonial domination will inevitably appear unconvincing; and (3) States continue to maintain their right to intervene on behalf of incumbent governments in this kind of conflict and therefore the question of the legitimacy of the separatists' claim will still arise in a roundabout fashion (not "Can I legally intervene on behalf of the claimants?" but "Can I legally aid those attempting to thwart the claim?").

A third solution, and the one that will be pursued here, seeks to maintain the underlying force of the self-determination principle and yet minimize the dangers to international peace and security by concentrating upon a method of ascertaining *legitimate* claims of this kind. Acknowledging that self-determination (insofar as it derives its strength from an innate urge to self-government coupled with a sense of the moral objections to alien domination resulting in exploitation, humiliation, and deprivation of human rights) is prima facie applicable to some but not all groups within independent States, the focus

of attention ought to be on determining which groups are entitled to
invoke the principle. Inevitably, this will involve an inquiry into the
nature of the group, its situation within its governing State, its prospects for an independent existence, and the effect of its separation on
the remaining population and the world community in general.
Taken as a whole, these considerations would evolve standards by
which the international community could ascertain instances of legitimate claims to separatist self-determination.

The probable benefits of this approach are significant. Most importantly, the international community would be given the chance to adjust its posture with regard to a particular separatist demand by virtue
of its ability to distinguish the legal merits of the claim. This might
permit a collective judgment, as was reached in the cases of Rhodesia
and South Africa, concerning the proper scope of outside States' behavior toward the situation. In addition, the norms of nonintervention
and proscription of force would again enjoy some protection under
this scheme. Unless specifically prohibited by an authoritative international decision, of course, intervention on behalf of the "legitimate"
party would still be possible and perhaps invited as enforcement of a
community standard; but then, even in the halcyon days before the
emergence of self-determination as a peremptory norm only a minority of jurists opposed *all* intervention. Jurists then purported to acknowledge that States interfere with the lives of other States for a variety of reasons (by request, for humanitarian purposes, as part of
collective self-defense, and so on), not all of which are legally objectionable. The problem with permitting intervention on behalf of a
people claiming a right of self-determination was that it opened the
door to a virtually unlimited freedom of intervention precisely because no one knew (within very broad limits) when the claimants, and
thus their would-be patrons, were legally entitled to invoke the principle. With the resolution of this basic uncertainty, other primary
norms of international behavior would no longer be endangered by
unrestricted, subjective decisions of third-party States regarding the
legality of their actions as furthering the principle of self-determination. These standards, whether specifically incorporated into the jurisprudence of an organization like the United Nations[1] (in the form of

1. For an interesting discussion of the emerging function of the United Nations "as a
dispenser of politically significant approval and disapproval of the claims, policies, and
actions of states, including ... their claims to status as independent members of the international system," *see* Claude, *Collective Legitimization as a Political Function of the United
Nations*, 20 INT'L ORGANIZ. 367 (1966).

a pronouncement similar to the 1970 *Declaration on Friendly Relations*), or whether remaining part of general international law, would constitute a basis for criticizing, and thus regulating, the conduct of outside States in a secessionist conflict.

It is undoubtedly true that the final decision regarding the jural legitimacy of some separatist claims could not be predicted in advance even with a fairly rigorous set of standards. Nevertheless, by promulgating such standards the world community might hope to influence the emergence and treatment of those claims for which the international reaction could be predicted with a reasonable accuracy. The secessionist pursuing a predictably "illegitimate" claim might hesitate to commence a struggle with his governing State, knowing that he would be unlikely to receive outside support or encouragement. This knowledge might conceivably influence him to cast his demands in the form of an appeal for minority rights or greater regional autonomy within the State rather than a call for complete territorial separation. Similarly, a governing State importuned by a manifestly "legitimate" claim might hesitate before committing itself to a bloody civil war in which it could expect no help from sister States and, indeed, could predict that its antagonists would enjoy an international blessing. At the very least, an educated guess at the reaction of the international community to an imminent claim to self-determination of this kind might make both unionist and secessionist more amenable to a negotiated settlement of their future political arrangement short of total independence for the claimants.

If the benefits of this approach are apparent, the proper method for selecting the relevant standards is decidedly not so. Obviously, the manner in which the various factors entering a calculation of legitimacy are chosen and weighted will be of crucial importance. It will reflect not only the selector's basic convictions about the proper structure of the international order (such as whether it should continue to stress the primacy of sovereign States or should permit other forms of political associations to participate in the international scheme), but also his beliefs regarding acceptable limits of international concern with the "internal" affairs of sovereign States. For our purposes, this latter issue queries the point at which the condition of a segment of a State's population triggers permissible collective interference to alter the State's treatment of its minority.

The response to these issues may require some serious rethinking of the accepted political and jurisprudential foundations of the international system. Before proposing a framework for the determination of secessionist legitimacy, therefore, it would be profitable to explore the two suggested models currently most in evidence. The first of these models, which now seems to enjoy a degree of international approval, is basically protective of the State-centered order, while the second results from a fundamental desire to accommodate the parochialist's demands. The significance of these two models, so clearly antipodal, lies in their willingness to strike a balance between the competing claims of the State's territorial integrity and the separatist's urge for self-government.

Remedial Secession—The Lex Lata

The demise of the "divine right" principle as the raison d'être of governmental authority forced rulers to justify their supremacy in far more mundane, utilitarian terms. Those who could, argued that their rule promoted certain tangible benefits for the ruled; and even those unable to find any positively beneficial side to their reign at least took comfort in the thought that by their very presence they were shielding "the people" from the nameless terrors of anarchy and chaos. Aside from the occasional anarchist, we have all to some degree accepted these explanations. Revolution is even now—more than two centuries after the Deity ceased speaking through kings and began endorsing the slogan *vox populi, vox Dei*—wisely shunned as an extreme and dangerous recourse. Inefficient or outright incompetent government is usually treated with a remarkable leniency; encroachments upon what were once thought to be "inalienable" liberties are generally borne with only mild protest; and even blatant displays of venality and corruption by those governing are rarely sufficient to induce a wholesale rejection of the basic system of government. But despite the apparent similarity between the situation of our ancestors being held in check by an appeal to a transcendent principle of divine right, and ourselves effectively curbed by the awesome thought of reforming a system of government once its deficiencies become manifest, there is one crucial difference. Whereas our predecessors, when aggrieved by massive tyranny, could only cast their eyes heavenward and ponder the veiled purpose behind investing so profane a candidate as their king with such a divine prerogative to rule, we have no equivalent theoretical bar to impeaching our governors. The nature of modern governmental authority is that it can, in principle, be altered or dissolved if it becomes an insupportable burden on those governed.

Recognizing the prevalence of these sentiments, the law of nations has carefully avoided being put in a position of guaranteeing the integrity of incumbent governors against the revolutionary demands of their own people. A ruler might be entitled (under the broad legal doctrine of noninterference) not to have his position subverted by other States for their own ends,[2] but he must manage his relationship with his own constituents without the support of international law. From this sound tradition, the secessionist must make one crucial leap. If international law makes no objection to the totality of the citizens of a State overthrowing their government when it becomes insupportable, why should it object to a segment of the population attempting to remove themselves from a regime which is particularly burdensome to them? Indeed, because the minority has no right to replace the government of the whole State (which might, after all, be acceptable to the majority), it must have recourse to neutralizing only that portion of the government's power directed at them—and that may entail separating themselves physically from the State. When the tyranny is universal, one speaks of the government being attacked; when the oppression is discriminatory, it is the State—meaning the territorial integrity of the State—which suffers the assault. In both instances, the secessionist would argue, the underlying principle is the same.

This image of the State as a privileged but not absolutely unassailable entity has apparently now been accepted by the international community. As we have seen, this theme is a logical extension of the "natural" right of resistance, it was implicit in the League of Nations' efforts to assure protection for minorities within heterogeneous States,[3] it receives strong support within juristic opinion,[4] and, significantly, it explains the unwillingness of the U.N. General Assembly (in the *Declaration on Friendly Relations*[5]) to ensure the territorial integrity of a State that does not possess a government "representing the whole people belonging to the territory without distinction as to race, creed or colour." Furthermore, the international reaction to a situation like Bangla Desh (and to a lesser extent Biafra) confirms the be-

2. Consider, for example, the recent uproar over the role of the United States Central Intelligence Agency in undermining the Allende regime in Chile.

3. This is true in the sense that secession lingered as an alternative should the international guarantees of minority rights prove inefficacious. *See* text accompanying notes 103, 104, chapter 2 *supra*.

4. *See, e.g.*, the opinions of Grotius, text accompanying note 21, chapter 2 *supra*; Cobban, text accompanying note 339 *id.*; Redslob, text accompanying notes 343–44 *id.*; Umozurike, text accompanying note 345 *id.*

5. Note 184, chapter 2 *supra*.

lief that the world community has accepted the legitimacy of secession
as a self-help remedy in cases of extreme oppression.

From the indications now available, therefore, the concept of "remedial secession" seems to occupy a status as the *lex lata*. The focus of
attention here is on the condition of the group making the claim. Remedial secession envisions a scheme by which, corresponding to the
various degrees of oppression inflicted upon a particular group by its
governing State, international law recognizes a continuum of remedies
ranging from protection of individual rights, to minority rights, and
ending with secession as the *ultimate remedy*. At a certain point, the severity of a State's treatment of its minorities becomes a matter of international concern. This concern may be evidenced by an international demand for guarantees of minority rights (which is as far as
the League was willing to go) or suggestions of regional autonomy,
economic independence, and so on; or it may finally involve an international legitimation of a right to secessionist self-determination as a
self-help remedy by the aggrieved group (which seems to have been
the approach of the General Assembly in its 1970 declaration).

As one approaches the extreme end of this continuum, the remedies not only become more severe; they also undergo a radical shift in
emphasis. There is a significant difference, for example, between the
international community using the coercive power of its collective
opinion in influencing a delinquent State to accord greater protection
for human rights, and the act of giving international legitimation to a
group *within* a State seeking to pursue self-help remedies. In the latter
case, the coercive effect results from what is actually a legal unleashing
of forces within the State.

Clearly, the doctrine of remedial secession is an unsatisfying solution when viewed from the perspective of the parochialist. It cannot
accommodate the desires of a group, for example, having a splendid
claim to cultural, historic, and linguistic distinctness and showing every sign of future viability as an independent entity, but lacking the
necessary quantum of oppression under their existing regime. The
parochialist would object that this approach allows the prejudices of
an oppressor to determine the nature of the "self," rather than some
innate qualities of the group concerned. Furthermore, remedial secession is geared to protect the present State-centered order; it implies
that every State has the ability to neutralize the right of any segment
of its population to separate self-determination merely by according a
measure of representative government, or protection of human rights.

It is therefore basically a conservative principle. What makes remedial secession appear so extraordinary an innovation and so seemingly radical a doctrine is simply that it was adopted by a body of States in which those possessing a truly representative government and adequate protection of human rights constituted a distinct minority.

In the end, one is left with the thought that remedial secession really has little to do with a positive doctrine of self-determination. It merely affirms a basic right of revolution by oppressed peoples; and this has long been thought to be one of those "inalienable" rights which the international community could neither bestow nor revoke. Perhaps most disturbing is that the doctrine of self-determination, which many assumed had at least some positive import for some "selves" somewhere, is thus reduced by the world community to a Damoclean sword menacing those States which fail to conform to certain minimum standards of representative democracy or protection of human rights. If the community intended by this to defuse the principle by conscripting it into the task of coercing (in an indisputably selective fashion) its own members, there are some who would have thought it a more honorable and less cynical course for the community to have openly disowned the principle of self-determination, in the postcolonial era, as a contentless, vestigial doctrine. After shouldering the hopes of so many from Woodrow Wilson on down, perhaps it deserved a decent burial.

The Parochialist's Model

As an alternative to remedial secession, the parochialist will offer a framework for ascertaining the legitimacy of separatist claims which has a wholly different focus. The parochialist would contend that the only really inescapable requirement for a legitimate claim to self-determination is the existence of a genuine "self" wanting to control its own political destiny. This self, he would argue, may be found not only in States that oppress their minorities (which, after all, is merely a symptom or confirmation that the group at least has a sufficient "selfness" to irritate its alien governors), but also in democratic, nondiscriminatory societies. The underlying force of the claim rests upon the urge to be governed by those like oneself; it is unconcerned with the relative merits of the alien rule because, as in the colonial context, the mere *fact* of alien domination is the basis of complaint. To be sure, extreme oppression of a segment of a State's population may intensify the basis of international concern, but it will not inevitably produce a "self" fit for the process of self-government. Conversely, the absence of such oppression does not necessarily belie the existence of this self.

The parochialist's model therefore emphasizes the elements of group identity to ascertain the legitimate self. His concern is with the historical, racial, cultural, linguistic, and religious distinctness of a people and the genuineness of their desire for political independence. To be a "self" and to desire the process of "determination," he would argue, is all that is needed to invoke the international principle of self-determination as the basis for a legitimate secession.

It goes without saying that the parochialist's suggestion is not at present widely accepted. There has never been a time when the pristine desire for self-government was itself sufficient to bridge the economic, political, and strategic chasms which must be crossed before an entity may be assured of a viable international existence. Moreover, the parochialist does not always argue from some tangibly evil effects of association within a heterogeneous State; his claim ultimately rests on the assertion of certain transcendent benefits which attend self-rule. There may in fact be such metaphysical advantages, but the international jurist is at a loss to know how they may be balanced against the grossly mundane detriments which often result from the dismemberment of established communities.

A FOREWORD

The gap that separates the doctrine of remedial secession from that of the parochialist results from a fundamental disagreement. The proponent of remedial secession is concerned with preserving the integrity of the sovereign State. He is willing to countenance the internal dismemberment of a State but only under the most extreme conditions and only when the State, by its outrageous behavior, has effectively forfeited its right to be free of international interference.[6] He justifies this prejudice by pointing out that the State is currently the accepted administrative unit in the international system: it is the State which undertakes international obligations, participates in international organizations, and so on. To suggest abandoning this accepted unit for some untried entity or entities, he warns, is to change

6. Compare, for example, the development of the United Nations rules in the area of human rights which suggest that only a *pattern* of racial, ethnic, or religious discrimination by a State will suffice to override the inhibition contained in article 2(7) of the Charter. *See* Buergenthal, *The United Nations and the Development of Rules Relating to Human Rights*, 59 AM. SOC. INT'L L. PROC. 132, 133–34 (1965).

horses in the middle of the race and consequently to jeopardize whatever stability has been achieved thus far. The parochialist, on the
other hand, does not share this abiding concern for international con-
venience, at least not when it conflicts with what he sees as the primordial demands of man's inner nature. In structuring political associations, he claims, final deference must be given to the ethnic,
regional, and cultural affinities of the people, for these are the stuff of
which a stable, natural world order is made. If this means dissolving
the artificial institution of States and replacing them with something
else, he urges, then by all means we should commence the process
now, in a relatively peaceful environment, rather than encourage violence as the only vehicle for attaining what he sees as the inevitable
result.

These two conflicting positions result from a difference in what
used to be called "first principles," that is, the basic theoretical prejudices that inevitably determine the character of the more detailed su-
perstructure. But are these the only first principles available, or does
the development of international law and relations during the last several decades permit the articulation of an intermediate principle between blind affirmation of the supremacy of the sovereign State and
total submission to parochial sentiment? From one perspective, the issue may be reduced to Matthew Arnold's question:

> Is there no life, but these alone?
> Madman or slave, must man be one?[7]

Secession and the Pursuit of World Order

An irrational commitment to either the form of the sovereign State
or the demands of parochial sentiment is unwholesome and unnecessary. Common sense requires that both be scrutinized for their underlying value and utility, and that neither be encapsulated in a dogmatic
sanctity. It makes no more sense to uphold the integrity of a State
when it no longer satisfies the fundamental purposes of a political association, than it does to glorify parochialism for the sake of parochialism as though this embodied a panacea for all the ills of the social
condition.

It might be objected, however, that this advice, although perhaps a
laudable course for States to follow as a matter of voluntary internal
management, cannot, solely by virtue of its own self-evident right-

7. Matthew Arnold, "A Summer Night."

eousness, become the basis for international interference with the structure of independent States. The major thrust of international law has historically been to regulate the intercourse of sovereign States and, given the characteristically bellicose nature of these entities, that has meant primarily the prevention of international war. Unquestionably, the common man benefited by the prevention of war; but this was an indirect, if pleasant, by-product of the paramount task of maintaining the inter-State order. Overall, it was felt that international law had quite enough to do in restraining the more violent habits of its unruly subjects without concerning itself with how they each treated their own individual subjects. The full realization that the condition of peoples within States strongly influences the inter-State order was painfully slow in coming. There are indisputable signs, however, that the international community has begun to perceive the sphere of its proper concern more broadly than could be expected under its traditional role of regulating the external relations of sovereign States.

At the present time, the self-imposed tasks of the international community can be seen as twofold: the maintenance of behavioral norms on the inter-State plane, and the promotion of standards regarding the protection and advancement of individuals and groups within States. The preamble of the United Nations Charter, for example, contains firm commitments not only to preserve the world order against future wars but also "to promote social progress and better standards of life in larger freedom"; "to reaffirm faith in fundamental rights, in the dignity and worth of the human person"; and "to employ international machinery for the promotion of the economic and social advancement of all peoples." These provisions, admittedly hortatory in nature, are supplemented by articles 55 and 56 of the Charter whereby all the members pledge themselves to take joint and separate action in cooperation with the organization to achieve certain goals, among which are "conditions of economic and social progress and development,"[8] and "universal respect for, and observance of, human rights and fundamental freedoms."[9]

By subscribing to these goals, the members of the United Nations have shown an appreciation for the close interrelationship between the general condition of peoples *within* States, and the delicate balance of the international order *among* States. To the extent that the Char-

8. U.N. CHARTER, art. 55(a).
9. *Id.* (c).

ter embodies a first principle, therefore, that principle would seem to be a maximization of international harmony coupled with a minimization of individual human suffering. In the case of war or inter-State strife, these two goals are entirely compatible; to inhibit the conflict is ipso facto to reduce the danger of individual human suffering. The case of a State depriving its citizens of basic human rights might not be as clear. By attempting to coerce the delinquent State, the community itself clearly disturbs the international harmony, but this is considered an acceptable risk in order to expunge the even more offensive (and dangerous) practice of disregarding fundamental human rights. The principle in these cases seems to be a maximization of international harmony consonant with the goal of promoting minimum conditions for individual and social development within States. When phrased in the more familiar negative fashion, this principle amounts to a doctrine of noninterference in the internal affairs of a State unless, by its treatment of its own subjects, the State transgresses a collective sense of the minimum requirements of human dignity and social order.

The phenomenon of secession presents the potential tension between these two goals even more starkly. Thus, the world community cannot indiscriminately advocate the disintegration of all polyethnic States, because to do so would create vast confusion in the current inter-State system and might well defeat its own purpose of promoting conditions for social and economic welfare by resulting in a proliferation of tiny ethnic communities lacking an economic base or viable political structure. Nevertheless, the continuance of polyethnic States containing two or more distinct "peoples," especially where one stands in an oppressive relationship to the other, will sometimes breed civil strife, injury to fundamental human dignity, loss of cultural identity, and the threat of outside intervention. To remain faithful to its first principles, the community must obviously balance these conflicting interests. What is significant here, however, is that this balancing must be carried on from a utilitarian viewpoint—albeit perhaps a utilitarianism with a basically conservative (State-centered) prejudice. Thus, it would seem possible to fashion a scheme whereby the institution of the existing State will be respected, unless to do so would contribute to more international disharmony than would result from legitimating the separation of a component group. Similarly, to use the perhaps unfortunate "quantitative" image, the secessionists' demands will be considered legitimate only in circumstances indicating that the general "amount" of world harmony would be increased by accepting the secession. Of course, any proposal for ascertaining legitimate claimants to self-determination in the secessionist context must carefully avoid encouraging disaffected groups who commence terrorist activities as a means of increasing the "disharmony" flowing from their present condition. Having elucidated the first principle to be applied in these situations, it remains to translate this frighteningly vague goal of "maximizing world harmony" into an operative framework for ascertaining legitimate secessionist claims.

The Nature of Legitimacy

A "legitimate" claim to secessionist self-determination under the above analysis must take into account several factors. First, the claimant must demonstrate that it is in fact a "self" (this much is implicit in the phrase self-determination) capable of independent existence or willing to annex itself to an existing, viable entity (an inescapable condition when the claim is for secessionist self-determination). Second, the claimant must show that acquiescence in its demand would be likely to result in a greater degree of world harmony (or less global and societal disruption) than would be the case if the existing union were preserved. As will be suggested below, these elements do not constitute a set of "necessary conditions" of legitimacy, to be satisfied by every claimant group to the same degree. A determination of legitimacy in a particular case can be reached by balancing the general interests of the world community and the remaining State against the strength of the claimants' argument for a right of self-determination.

THE INTERNAL MERITS OF THE CLAIM

The doctrine of self-determination has never been interpreted to mean that *any* group wishing to adopt the title of a "self" has a right to political independence. Throughout its checkered career, the doctrine has always been understood, variously but consistently, to require a nation, or a people, or a colonial people, or some other category with a similar ethnological basis. It has never been intended to encompass a group of people, for instance, united only by a common economic advantage but otherwise entirely fungible with the other members of their society. This limitation of the principle, although somewhat arbitrary, is nonetheless sound. The force of the parochialist argument rests upon two observable "facts." First, people are generally more likely to consent to be governed by individuals like themselves (in a racial, cultural, linguistic, historical sense); and, second, history teaches that government of a distinct group by an alien population has often (but not always) resulted in oppression, humiliation, and exploitation. By requiring elements of group identity, therefore, the doctrine of self-determination seeks those factors which give rise to a parochial sentiment and which are thus likely to produce government based on consent. The limitation of the principle to distinct selves is consequently a useful and realistic restriction. Fortunately, there has been no shortage of discussion over what constitutes group distinctness. The students of nationalism have long pursued their self-appointed task of defining the characteristics of the "nation" and some (but not all) of their labor will be relevant to the present issue. As a convenient example, the Permanent Court of International Justice in the *Greco-Bulgarian "Communities"* case identified a "community" as a thing possessing both objective and subjective distinctness. A community, they thought, is "a group of persons living in a given country or locality, having a race, religion, language and traditions of their own, and united by the identity of such race, religion, language and traditions in a sentiment of solidarity."[10]

Assuming that group distinctness may be demonstrated by reference to cultural, racial, linguistic, historic, or religious factors, several caveats are nevertheless in order. First, the doctrine of self-determination cannot be stretched to require that all of these elements be present in every self—only a reasonable showing of distinctness seems to be necessary. Second, there is an equal danger in trying to implement the doctrine by emphasizing one factor to the exclusion of others. Harold Nicolson cogently reminds us, for example, that during the Paris Peace Conference of 1919 when the question of the emphasis to be placed on "historical" claims for self-determination was raised, the Italians "showed a marked predeliction for the Empire of Hadrian."[11] Finally, in a claim for secessionist self-determination, it seems inescapable that the claimant group must occupy a distinct territory.[12] It is conceivable that a particular group widely intermixed with the ambient population (such as the European Jews or American Blacks) or one leading a nomadic existence (such as the Gypsies) might wish to secede from the governing population politically but not territorially. This would result in a kind of dual sovereignty similar to that once practised on the island of Cyprus, without any territorial division of

10. [1920] P.C.I.J., ser. B, No. 17, at 33.
11. H. NICOLSON, PEACEMAKING 1919, at 130 (1944).
12. For a discussion of whether a territory is necessary for the growth of nationalistic sentiment see HERTZ, chapter 1, note 1, at 146–51 *supra*.

the country. Examples of this kind of relationship are very rare and it appears that the practical problems involved in having two intermixed populations, each responsible to a different political and legal order, are insurmountable. Where the group lacks a geographical homeland, therefore, the problem is more amenable to a solution involving minority protections within the existing framework than to a "political" secession.

The second aspect of the internal merits of the separatists' claim — that the claimant be capable of an independent existence after the secession — can also be empirically verified.[13] The minimum requirements for economic viability and the prospects for some basic political structure are of course the first considerations here. In addition, the claimant group ought to be able to demonstrate a basis for the future cohesiveness of its population. To some extent, the evidence of cohesiveness will utilize the same factors of racial, linguistic, religious, and cultural identity which established the group's "selfness," but it may also include, for instance, proof of the community's unique economic interdependence. Where a group's claim for secession results primarily from the persecution it suffers at the hands of its present governors, however, the internal cohesiveness of the people may evaporate as soon as the external irritant is removed. To permit a secession on this basis alone is to court the danger of "indefinite divisibility," that is, the possibility of a further fracturing of the new entity into unrealistically small segments shortly after the secession. Obviously, where the group avows its intention of uniting itself to an established, viable State soon after the separation (as do, for example, the Somali-inhabited portions of Kenya and Ethiopia), then the burden of showing future viability is greatly reduced.

Finally, three remaining areas of uncertainty must be addressed here. First, the requirements for a viable, independent entity are not necessarily identical with those traditionally needed for Statehood. The issue of whether a secession *must* result in the separating province becoming a fullfledged State will be discussed below. It is sufficient at this point to note that an international endorsement of a scheme for ascertaining secessionist legitimacy may involve an acceptance of polit-

---

13. The suggestion that these factors are capable of empirical verification and quantification can be carried to an extreme. *See, e.g.,* Dodd, *The Scientific Measurement of Fitness for Self-Government,* 78 SCIENTIFIC MONTHLY 94 (Feb. 1954) for a suggestion that a dependent peoples' capability for self-government can be measured by weighing 350 indices of fitness for self-government derived from an equal number of "objectively observable phenomena."

ical units with some but not all of the characteristics and obligations of the traditional State. Second, no undue emphasis should be placed on the adjective "independent" in the phrase "viable, independent entity." The entity must of course be viable without its present governing State (and so in that sense independent) but it need not possess, for instance, the attribute of economic independence. In today's world, this latter form of independence is a rare occurrence indeed and one which the vastly interdependent world community could hardly ask of a seceding province.[14] A similar conclusion must be reached in the area of military defensibility; except for a few States, the current modus operandi for protecting oneself militarily is to participate in defensive alliances. Very few States can imagine their own military capability, by itself, as constituting an effective deterrent against aggression. Third, one cannot, under the guise of requiring evidence of future viability, demand proof of future affluence. That is, the standard for viability must be minimal; it is not significant that the people of the seceding entity may suffer a reduction in their standard of living or some other inconveniences after the separation. In short, the international community might reasonably seek to prevent a group from committing social suicide (because it will inevitably be left with the problem of disposing of the corpse), but it cannot forcibly prevent a self-inflicted, nonlethal wound where this is the freely chosen decision of the people involved.

THE DISRUPTION FACTOR

Even after identifying the "self" and ascertaining that it *can* have an existence apart from its present governing State, we still must inquire into whether it *ought* to be permitted such an independent existence. To answer this question in light of the first principles discussed above, we must know whether acquiescence in the secession would serve to promote general international harmony—an issue involving both the concerns of the inter-State order and the goal of fostering conditions conducive to social development and the protection of human dignity. Because secession inevitably involves a change in the status quo and

14. An examination of the condition of existing States might suggest that many could not satisfy any reasonable test of economic viability. Nevertheless, this ought not, by itself, to prevent the international community from employing a somewhat stricter standard for judging the viability of seceding entities. In one sense, the fact that international charity is already heavily burdened by States in economic difficulties is precisely what heightens the world community's anxiety over increasing this strain by legitimating any new claimants.

any such change is a disturbance of sorts, it would be more realistic to approach this question from the perspective of whether secession, or a continuation of the present union, would be more disruptive of the general international harmony. Furthermore, only by balancing the amount of disruption likely to occur if the secession is accepted against the current disruption resulting from the condition of the claimant group within its governing State can the international community accurately calculate this factor.

The nature of the disruption likely to ensue from a successful secession will be of two kinds: (1) the effects of the separation on the remaining State and other States indirectly concerned, and (2) the effects on the general international order. A secession will by definition have the result of diminishing the land mass and population of the original State. In determining the effect of this loss one must inquire into factors such as the economic significance of the seceding province to its former partners, and the strategic value of the territory and population. The amount of disruption will obviously be high if the secession threatens to remove the economic base of the country (as in the secession of the Katanga); expose the remaining State to aggression from a hostile neighbor; split the State in two geographically by the creation of a new entity between remaining regions; jeopardize access to ports or facilities for external trade and communication, and so on. Of course, the original State clearly cannot argue that the separation of a province will injure its economic life simply because it had enjoyed the privilege of exploiting that province during the period of union. Apart from its effect on the remaining country, the separation may also seriously alter the balance of power or customary trading patterns in the area, causing concern to third-party States. Should the secession be likely to induce intervention or other hostile acts to redress this balance, and where the international community is not prepared to resort to adequate measures of prevention, this fact must be acknowledged as a possible source of disruption.

The probable effect of the secession on the general international order is the second area of concern here. This issue is closely related to the ability of the seceding entity to maintain an independent existence after the separation. Where it cannot, and international charity is liable to become the instrument for maintaining its economic life, the world community has a justifiable ground for anxiety. Other bases of international concern might be the presence of "trapped" minorities within the seceding entity, the willingness of the government of the new entity to accord respect for human rights, and its attitude toward the other fundamental norms of international behavior.

Finally, the international community must prepare for the effect upon its own structure of the new entities likely to arise by operation of a doctrine of secessionist legitimacy. It seems clear that, where the new entity does not have the characteristics normally required for Statehood, a legitimation of the secession must imply an international acceptance of some other unit of political association. An accommodation of this change in the structure of the international order need not be as drastic as it initially appears. First, the international system is not unfamiliar with nonsovereign entities; it has historically accepted designations such as protectorates, colonies, free cities, mandates, trusteeships, and associated States, as the need arose. Second, the concern with keeping the global map free of entities that do not possess the traditional requirements of Statehood — such as a secure resource base, a significantly large population, and sovereign independence — no longer appears very forceful. These classic indicia of Statehood have been diluted nearly to the point of oblivion by the post-1960 proliferation of numerous tiny entities which have sought, and been granted, recognition as States by the international community. The League of Nations, of course, had originally set a precedent of not admitting territories such as Lichtenstein and San Marino because they were too small.[15] Demonstrating a much greater elasticity in this regard, the United Nations has, since 1961, accorded pro forma recognition to territories of minute geographical size, many with a population of less than 1,000,000 — and some less than 100,000 — without a secure economic base, and lacking any significant amount of "independence." Indeed, it is now difficult to imagine a territory so small and so fragile that it could not be recognized as a State under the present standards. Third, the transmogrification of the concept of the State resulting from its extension to encompass these tiny units has led to a serious concern with the problems and status of such "ministates" and "microstates" within the contemporary international order,

15. Both the League and the United Nations attempted to articulate criteria for determining when a territory is fit for self-government. For the League's conditions regarding the termination of a mandate see LEAGUE OF NATIONS, PERM. MANDATES COMM'N, 20th sess. 228–29, League Doc. C. 422. M. 176 (1931). For the United Nations effort see G.A. Res. 742, Annex, 8 U.N. GAOR, Supp. 17, at 21, 22–23, U.N. Doc. A/2630 (1953), entitled "Factors indicative of the attainment of independence or of other separate systems of self-government."

and their effect upon that order.[16] In short, we are not wholly unpre-
pared for the transition to an international structure accommodating
territorial units that are not sovereign States in the classic sense. Entities resulting from the operation of a doctrine of secessionist legitimacy, therefore, could either be granted the titular status of "States"
under the current expansive use of that term or, more realistically, be
placed in a category such as that of an "associated State" for purposes
of participation in the international arena.[17]

At a certain point, it might be objected, a loose concept of associated Statehood becomes virtually indistinguishable in operation from
a wide grant of regional autonomy within a unified State. A question
therefore arises regarding the *minimum* obligations such an "associated
State" will have to fulfill to be a separate international entity. The only
inescapable requirement in this regard, I suggest, is that the entity exercise effective jurisdiction and control over its own territory. The utility in maintaining a separate international existence for *some* purposes
rests in the ability of the entity to extend its sphere of independence
should its associated partner abuse the authority granted it in areas
such as monetary affairs, international representation, diplomatic
duties, and defense. Furthermore, the knowledge that the weaker
partner may assume greater responsibility for its own affairs is likely
to chill any temptation for the dominant partner to abuse its position.

A more interesting situation is presented if the seceding entity
openly abjures any intention of seeking international recognition as a
State or even any lesser gradation of statehood. It may wish to exist in
isolation from international life, neither seeking to participate in international affairs nor welcoming international interference in its own.
Although this sentiment is a curious reversal of the typical anxiety of
small territories that they will not be accorded *enough* recognition, it

---

16. *See, e.g.,* S. SMITH, MICROSTATES AND MICRONESIA (1970); PROBLEMS OF SMALL
TERRITORIES (B. Benedict ed. 1967); UNITED NATIONS INSTITUTE FOR TRAINING AND RE-
SEARCH, STATUS AND PROBLEMS OF VERY SMALL STATES AND TERRITORIES (UNITAR Ser.
No. 3, 1969); Keohane, Book Review, *Lilliputian's Dilemmas: Small States in International
Politics,* 23 INT'L ORGANIZ. 311 (1969); Mendelson, *Diminutive States in the United Nations,*
21 INT'L & COMP. L.Q. 609 (1972); Panel: *The Participation of Ministates in International
Affairs,* 62 AM. SOC. INT'L L. PROC. 155 (1968).

17. *See, e.g.,* W. REISMAN, PUERTO RICO AND THE INTERNATIONAL PROCESS: NEW ROLES
IN ASSOCIATION 9–20 (1975) where the author asks in passing, "If association were made
more explicit, might not erstwhile secessionist movements such as Biafra and the South-
ern Sudan have been resolved more quickly and peacefully?" *Id. 20. See also* K. DEUTSCH,
NATIONALISM AND ITS ALTERNATIVES (1969); Broderick, *Associated Statehood: A New
Form of Decolonisation,* 17 INT'L & COMP. L.Q. 368 (1968).

does not present any insuperable problems to world order. The international community might reasonably insist that even a nonparticipatory entity must act in accordance with certain basic normative principles such as the proscription of the use of force, just as that entity would itself benefit from the general international regulation of offensive conduct involving the use of force. Furthermore, to the extent that the entity *does* accept intercourse with the outside world in the form of trade contacts, requests for developmental assistance, allowing aliens to reside in the territory, and the like, it must undertake to respect the international standards involved in such activities. Within these limits, however, the simple existence of nonparticipatory entities does not constitute a matter for excessive international concern.

Finally, the danger of the "demonstration effect" (the recognition of one secession tending to foment other movements elsewhere) should not contribute to the assessment of future disruption. The very existence of a scheme for determining secessionist legitimacy would limit the precedential effect of such a recognition by rendering it explicable in terms of the standards articulated by the international community. It is only when a particular claim is recognized without specifying the circumstances which made it acceptable to the community that other, dissimilar, movements might feel encouraged by the decision.

It would be a serious mistake to end our inquiry after calculating the amount of future disruption likely to be engendered by the secession. If the significance of this factor is to be accurately assessed, the amount of future disruption must be balanced against the degree to which international harmony is currently disrupted by the presence of the group within its governing State. This latter disturbance would, after all, be removed by accepting the group's secession and would thus operate as a positive benefit to the world order. Current disruption in this sense may arise from several sources. Should the group be the victim of discriminatory oppression involving for example the deprivation of human rights and political freedoms, the international community, with its recent sensitivity to such behavior, might find the situation inherently offensive. Should individual States react similarly, they might attempt to redress the group's condition by intervention or external pressure. The group itself might pursue a self-help remedy of armed rebellion against its oppressors, thus forcing the country into civil war involving risks of third-party interference or escalation into global conflict. Even where the group does not suffer any severe persecution and is unlikely to follow a course of armed rebellion, the simple presence of an unsatisfied nationalism or the unfulfilled desire of an ethnic group for self-government is to a limited extent a cause of international concern.

One important caveat must be noted here. A people may not fabricate the appearance of oppression or deliberately endeavor to increase the disruptive character of their present situation by antagonizing their governors into taking police action against them. A group living in a democratic, nondiscriminatory society that undertakes a campaign of terrorism merely to draw attention to its claim or to coerce its governors into accepting its demands—thus compelling the authorities to enforce security measures—cannot be seen as the victims of "oppression." For purposes of the "current disruption" element, the situation of the group must be viewed from the perspective of its normal condition within the society, that is, in the absence of any violent antagonism of its governors. Only in cases where this normal condition is one of such harsh oppression that the group justifiably resorts to a course of self-defense may the disturbance resulting from its action be acknowledged as a factor in the calculation of current disruption. The alternative to this limitation is obviously intolerable. It would place a premium upon the people's willingness and ability to pursue a policy of indiscriminate terrorism against their governors (or for that matter other States as well) when they themselves are not the victims of forceful persecution, in order to render their case a "disturbing" one in the eyes of the world community. Furthermore, it would allow a small number of extremists to upset the international scheme for ascertaining a legitimate claim by producing violent manifestations of a discontent not shared by the majority of the people involved. Rather than be considered as a symptom of gross irresponsibility, thus casting doubt upon the group's ability to comport itself in a civilized manner once independent, this alternative would dangerously reward the willingness of a group to commit acts of unbridled savagery.

This limitation raises a very important related issue. Where a claimant group actually resorts to violence as a forceful method of achieving its goal, when can the disorder arising from the ensuing conflict be considered as a factor in current disruption? Clearly, the mere fact of internecine fighting cannot always be an element of current disruption. This would allow, indeed, encourage, every group to use force as a method of increasing the international community's perception of the disruptive nature of their situation. Furthermore, there is little basis in international law for denying the right of sovereign States to undertake suppression of secessionist activity in the absence of a collective international judgment affirming the legitimacy of the group's claim to self-determination. On the other hand, to say that fighting ought never to be a factor in the determination of current disruption is highly unrealistic. Where the claimant group is the victim of severe oppression or persecution, its decision to pursue a self-help remedy may be seen as an exercise of a fundamental right of resistance. Certainly the danger that a group will be forced to resort to violence as a method of self-defense against a brutal governing regime is a *risk* that ought to be considered in evaluating current disruption. Once the danger becomes a reality, that is, once they do resort to forceful self-defense, the resulting disorder is a direct consequence of their condition within the governing State and should affect the calculation of current disruption.

The best rule therefore would seem to be this: where the claimant group has not been driven to utilize violence as a justifiable means of self-defense against an oppressive State (that is, where the secessionists have unnecessarily and without adequate provocation adopted violence as a means of attaining their goal) then the State may exercise its prerogative of attempting to suppress the secession without the resulting disturbance becoming a factor in the calculation of current disruption. However, should a governing State in this position engage in a savage campaign needlessly causing injury to the lives, property, and human dignity of the insurgents (as was the case for instance in Bangla Desh), then the fact of this excessive brutality, above that excusable as reasonably necessary to counter the secession, will enter the calculation. A State that compels its citizens to resort to forceful self-help remedies must bear the risk that this disorder and its attendant danger of external intervention and escalation will contribute to an assessment of current disruption. Clearly, some argument will center upon the issue of when a group is justified in resorting to violence as a method of self-defense. Although this will not always be clear, the international community has been able in the past to agree on the illegal nature of a regime (Rhodesia, Namibia) and express its distaste for regimes inflicting severe oppression (Chile, Greece under the colonels). There is no reason, therefore, to think that the question of justifiable self-defense in this context will always be hopelessly clouded.

The basis for these restrictions is apparent. One of the benefits of developing a rational scheme for the determination of secessionist legitimacy is that the international community has a unique opportunity to structure its guidelines so as to avoid placing a premium upon an unnecessary resort to violence by either party. The assessment of current disruption can sometimes offset the international concern for the future disruption likely to result from secession and, under this analysis therefore, a greater amount of present disturbance operates to the advantage of the secessionist's claim. The scheme consequently inhibits a State's willingness to inflict oppression upon its minorities. Nevertheless, care must be taken that these standards do not place a premium on a group's adoption of terrorism or violent secession where this is not a justifiable remedy of last resort. Finally, even where the State may legitimately employ force to counter a secessionist attempt, the scheme may hope to moderate and discipline the use of such force by considering any unnecessary brutality or savagery by the central government's agents as tending to heighten the current disruptive consequences of the situation.

THE CALCULATION OF LEGITIMACY

The final decision regarding the legitimacy of a particular secessionist claim must result from the balancing of the internal merits of the claimants' case against the justifiable concerns of the international community expressed in its calculation of the disruptive consequences of the situation. By balancing these two aspects, the community will avoid being forced to articulate a single, immutable standard of legitimacy, to be applied with arithmetical remorselessness against each and every group in the same way. As we have seen, both the principle of remedial secession and the parochialist model suffer from an essentially linear character. In the former, legitimacy is determined by locating the condition of the claimant group upon a line representing the gradations of oppression capable of being inflicted by a governing State. In the latter, this line represents the spectrum of "group distinctness," the legitimate claimant being one that can demonstrate a sufficient quantum of "selfness." Remedial secession cannot accommodate the plea of an unquestionably valid "self," capable of separating from its present regime with very little disruption to itself, its governors, or the international community but presently living within the borders of a State not given to inflicting undue oppression. On the other hand, the parochialist model must apparently accept the legitimacy of a distinct "self" even when the secession would operate to wreak vast disruption on the remaining State or the international order; and it would deny legitimacy to a group possessing a weaker claim to selfhood but whose separation would not increase, and might diminish, the general amount of societal and global disruption.

If the international community is to be capable of accommodating the wide disparities in the nature and circumstances of secessionist movements, it must employ a more flexible method for ascertaining legitimacy. Using the criteria set out above, the various elements relevant to a determination of legitimacy can be reasonably accounted for by balancing what I have called the "internal merits of the claim" against the items contributing to the "disruption factor." These are, after all, the two competing claims in this area. Where the legitimate interests of the world community (as expressed in the disruption factor) are threatened by a proposed secession, it is reasonable to require exceptionally strong evidence of the group's claim to selfhood. However, where these concerns are not seriously threatened or are jeopardized to an even greater extent by the present situation of the group, ipso facto, the basis for a cautious handling of the claim is removed, and the standards of group selfhood need not be as strict. As we have seen, when neither the integrity of sovereign States nor the self-governing urge of particular communities is taken as an absolute value, the justifiable concerns of separatist groups, unified States, and the general international order may all be balanced to achieve the most rational solution.

This calculation might be undertaken in the following way. After forming its prognosis regarding the probable disruptive consequences of allowing the secession, the international community (or that body entrusted with advising on the legitimacy of these claims), must balance this factor against its assessment of the current disturbance flowing from the position of the claimant group within its governing State. The result of this balancing — the disruption factor — will be high where the future danger of permitting the secession outweighs the risk of maintaining the status quo. It will be considered "even" when neither of these alternatives is likely to produce a measurable increase in disruption; and it will be low when *either* (1) the risk of future disruption is minimal but there is some measure of current disruption, *or* (2) the risk of future disruption, although significant, is nevertheless outweighed by a serious amount of current disruption. Obviously, the disruption factor as used here is a term of art. It offends one's common sense instinct to say that a significant amount of future disruption *plus* a current situation with vastly disruptive consequences may together produce a calculation of a "low" disruption factor. This curious result is, however, necessary to allow flexibility in accounting for the possibly disruptive consequences of forcing the claimant to remain with its governing State.

The second preliminary evaluation concerns the internal merits of the particular claim. As we have seen, this measurement must take into account the strength of the group's case for selfness within the commonly accepted dimensions of that category, and the group's prospects for being a viable entity once separated from its present governors. The final determination of legitimacy, therefore, will result from the relationship of the disruption factor to the internal merits of the claim. The relationship between these two factors may be represented graphically as is done, for the sake of visualization, in appendix 2. Obviously, by suggesting that this calculation may be described on a graph I do not mean to imply that these matters admit of a scientific or mathematical solution, or that such vague and controversial items as a group's "distinctness" or the probable disruptive effects of a secession can be quantified in a precise manner. The utility of a scheme such as this lies in its function as a basis for argument—never a mathematically precise art, but the customary one for adjudicating conflicts within the imprecise field of human affairs. The use of a graph, therefore, although somewhat ingenuous, is nevertheless helpful in clarifying the bounds of argument.

Referring to appendix 2, the disruption factor, resulting from a balancing of current and future disruption, is represented by the x axis. It should be apparent that the balancing required to ascertain this factor involves more than a simple subtraction of the current from the future disruption. An assessment that utterly disastrous consequences would flow from a secession cannot be ameliorated by subtracting some amount of minor current disruption, just as a surgeon does not alter his opinion regarding the dangers of undertaking an operation with a high probability of patient mortality, merely because it will relieve an uncomfortable (but nonlethal) condition. The designation of gradations less than "even" on the x axis is of course necessary to account for situations in which the quantum of future disruption, if any, is outweighed by the disruptive consequences of the status quo. The decision regarding the internal merits of the claim, represented by the y axis, is graded on an increasing scale from poor to fair to excellent.

In order to ascertain whether a particular claim, once plotted on the graph, is in fact legitimate (a relative and not absolute standard), the international community must establish broad guidelines below which it will not consider a claim to be a legitimate invocation of the right to self-determination. This judgment, in effect the international threshold of legitimacy, is represented on the graph by line ab. Obviously, this line may be drawn at any angle and need not bisect the field, as it does in appendix 2. The area above this line represents the field of legitimate claims, and that below illegitimate. By establishing conditions bringing line *ab* nearer to the *y* axis, the community increases the difficulty of achieving recognition as a legitimate claim.

The basic principles and operation of this scheme can be easily illustrated on the graph. Where the disruption factor is high, the claimant must make out an extraordinarily good case for its entitlement to self-determination. In other words, the higher the disruption factor, the more will be required by way of demonstrating selfness and future viability. Where little disruption is liable to ensue from the secession, or where the amount of current disruption outweighs the future risk, the community can afford to be less strict in its requirements for selfhood simply because the basis for its anxiety (including its concern for the effect on the remaining State) will be alleviated or else outweighed by its concern for the present situation. It may therefore accommodate to a greater extent the self-governing wishes of a particular people who cannot offer overwhelming proof of their racial, historical, or linguistic distinctness.

Because a weakness in the claimant's case for future viability is liable to be closely tied with an increase in the probable future disruption resulting from the separation, a low assessment of future viability will usually entail a higher estimate of the disruption factor. To some extent, of course, this can be offset by a particularly strong case for selfness—the other factor in the internal merits calculation. The one important exception to this rule obtains where the secession, although liable to cause a significant amount of future disruption, is undertaken to remedy the extremely disturbing consequences of leaving the group under its present regime. In such a case, the current outweighs the future disruption, resulting in a low overall disruption factor. For such a situation, therefore, the community will accept a relatively low showing of internal merits. This means, in effect, that the community is willing to risk legitimating an entity requiring international aid for its survival and/or lacking an irrefutable case for selfness, because of the more disturbing consequences of allowing it to remain within the clutches of its present governors.

An example of how this conceptual framework would operate in practice might be helpful here. Let us take the claim of East Pakistan (Bangla Desh) just prior to the outbreak of the Indo-Pakistan War of 1971 and briefly sketch the procedure by which its legitimacy would be analyzed under this scheme. First, the disruption likely to result from allowing the secession was clearly significant. East Pakistan had a notoriously weak economic base and by no stretch of the imagination could it be anticipated to survive as a self-supporting entity immediately after independence. Furthermore, the secession would have resulted in removing more than half of Pakistan's population (although, overall, West Pakistan seemed capable of standing alone). Finally, the presence of large non-Bengali minorities, such as the Biharis, within East Pakistan constituted a serious matter for international concern. Balanced against this, of course, was the amount of current disruption resulting from the condition of East Pakistan within the union. As we have seen, it had been the victim of serious discrimination and exploitation at the hands of the West since independence. In addition, the extreme brutality of the West Pakistani army after March 26, 1971—involving massive, unjustifiable loss of life and injury to human dignity—resulted in large-scale refugee problems and an imminent danger of intervention by India (which bore close ethnic affinities with the East Bengali people). The conduct of the West Pakistani forces, going far beyond even an expansive interpretation of a State's "permissible" behavior in subduing a secession (assuming that an outright secessionist attempt was imminent on March 26), was even such as to risk an international war between India and Pakistan. In short, the amount of current disruption, measured both by the international concern with individual human dignity, and by the threat to the inter-State order, was very great. Even when balanced against the admittedly significant amount of future disruption, therefore, it heavily outweighed the future risk and thus permitted an overall calculation of a low disruption factor.

On the other side of the calculation, of course, would be the internal merits of the claim by the East Pakistani people for a right of secessionist self-determination. First, as we have seen, they had a very poor case for their future viability without massive international aid. Furthermore, although they had just completed political elections, they were at best novices in conducting "the affairs of State" which had traditionally been almost the exclusive prerogative of the West wing. Offsetting to some extent this poor showing of future viability, was the strong claim of the East Pakistani people to selfhood. Aside from religion (which they shared in common with the West wing), they were culturally, racially, historically, and linguistically distinct from the people of West Pakistan. Accordingly, their general case for the internal merits of their claim under this analysis, containing one strong and one weak element, might be assessed as fair.

When located on the graph contained in appendix 2, therefore, the Bangla Desh claim would fall in a position close to the point marked (i). Should the international community establish a threshold of legitimacy represented in the form of a line *ab* running anywhere *below* point (i), then the claim would be considered legitimate. If the standards for legitimacy were stricter, this would force line *ab* to approach the *y* axis and thus leave point (i) within the illegitimate field. If we are correct in thinking that the international community as a whole *did* accept the legitimacy of Bangla Desh's claim, then they reached a decision accepting the emergence of a nonviable entity, dependent upon international charity, in order to alleviate the intolerable disruption flowing from the situation of East Pakistan.

How might this result have been affected by an alteration of circumstances? First, without the overwhelming force of current disruption, the element of probable future risk in allowing the secession would have resulted in an overall calculation of "high" on the *x* axis. Had all the other factors remained constant, this would have placed the claim close to point (ii)—almost certainly within the illegitimate field. Second, had there been little or no danger of future disruption, then the significant amount of current disturbance would have moved the claim well below "even" to a point closer to the extreme left end of the *x* axis. This would have produced a claim in the area of point (iii)—probably well within even a narrow field of legitimacy.[18]

Finally, let us assume that everything else in the Bangla Desh case remained the same, but that the people of East Pakistan were not a distinct "self." That is, they did not share any significant bonds of religion, culture, or history but represented a mixed lot of people with differing backgrounds, indistinguishable as a group from the general population of the heterogeneous State. For purposes of the present analysis, this would have meant that both the selfness and viability elements of their claim would be assessed as poor. On the graph, therefore, the claim would be plotted somewhere near point (iv)—unlikely to be within a legitimate range unless line *ab* were established unrealistically close to the *x* axis. The result in this situation is enlightening. The international community would have made a decision that the oppressed situation of the people concerned represented a significant disruption to the present world order. Nevertheless, despite the fact that international concern for their plight was sufficient to overcome

18. Of course, except in cases where the seceding province seeks to join with an existing viable State, the assessment of a low future disruption implies that the internal merits of the claim would also be improved because of the better chances for future viability. Thus, in this situation it is probable that the claim would be located even higher on the *y* axis and thereby increase its chances for a determination of legitimacy.

the basic prejudice of noninterference in the internal affairs of States, the community could not legitimate a right to secessionist self-deter mination as a remedy simply because there was no genuine self to exercise this right. Realistically, the community would therefore be compelled to employ a remedy that did not require the precondition of a self in the sense of self-determination. Such a remedy might involve seeking international guarantees for human rights, political freedoms, and minority rights; international suggestions of greater regional autonomy, economic freedom, or religious liberty, and so on, as the situation required. To generalize, where the condition of a people within a State constitutes a matter of sufficient international concern to remove it from the category of a "domestic affair," but the circumstances of the people do not warrant the conclusion that they are a self and thus a candidate for the remedy of self-determination, the community must resort to less extreme remedies which operate within the framework of the existing State.

Even given a framework such as that sketched above, one is left with the issue of where to establish the minimum requirements for legitimacy. The outer limits of this question seem to be clear; to establish too strict a standard (that is, to draw line ab too close to the y axis) is to remand the matter back to its present unregulated, or at least obscurely regulated, condition. Neither secessionist groups nor outside States wishing to intervene on their behalf will credit a scheme that purports to balance the competing claims of unionist and secessionist but in reality forces the claimants to strive for an impossibly high standard of legitimacy. On the other hand, to accord legitimacy too readily (to draw line ab too close to the x axis), puts the community in the position of affirming the rights of groups with relatively weak claims or whose secession would result in significant disruption to the remaining State and the international order. Neither independent States containing separatist movements nor their sister State supporters will recognize the force of a scheme that would so flaunt their basic sense of order and self-preservation.

To be effective, the standard must be reasonable. It may have some conservative bent, but it should not completely ignore the wishes of genuine "selves" for self-government where this is feasible without undue disruption of global and societal order. Furthermore, the standard should be broadly articulated in advance rather than rely on an ad hoc determination under the political pressures of concrete situations. Such a scheme would allow for flexibility and argument; the basic decision of how much will be required for legitimacy, within a reasonable scope, can and ought to be made in advance. The most fruitful approach to this task would seem to be the establishment of broad guidelines similar to the 1970 *Declaration on Friendly Relations*. There are two benefits to this approach. First, the collective judgment of the community could be formed without some States being compelled to vote, in effect, for the dismemberment of an ally or protégé. Second, a published standard would allow claimants and unionists to evaluate the strength of their respective positions and would perhaps induce them to settle on alternative solutions to their difficulties. There is, of course, some risk for independent States in publishing a framework that might one day operate against them, and, realistically, they are unlikely to undertake such a task merely to promote the good, the beautiful, and the true. Nevertheless, more cogent reasons can be marshalled to support this suggestion. By establishing the standards in advance, members of the world community can, if they wish, give the scheme a somewhat conservative tone. Although it may operate to their future distress, the scheme is equally liable to furnish them with a legal justification for their nonrecognition of certain claims within their borders. Of equal importance under a "realistic" appraisal of State motivations, the scheme could justify their request for outside aid in certain secessionist conflicts and provide a basis for condemning anyone aiding their antagonists.

Without question, States will continue to be importuned by separatist movements with or without a rational scheme for determining the legitimacy of these claims. By publishing such a scheme, the world community might hope to impose a reasoned, predictable order upon so dangerous an area of societal and international discord. It is suggested, moreover, that it is in the enlightened self-interest of individual States to further this effort. Surely it is wiser, and in the end safer, to raise secessionist claims above the present "force of arms" test and into a sphere in which rational discussion can illuminate the legitimate interests of all concerned.

Appendix 1   The Principle of Equal Rights and Self-Determination of Peoples*

[1] By virtue of the principle of equal rights and self-determination of peoples enshrined in the Charter of the United Nations, all peoples have the right freely to determine, without external interference, their political status and to pursue their economic, social and cultural development, and every State has the duty to respect this right in accordance with the provisions of the Charter.

[2] Every State has the duty to promote, through joint and separate action, realization of the principle of equal rights and self-determination of peoples, in accordance with the provisions of the Charter, and to render assistance to the United Nations in carrying out the responsibilities entrusted to it by the Charter regarding the implementation of the principle, in order:

(a) To promote friendly relations and co-operation among States: and
(b) To bring a speedy end to colonialism, having due regard to the freely expressed will of the peoples concerned;

and bearing in mind that subjection of peoples to alien subjugation, domination and exploitation constitutes a violation of the principle, as well as a denial of fundamental human rights, and is contrary to the Charter.

[3] Every State has the duty to promote through joint and separate action universal respect for an observance of human rights and fundamental freedoms in accordance with the Charter.

[4] The establishment of a sovereign and independent State, the free association or integration with an independent State or the emergence into any other political status freely determined by a people constitute modes of implementing the right of self-determination by that people.

*From the General Assembly's 1970 *Declaration on Friendly Relations, supra,* chapter 2, note 184.

[5] Every State has the duty to refrain from any forcible action which deprives peoples referred to above in the elaboration of the present principle of their right to self-determination and freedom and independence. In their actions against, and resistance to, such forcible action in pursuit of the exercise of their right to self-determination, such peoples are entitlted to seek and to receive support in accordance with the purposes and principles of the Charter.

[6] The territory of a colony or other Non-Self-Governing Territory has, under the Charter, a status separate and distinct from the territory of the State administering it; and such separate and distinct status under the Charter shall exist until the people of the colony or Non-Self-Governing Territory have exercised their right of self-determination in accordance with the Charter, and particularly its purposes and principles.

[7] Nothing in the foregoing paragraphs shall be construed as authorizing or encouraging any action which would dismember or impair, totally or in part, the territorial integrity or political unity of sovereign and independent States conducting themselves in compliance with the principle of equal rights and self-determination of peoples as described above and thus possessed of a government representing the whole people belonging to the territory without distinction as to race, creed or colour.

[8] Every State shall refrain from any action aimed at the partial or total disruption of the national unity and territorial integrity of any other State or country.

Appendix 2   The Calculation of Legitimacy

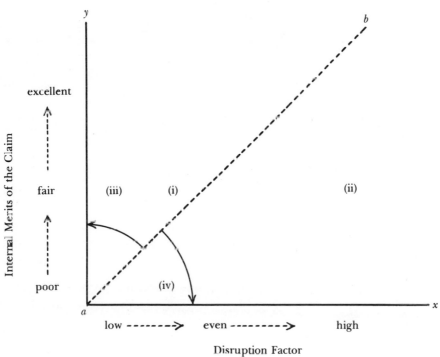

Index